OpenOffice.org For Dummies

W9-BAS-639

Function Toolbar Buttons

Button	Name	Function
	Load URL	This drop-down list opens recently used documents, files, and help pages.
	New	Opens a new OpenOffice.org document. Click the button, and you can choose to open any OpenOffice.org document as well as to access templates.
	Open File	Displays the Open dialog box, where you can find any file that the application can open.
	Save Document	Saves your document. The first time that you save a document, the Save As dialog box opens so that you can name the file and choose a location.
	Edit File	Used if you are working on a read-only file (a file that you cannot change, such as a file where you do not have the required permission).
	Export Directly as PDF	Opens the Export as PDF dialog box, where you can save the file in Adobe Acrobat Reader (PDF) format.
	Print File Directly	Prints the file.
	Cut	Moves selected data from your current file (where it is deleted) to the clipboard.
	Copy	Copies selected data from your current file to the clipboard.
	Paste	Inserts data from the clipboard to the location of the cursor in your current document.
	Undo	Undoes the last command.
	Redo	Redoes the last command that you undid.
	Navigator On/Off	Opens and closes the Navigator window.
	Stylist On/Off	Opens and closes the Styles window, shown in Figure 1-7. Styles are groups of formatting instructions. For more information, see Chapter 4.
	Hyperlink Dialog	Opens the Hyperlink dialog box, where you can assign a hyperlink to selected text.
	Gallery	Opens the Gallery, a graphics and sound collection and organizer.

Wiley, the Wiley Publishing logo, For Dummies, the Dummies Man logo, the For Dummies Bestselling Book Series logo and all related trade dress are trademarks or registered trademarks of John Wiley & Sons, Inc. and/or its affiliates. All other trademarks are property of their respective owners.

For Dummies: Bestselling Book Series for Beginners

OpenOffice.org For Dummies®

Main Toolbar Buttons

You can turn any fly-out toolbar into a floating toolbar. Click almost any button on the Main toolbar and hold down the mouse button for a second. You can then drag the fly-out toolbar from its title bar to any location on the screen.

Button	Name	Function
	Insert	Opens a fly-out toolbar from which you can insert frames, graphics, tables, another document, footnotes, endnotes, special characters, sections, index markers, and bookmarks.
	Insert Fields	Inserts date, time, page number, and other fields into your document.
	Insert Object	Inserts a chart, formula (from OpenOffice.org Math), OLE object, and several other objects.
	Show Draw Functions	Opens a fly-out toolbar that you can use to include drawing objects in your documents. See Chapter 5 for more details.
	Show Form Functions	Opens a fly-out toolbar that you use to create forms. You use forms to enter and edit data in a database.
	Edit Auto Text	Opens the Auto Text dialog box, where you can create and edit Auto Text. The Auto Text feature enables you to create shortcuts for longer text items.
	Direct Cursor On/Off	Toggles the Direct Cursor on and off. The Direct Cursor allows you to quickly align and position text, images, tables, and other objects.
	Spellcheck	Opens the Spellcheck dialog box so that you can check your spelling.
	Auto Spellcheck On/Off	Toggles ongoing Spellcheck on and off. When turned on, misspelled words (that is, words that are not in one of Spellcheck's dictionaries) are underlined with a wavy, red line. Right-click the word to display spell-checking options. (See Chapter 3 for more details.)
	Find On/Off	Opens and closes the Find & Replace dialog box, where you can find and replace text. See Chapter 4 for more information.
	Data Sources	Opens the Data Sources window that you use to work with databases. You can use a data source to create personalized documents (mail merge). For more details, see Chapter 5.
	Nonprinting Characters On/Off	Displays and hides nonprinting characters such as spaces, paragraphs (returns), and tabs. You can display nonprinting characters when you are trying to determine why a document doesn't look right.
	Graphics On/Off	Toggles the display of graphics on and off. Turn off graphic display when you find that it slows the display on your screen, especially while you navigate through your document.
	Online Layout	Displays your document as it would look as an HTML document.

Copyright © 2004 Wiley Publishing, Inc. All rights reserved.
Item 4222-2.
For more information about Wiley Publishing, call 1-800-762-2974.

For Dummies: Bestselling Book Series for Beginners

OpenOffice.org FOR DUMMIES®

by Ellen Finkelstein, Gurdy Leete, and Mary Leete

WILEY

Wiley Publishing, Inc.

OpenOffice.org For Dummies

Published by
Wiley Publishing, Inc.
111 River Street
Hoboken, NJ 07030-5774

Copyright © 2004 by Wiley Publishing, Inc., Indianapolis, Indiana

Published by Wiley Publishing, Inc., Indianapolis, Indiana

Published simultaneously in Canada

No part of this publication may be reproduced, stored in a retrieval system or transmitted in any form or by any means, electronic, mechanical, photocopying, recording, scanning or otherwise, except as permitted under Sections 107 or 108 of the 1976 United States Copyright Act, without either the prior written permission of the Publisher, or authorization through payment of the appropriate per-copy fee to the Copyright Clearance Center, 222 Rosewood Drive, Danvers, MA 01923, (978) 750-8400, fax (978) 646-8600. Requests to the Publisher for permission should be addressed to the Legal Department, Wiley Publishing, Inc., 10475 Crosspoint Blvd., Indianapolis, IN 46256, (317) 572-3447, fax (317) 572-4447, e-mail: permcoordinator@ wiley.com.

Trademarks: Wiley, the Wiley Publishing logo, For Dummies, the Dummies Man logo, A Reference for the Rest of Us!, The Dummies Way, Dummies Daily, The Fun and Easy Way, Dummies.com, and related trade dress are trademarks or registered trademarks of John Wiley & Sons, Inc. and/or its affiliates in the United States and other countries, and may not be used without written permission. All other trademarks are the property of their respective owners. Wiley Publishing, Inc., is not associated with any product or vendor mentioned in this book.

THE PUBLISHER AND THE AUTHOR MAKE NO REPRESENTATIONS OR WARRANTIES WITH RESPECT TO THE ACCURACY OR COMPLETENESS OF THE CONTENTS OF THIS WORK AND SPECIFICALLY DIS-CLAIM ALL WARRANTIES, INCLUDING WITHOUT LIMITATION WARRANTIES OF FITNESS FOR A PAR-TICULAR PURPOSE. NO WARRANTY MAY BE CREATED OR EXTENDED BY SALES OR PROMOTIONAL MATERIALS. THE ADVICE AND STRATEGIES CONTAINED HEREIN MAY NOT BE SUITABLE FOR EVERY SITUATION. THIS WORK IS SOLD WITH THE UNDERSTANDING THAT THE PUBLISHER IS NOT ENGAGED IN RENDERING LEGAL, ACCOUNTING, OR OTHER PROFESSIONAL SERVICES. IF PROFES-SIONAL ASSISTANCE IS REQUIRED, THE SERVICES OF A COMPETENT PROFESSIONAL PERSON SHOULD BE SOUGHT. NEITHER THE PUBLISHER NOR THE AUTHOR SHALL BE LIABLE FOR DAMAGES ARISING HEREFROM. THE FACT THAT AN ORGANIZATION OR WEBSITE IS REFERRED TO IN THIS WORK AS A CITATION AND/OR A POTENTIAL SOURCE OF FURTHER INFORMATION DOES NOT MEAN THAT THE AUTHOR OR THE PUBLISHER ENDORSES THE INFORMATION THE ORGANIZATION OR WEBSITE MAY PROVIDE OR RECOMMENDATIONS IT MAY MAKE. FURTHER, READERS SHOULD BE AWARE THAT INTERNET WEBSITES LISTED IN THIS WORK MAY HAVE CHANGED OR DISAPPEARED BETWEEN WHEN THIS WORK WAS WRITTEN AND WHEN IT IS READ.

For general information on our other products and services or to obtain technical support, please contact our Customer Care Department within the U.S. at 800-762-2974, outside the U.S. at 317-572-3993, or fax 317-572-4002.

Wiley also publishes its books in a variety of electronic formats. Some content that appears in print may not be available in electronic books.

Library of Congress Control Number: 2004100689

ISBN: 0-7645-4222-2

Manufactured in the United States of America

10 9 8 7 6 5 4 3 2 1

1B/RY/QS/QU/IN

WILEY

About the Authors

Ellen Finkelstein has written numerous best-selling computer books on AutoCAD, PowerPoint, and Flash. She consults on Web site and presentation content and organization, and maintains a Web site of free tips and tutorials at www.ellenfinkelstein.com. She works at home so that she can help her kids with their homework between paragraphs of her current book.

Gurdy Leete is an assistant professor of art and the director of the programs in digital media at Maharishi University of Management, where he has taught computer graphics and animation for the past 11 years. Gurdy has written extensively on computers, graphics and software. He is also an award-winning graphics software engineer, and is a coauthor of the Multitile plug-in for the free GNU image manipulation program, the GIMP. A selection of Gurdy's computer art is available for download under the terms of the free software license, the GNU GPL, from his Web site, www.infinityeverywhere.net.

Mary Leete has published widely on computers and other subjects. She has a masters degree in Professional Writing and has taught writing at the university level. She also has.a B.S. in computer science from Rutgers University and worked for several years as a database and spreadsheet programmer. Mary used OpenOffice.org exclusively to help design and build the Leetes' new home. She used Draw to create numerous plans, Calc for budgets and expense accounting, Writer for endless correspondence and Impress to give seminars on the joy of being your own contractor after it was all finished.

Dedication

To MMY, who showed us that life is a lot like open-source software — unrestricted.

Acknowledgments

We'd like to thank Terri Varveris who was our very competent acquisitions editor at Wiley. We feel very fortunate to be able to write this book and we appreciate her support. Thanks to Pat O'Brien, our project editor, for his careful review of the book and for keeping track of the numerous details that go into the production of any book. John Edwards did a thorough job of editing our text to make sure that everything we wrote was clear and consistent so that you wouldn't be confused. We'd also like to thank Tim Kampa, our technical editor.

Publisher's Acknowledgments

We're proud of this book; please send us your comments through our online registration form located at www.dummies.com/register/.

Some of the people who helped bring this book to market include the following:

Acquisitions, Editorial, and Media Development

Project Editor: Pat O'Brien

Acquisitions Editor: Terri Varveris

Copy Editor: John Edwards

Technical Editor: Tim Kampa

Editorial Manager: Kevin Kirschner

Media Development Specialist: Laura Moss

Media Development Manager: Laura VanWinkle

Media Development Supervisor: Richard Graves

Editorial Assistant: Amanda Foxworth

Cartoons: Rich Tennant (www.the5thwave.com)

Production

Project Coordinator: Courtney MacIntyre

Layout and Graphics: Seth Conley, Andrea Dahl, Stephanie D. Jumper, Michael Kruzil, Lynsey Osborn, Heather Ryan, Jacque Schneider

Proofreaders: John Greenough, Andy Hollandbeck, Paula Lowell, Carl William Pierce, Dwight Ramsey, Charles Spencer

Indexer: TECKBOOKS Production Services

Special Help
Andrea Dahl

Publishing and Editorial for Technology Dummies

> **Richard Swadley,** Vice President and Executive Group Publisher
>
> **Andy Cummings,** Vice President and Publisher
>
> **Mary C. Corder,** Editorial Director

Publishing for Consumer Dummies

> **Diane Graves Steele,** Vice President and Publisher
>
> **Joyce Pepple,** Acquisitions Director

Composition Services

> **Gerry Fahey,** Vice President of Production Services
>
> **Debbie Stailey,** Director of Composition Services

Contents at a Glance

Table of Contents

Introduction

● ●

*W*elcome to *OpenOffice.org For Dummies,* your friendly companion to the free office suite. In this book, we explain in plain English how to make the most of this feature-rich office suite. *OpenOffice.org For Dummies* aims to give you all the information you need to start using OpenOffice.org right away — with no hassle.

About This Book

As though you hadn't guessed, *OpenOffice.org For Dummies* covers the OpenOffice.org office suite of programs, including Writer (word processor), Calc (spreadsheet), and Impress (presentation program). We also explain how to use the HTML editor and Draw, the drawing program.

We comprehensively explain OpenOffice.org's features, including

- ✔ Switching to OpenOffice.org from other office suites
- ✔ Creating, editing, and formatting documents in Writer
- ✔ Creating form letters
- ✔ Working with graphics in all the OpenOffice.org applications
- ✔ Creating Web pages with the HTML editor
- ✔ Creating, editing, and formatting a spreadsheet in Calc
- ✔ Calculating and using functions
- ✔ Manipulating data
- ✔ Creating, editing, and formatting presentations in Impress
- ✔ Animating a presentation
- ✔ Creating graphics in Draw

How to Use This Book

You don't have to read this book from cover to cover. *OpenOffice.org For Dummies* provides just the information you need, when you need it. If you need the spreadsheet, start with Part III, "Using Calc — The Spreadsheet." If you need to draw something, go to Part V, "Using Draw — The Graphics Program." Read what you need and save the rest for later.

For extra information, don't pass up Part VI, "The Part of Tens," where we explain ten reasons to use OpenOffice.org and ten places to look for support. Our appendixes help you install and configure OpenOffice.org.

Keep *OpenOffice.org For Dummies* by your computer while you work. You'll find it to be a loyal helper.

Foolish Assumptions

We assume that you know at least a little about what a word processor, spreadsheet, and presentation program help you accomplish. We also assume that you know the operating system you use. We wrote this book to cover Windows, Linux, and the Mac OS, all at the same time. Talk about foolish! At any rate, we assume that you can get over any minor differences due to your operating system.

Conventions Used in This Book

Sometimes it helps to know why some text is bold and other is italic so that you can figure out what we're talking about. New terms are in *italics* to let you know that they're new. Messages and other text that come from OpenOffice.org are in a `special typeface, like this`.

When we say something like "Choose File⇨Save As," it means to click the File menu at the top of your screen and then choose Save As from the menu that opens. When we want you to use a toolbar or toolbox button (or tool), we tell you to click it or choose it.

How This Book Is Organized

We start by introducing you to OpenOffice.org and its environment. We also give you some tips about switching to OpenOffice.org from another office suite. Then we plunge right in and start telling you about each application.

To be more specific, this book is divided into six parts. Each part contains two or more chapters that relate to that part. Because some features of OpenOffice.org apply to all the applications, you may find more detail in the part on Writer, which comes early in the book. For example, we don't explain how to spell check three times; instead, we explain it once and then refer to the first mention later on.

Part 1: Introducing OpenOffice.org

Part I contains important introductory information about OpenOffice.org, including why it sounds like a Web site, why it's free, how to get it (it's on the CD-ROM that accompanies this book), how it looks, and what applications it includes.

Chapter 2 explains what OpenOffice.org can do for you at home and at work, how OpenOffice.org compares to the other office suites out there, and how to get help.

Part II: Using Writer — The Word Processor

Part II covers everything you need to know about Writer. Chapter 3 explains the basics of opening a document, laying out the page, entering and editing text, navigating through a document, changing views, spell checking, saving, and printing.

Chapter 4 goes more deeply into formatting, including how to use templates and styles, choosing fonts, setting up paragraphs, as well as adding numbered or bulleted lists. Chapter 5 covers how to create complex documents, including setting up personalized form letters (mail merge); adding borders, frames, and graphics; creating tables of contents and indexes; and dividing a page into columns or tables.

Chapter 6 explains how to add hyperlinks and track changes to documents when you collaborate with others. Chapter 7 covers the HTML editor that you use to create Web pages. There's an extra chapter on the CD-ROM with information on setting options, configuring preferences, and making macros.

Part III: Using Calc — The Spreadsheet

Part III covers the Calc application, which enables you to crunch all the numbers in your life. Chapter 8 explains how to input data, navigate around your huge spreadsheets, and save them for posterity. Chapter 9 explains how to select, move, and copy data as well as how to format your data. Chapter 10 is all about printing. Chapter 11 tells you how to make your data look good. Chapter 12 covers the details of calculating formulas and using Calc's built-in functions. On the CD-ROM, a bonus chapter explains how to use Calc to analyze data.

Part IV: Using Impress — The Presentation Package

Part IV explains how to create impressive impressions using Impress. Chapter 13 gives you the basics of creating a new presentation, using the various views, adding slides, and saving. Chapter 14 covers editing and formatting. Chapter 15 explains how to add images, create backgrounds, and work with 3-D effects. Chapter 16 is all about animation. Chapter 17 covers the process of delivering your slide show and printing. On the CD-ROM, a bonus chapter gives you some tips for setting up Impress.

Part V: Using Draw — The Graphics Program

Draw creates great graphics that you can use alone or insert into the other OpenOffice.org applications. Chapter 18 explains the basics of creating and editing shapes. On the CD-ROM, a bonus chapter explains layers, curves, fills, special effects, and 3-D.

Part VI: The Part of Tens

No *For Dummies* book is complete without its Part of Tens — it's a tradition! Chapter 19 gives you ten reasons to use OpenOffice.org, if you're not already convinced. Chapter 20 provides ten places to look for support, in addition to this book, of course.

Part VII: Appendixes

Last, but not least, we come to the appendixes. They add some valuable information to the end of this book, including instructions on installing and configuring OpenOffice.org.

About the CD-ROM

Don't forget to check out the CD-ROM. It contains OpenOffice.org for Windows, Linux and Mac OS X, so you don't have to go far to get it. We make it easy!

Icons Used in This Book

If you see little pictures in the margins, you have found an icon. Icons point out special information in the text and quickly let you know if you need to pay attention or can ignore it.

This icon alerts you to information that you need to keep in mind to avoid wasting time or falling on your face.

OpenOffice.org has some advanced features you may want to know about — or skip over entirely. This icon lets you know when we throw the heavier stuff at you.

Tips help you finish your work more easily, quickly, or effectively. Don't miss out on these.

Uh-oh! "Watch out here!" is what this icon is telling you, or else you never know what may happen.

Where to Go from Here

If you don't already have OpenOffice.org installed, get out the CD-ROM and install it. Complete instructions for your operating system are in Appendix A. Then open OpenOffice.org, turn to Chapter 1, and take the plunge.

Enough of all this talk. Let's move into the real content of this book and start using OpenOffice.org!

Enjoy!

Part I
Introducing
OpenOffice.org

In this part . . .

Part I introduces you to OpenOffice.org. If you're new to OpenOffice.org, read this part to understand the whole framework of open source software and how OpenOffice.org fits in (and where you fit in, too). This part explains what OpenOffice.org is, how to get started, and how you can use OpenOffice.org.

Chapter 1

Getting to Know OpenOffice.org

*O*penOffice.org is an exciting new Office suite program that is extremely powerful and completely free to everyone. It operates on Windows, Linux, Macintosh, and Solaris, and it can easily read and write a plethora of file formats, including Microsoft Office. It is currently available in more than 30 languages, and people all over the world are migrating to OpenOffice.org for their entire office suite needs. Over sixteen million people currently use the program, and the total is increasing daily!

You don't have to pay a single dime to use OpenOffice.org — either now or in the future! Sounds too good to be true? The more you learn about OpenOffice.org, the more fascinated you'll become.

What Is OpenOffice.org?

OpenOffice.org, the Office suite, includes the following four major applications:

- **Writer:** A full-featured word processor that also includes an HTML editor for designing Web pages
- **Calc:** An extremely capable spreadsheet program that also allows you to link to corporate databases
- **Draw:** An excellent drawing and graphics program for both 2-D and 3-D
- **Impress:** A very capable presentation program for creating electronic slide shows

As its name suggests, OpenOffice.org is also a Web site. The Web site, at www.openoffice.org, is the home of the project that creates, markets, and distributes the applications.

What is Writer?

What do you use your word processor for? Jotting down notes to yourself? Writing letters? Or publishing an entire book with style sheets, automated indexing and table of contents generation, as well as bibliographies? Whether your needs are large or small, Writer is up to the job. Figure 1-1 is an example of a Writer document. Look familiar? This book was written in OpenOffice.org.

Of course, Writer does all the basic things that word processors do, but it also allows you to do much more including:

- Design and create your own Web pages.
- Create forms for automatically inputting data into databases.
- Create personalized documents with Mail Merge, and link to your email address book or external database.

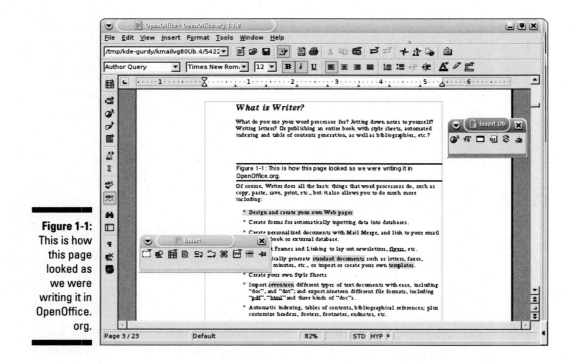

Figure 1-1: This is how this page looked as we were writing it in OpenOffice. org.

- Use Text Frames and Linking to lay out such documents as newsletters and flyers.
- Automatically generate standard documents such as letters, faxes, agendas, minutes, or import or create your own templates.
- Create your own Style Sheets.
- Import seventeen different types of text documents with ease, including "doc", and "dot"; and export nineteen different file formats, including "pdf", "html" and three kinds of "doc"s.
- Automatic indexing, tables of contents, bibliographical references; plus such details as custom headers, footers, footnotes, and endnotes.
- Track changes; compare documents, Automatic outlining, Spellchecking, and Thesaurus.
- Automatically correct words, or automatically complete words as you type. (This is all completely customizable, of course.)
- Insert Dynamic fields (such as date and time) and hyperlinks.
- Connect to email software.
- Create and use macros.

What is Calc?

Calc can calculate anything you hand it. It's a full-featured spreadsheet program with all the great bells and whistles you'd expect from the best. While Calc is super at doing all the basic spreadsheet things, such as adding, sorting, manipulating rows and columns, and inserting graphics, Calc also lets you do the following:

- Link to external databases, such as dBase and MySQL (or even your email address book) and view, query, sort, filter, generate automatic reports and more, as well as input data.
- Use an intuitive graphical interface to organize your data from your spreadsheets or database.
- Filter your spreadsheet or database data to locate information quickly.
- Use automatic subtotaling with outlining capabilities to give you instant information of the big picture, whenever you need it.
- Use any and all of 364 built-in functions for financial, mathematical, statistical, database and other purposes. Or create your own formulas.
- Use extensive formatting capabilities, including autoformatting, style sheets, graphical backgrounds, fancy borders, as well as conditional formatting.

- ✔ Freeze headings, create multiple sheets for a 3D spreadsheet, use split sheets, floating frames....
- ✔ Validate data (for example, require a specified format, such as a date).
- ✔ Save, print, and import and export a variety of formats (including your favorites).
- ✔ Generate 3-D charts, try out goal seeking, protect your documents, create macros, and lots more.

What is Impress?

Impress creates presentations (also known as slide shows) that you display from your computer, often with a projector, so that people can see what is on your screen. Each page of a presentation is called a *slide*. You add slides to a presentation and then add text and graphics to each slide. You also have all you need to create a masterful presentation. Impress allows you to do the following:

- ✔ Create a presentation quickly with AutoPilot or a template.
- ✔ Add notes to each slide that are just for the presenter.
- ✔ View your presentation in several ways using the Drawing, Outline, Slide, Notes, Handout, and Slide Show views.
- ✔ Save, print, and export and import in several formats (including your favorites).
- ✔ Format text characters and paragraphs.
- ✔ Create bulleted and numbered lists.
- ✔ Control the look of the presentation with a master slide.
- ✔ Insert graphics and control them using layers.
- ✔ Create your own graphics, including 3-D graphics.
- ✔ Add text animation and slide transitions.

What is Draw?

Draw is well integrated with the other OpenOffice.org programs but stands completely on its own as well. It's a great drawing program. Of course, it offers the basic drawing functions, such as the ability to automatically create lines, curves, circles, squares, 3-D spheres and more, but you can also use the following more advanced features with Draw:

- Customize your own glows, transparencies, gradients, bitmaps, or use ready-made gradients and import bitmaps.

- Use floating toolbars for easy access to create shapes, curves, lines, arrows, dimensional brackets, and more.

- Merge, subtract, intersect, rotate, and flip your graphics and otherwise modify them in many ways.

- Edit points to fine-tune curves and polygons.

- Cross-fade images for animated dissolves and morphing.

- Create text animation for livening up your Web pages or presentations.

- Use smart connectors to create flow-charts and organizational charts.

- Add shadows and 3D effects; create 3-D objects from 2-D objects. (Careful, this is addicting.)

- Add shading, texture, lighting, and materials to 3-D graphics; rotate 3-D objects in three dimensions.

- Use layers and groups.

- Import and export many formats, including SWF Flash Player format.

Why is OpenOffice.org free?

A few years ago, Sun Microsystems, Inc. noticed that it was paying Microsoft millions of dollars for the use of its software, and at the same time, Sun needed office tools for its Solaris operating system. Sun then bought a company called StarDivision, which had created an office suite that was competitive in features with Microsoft Office, with one important difference — the suite ran on GNU/Linux and Solaris operating systems as well as Windows. The product was called StarOffice.

Sun released the StarOffice programmers' source code as an open source program and called it OpenOffice. At the same time, Sun also sells StarOffice as a proprietary program, because some clients requested that Sun provide guarantees and support for the software. StarOffice adds a few proprietary features to OpenOffice, such as licensed templates, extra clip art, and the Adabas D database, along with 24-hour support from Sun, and Sun offers StarOffice at a reasonable price.

By making OpenOffice.org "Open Source", Sun generated a community of about 100,000 computer programmers and enthusiasts to create new features, improved documentation, and provide great support for the program — and all for free! Everyone is excited about OpenOffice.org and wants to be a part of this historic endeavor.

Everyone is welcome to participate in the project if you want. If you are a programmer, or even just an OpenOffice.org enthusiast, you might find helping out to be almost irresistible.

If you would like a new feature, you can go to OpenOffice.org, the Web site, and request it. If you're a programmer, you can even contribute a new feature of your own.

What is open source software?

In *open source software,* the source code of the software is freely available to users. If you are a programmer, you can use, modify, and redistribute the code. (The distribution part has a few rules.) You are encouraged to participate in the OpenOffice.org project (actually, one of its many projects) by contributing to the project — writing new code, issuing bug reports, writing documentation, and so on. (You don't need to be a programmer to contribute.) You can also join mailing lists to read about various aspects of the project on a regular basis.

The OpenOffice.org Web site shows you the many ways that you can contribute to the project and lets you know how to join one or more of the mailing lists.

OpenOffice.org, the organization, asks that all public communications use OpenOffice.org when referring to the suite of applications, even though simply using OpenOffice seems to make more sense. Leave it to the lawyers and trademark laws to complicate things, but that's okay, this way we can always remember where to go for our free upgrades and online support.

Can OpenOffice.org replace my current office suite?

With OpenOffice.org you can most likely do everything you currently do with your office suite, and maybe even lots more. You may find OpenOffice.org to be even more handy than your current Office suite. Users report that OpenOffice.org is extremely robust and can handle very large, complex documents with ease. And many users are fond of having their files take up 25 to 60 percent less space than that of the leading office suite. Also since OpenOffice.org is open source, any security holes are dealt with extremely quickly. Anyone in the OpenOffice.org community can find and fix any problem or potential problem in a flash! No waiting for one company to get around to it. This means it is much less likely that anyone could take over your computer from another location without your knowledge and consent through OpenOffice.org.

OpenOffice.org was created as a Microsoft Office clone, so Microsoft Office users generally experience little or no difficulty making the transition. However some situations do exist where it is not recommended that you switch to OpenOffice.org. They are as follows:

- ✔ If your business requires the Exchange Server capabilities of Microsoft Outlook, This feature allows you to have shared workspaces with other people on other computers. OpenOffice.org has no substitute for it — at least not on Windows or Mac.

- ✔ VBA macros written in Microsoft Office, as well as other macros from other office suites do not convert into OpenOffice.org and must be re-programmed. (It is estimated that this may affect five percent of office suite users.)

In other words, unless you are a power-user of another office suite with special needs, converting to OpenOffice.org should be no problem. Chapter 2 explains more about switching to OpenOffice.org.

To write this book with OpenOffice.org, we needed perfect compatibility with Microsoft Word, because the publisher automatically converts Word text and formatting into QuarkXPress to print the book that you are reading. We imported Wiley's custom Word template into OpenOffice.org and wrote the entire book in OpenOffice.org. We checked the document in Microsoft Word. Occasionally, we had to change the document formatting to match what the publisher wanted in Word. However, the actual text transferred perfectly from OpenOffice.org to Word.

Getting Started with OpenOffice.org

Most people who use OpenOffice.org download the program from the Web site of the same name. Other people get it from their friends. But you don't have to do either. The CD-ROM with the complete program for Windows, Mac, and Linux accompanies this book. Check out Appendix A for Installation Instructions.

If you need to go to Appendix A, go ahead. We'll wait for you. Then come back here to continue reading about opening and working in OpenOffice.org.

Once you have OpenOffice.org installed on your system, you are ready to open it and get to work!

To open OpenOffice.org, follow these steps:

- ✔ **Windows:** Choose Start⇨Programs (or All Programs)⇨OpenOffice 1.1, and then choose the application that you want from the submenu. For example, to open the word processor, choose Text Document.

- ✔ **Linux:** The procedure depends on the Linux distribution that you have.

Linux has several different desktop environments. If you are using KDE, then choose K➪OpenOffice.org 1.1.0 and then choose the application that you want from the submenu. If you are using Gnome, then choose Applications➪Office and then choose the application that you want from the submenu. Most Linux desktop environments have a relatively straight-forward way of finding OpenOffice.org.

✔ **Macintosh:** Navigate to the folder that contains OpenOffice.org (which should be called `OpenOffice.org1.0.1`), and double-click the Start OpenOffice.org icon to open a blank Writer document. To open another application, choose File➪New and choose the type of document that you want to open.

Of course, you can place an alias on your desktop and double-click that or drag the alias to your dock.

The first time you open OpenOffice.org, you see the OpenOffice.org Registration dialog box. To register, choose Register Now and click OK. The OpenOffice.org Web site opens, so that you can register.

Facing the Interface

Each application in OpenOffice.org has a somewhat different look, of course, but many features of the interface are common throughout the suite of applications.

In the following sections, we use Writer, the word processor, as an example. However, the principles apply to all the applications. For more details, refer to the parts of this book that explain the applications that you want to use.

Tooling through the toolbars

A *toolbar* is a bar of small buttons with pictures on them that you click to exe-cute commands or otherwise complete the task that you are working on. All applications have three commonly used toolbars: the Function Bar, Main tool-bar, and Object Bar, as shown in Figure 1-2. The toolbar buttons are shown on the Cheat Sheet at the front of this book.

The following sections describe OpenOffice.org's three main toolbars.

Function Bar

The Function Bar is the most similar toolbar across all the applications. This toolbar contains basic commands that apply to most types of tasks. You can find the toolbar at the top of the OpenOffice.org application window.

Main toolbar   Object bar   Function bar

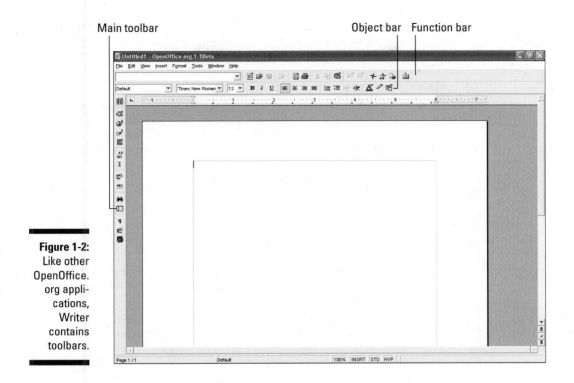

Figure 1-2:
Like other
OpenOffice.
org appli-
cations,
Writer
contains
toolbars.

When you open a window, such as Navigator, Stylist, Gallery, or Preview (in Impress), you can let it float on the desktop or you can *dock* it. The following points explain docking and undocking:

- ✔ To dock a window, press Ctrl and drag the window by its title bar to the right side of the application window.

  When docked, you can use the arrow icon in the window to collapse the window to a tiny bar that takes up little screen space. Click the arrow again when you need to see the window.

- ✔ To undock a window, use the same procedure (press Ctrl and drag the window by its top toolbar).

- ✔ You can also click the Pin icon in the window to change the window from floating to *stick* (docked).

Main toolbar

The Main toolbar resides along the left side of your screen and contains many often-used commands.

You can turn any fly-out toolbar into a floating toolbar. Click the Insert button on the Main toolbar and hold down the mouse button for a second. You can then drag the fly-out toolbar from its title bar to any location.

Object Bar

The Object Bar changes depending on the type of objects that you have in your document or have selected. In general, the Object Bar has tools for formatting objects. In Writer, you usually see the Text Object Bar, because you most often work with text in Writer. The purpose of the Text Object Bar is to help you format text. Other Object Bars have tools for formatting other types of objects, depending on the application that you are using and the object that you have selected.

Other toolbars

OpenOffice.org has the following additional toolbars:

- **Hyperlink Bar:** Use the Hyperlink Bar to search the Internet or edit existing hyperlinks. To display or hide the Hyperlink Bar, choose View⇨Toolbars⇨Hyperlink Bar.

- **Formula Bar:** Use the Formula Bar to create formulas in your documents. For example, you can create a table, enter numbers, and then add the numbers. To display or hide the Formula Bar, choose View⇨Toolbars⇨Formula Bar or press F2.

- **Status Bar:** The status bar at the bottom of the screen displays information about your current document. You can change your display zoom, change from insert to overwrite mode, and so on. If you have made changes to your document since you last saved, you see an asterisk on the status bar. You can display or hide the status bar by choosing View⇨Status Bar.

Working with toolbars

You can add buttons to or remove buttons from any toolbar so that you can more easily find the tools that you need quickly. The easiest way to add or remove buttons is to right-click the toolbar that you want to modify; then choose Visible Buttons from the submenu that appears. Figure 1-3 shows the menu's button options for the Text Object Bar in Writer. You can see, for example, that you could add buttons for line spacing.

You can add your own buttons and create your own toolbars. For more information about customizing toolbars, see the bonus Chapter on the CD-ROM, "Writer: Fine Tuning Your Preferences."

Using the menus

A few details may help make your menu experience more fruitful. The following menu items are standard across all the programs:

- ✔ **File:** Provides functions for the file as a whole, including open, save, print, export, AutoPilot, and templates

- ✔ **Edit:** Provides editing functions, including cut, copy, paste, undo, redo, AutoText, and Find & Replace

- ✔ **View:** Provides functions for viewing your document, including zoom, the ruler, toolbars, and nonprinting characters

- ✔ **Insert:** Inserts such items as page breaks, special characters, hyperlinks, headers, footers, tables of contents, indexes, tables, and graphics

- ✔ **Format:** Formats characters, paragraphs, and pages; adds numbering or bullets; changes case (as in uppercase or lowercase); and specifies styles (collections of formatting instructions)

- ✔ **Tools:** Provides Spellcheck, the thesaurus, hyphenation, AutoCorrect, the Gallery, data sources, mail merge, macros, and customization

- ✔ **Window:** Switches among open documents so that you can see what is in documents, copy data from one document to another, and so on

- ✔ **Help:** Get help!

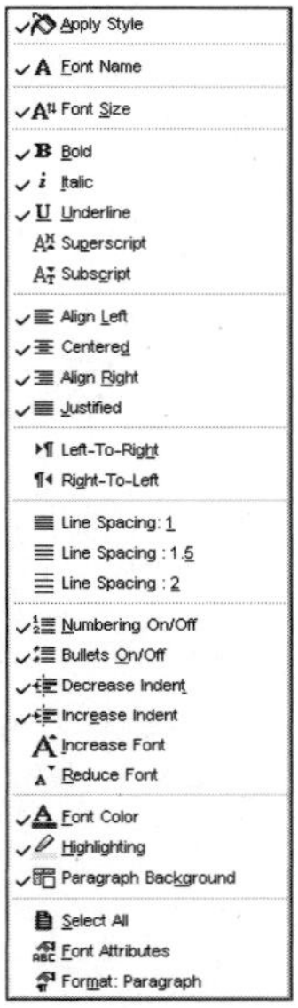

Figure 1-3:
You can add buttons to or remove buttons from toolbars by clicking one of the items on the Visible Buttons submenu.

Each major application has an additional menu, described as follows:

- Calc has a Data menu for sorting, filtering, and analyzing the data in your spreadsheet.
- Impress has a Slide Show menu for specifying how your presentation runs when you deliver it full-screen.
- Draw has a Modify menu for rotating, flipping, aligning, and otherwise changing your drawing objects.

When you open a menu, you can tell whether a menu item has a submenu, opens a dialog box, or simply executes a command, as shown in Figure 1-4.

Cutting it short with keyboard shortcuts

OpenOffice.org has a huge selection of keyboard shortcuts; you can also create your own shortcuts. Keyboard shortcuts are especially useful in Writer, where your hands are on the keyboard most of the time.

When you open a menu, you can see the keyboard shortcuts listed along the right side of the menu. For example, in Figure 1-4, you can see that pressing Ctrl+F10 toggles nonprinting characters on and off.

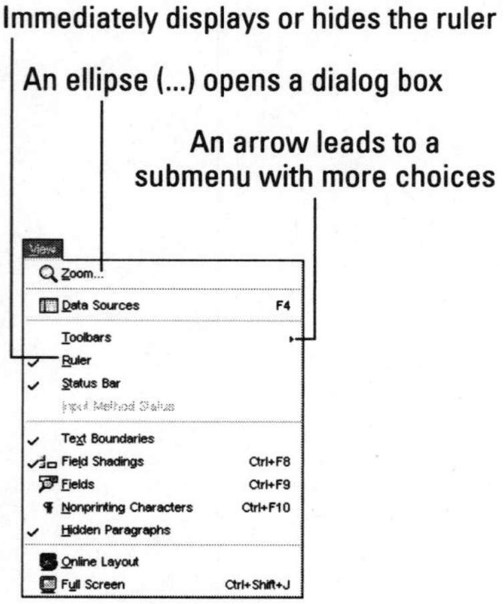

Immediately displays or hides the ruler

An ellipse (...) opens a dialog box

Figure 1-4:
A menu item can lead to a submenu with more choices, open a dialog box, or immediately execute a command.

An arrow leads to a submenu with more choices

View	
Q Zoom...	
Data Sources	F4
Toolbars	▸
Ruler	
Status Bar	
Input Method Status	
Text Boundaries	
Field Shadings	Ctrl+F8
Fields	Ctrl+F9
Nonprinting Characters	Ctrl+F10
Hidden Paragraphs	
Online Layout	
Full Screen	Ctrl+Shift+J

Closing OpenOffice.org

When you have finished creating a document, spreadsheet, or presentation, you can close OpenOffice.org. It will be waiting for you when you return.

To close OpenOffice.org, do one of the following:

- ✔ Choose File➪Exit.
- ✔ Press Ctrl+Q.
- ✔ Click the Close button at the upper-right corner of the window.

Chapter 2

Switching to OpenOffice.org

*1*f you are using another office suite — a set of programs that includes a word processor, spreadsheet, and probably a presentation program — how easy is it to switch to OpenOffice.org. Do you have to learn a whole new way of working? Does OpenOffice.org have as many features as Microsoft Office, WordPerfect Office, or StarOffice? Finally, if you have questions about how to accomplish a certain task, how do you get answers?

What OpenOffice.org Can Do for You

What does any office suite do for you? You need to write letters, reports, and memos. You have to crunch numbers for your budget or sales projections. You put it all into a presentation to show employees, prospective customers and investors, or colleagues. OpenOffice.org can do all this and more.

Using OpenOffice.org at home

Unfortunately, you often need to take work home from the office. Or, fortunately, you work at home all the time, but you need to e-mail documents, spreadsheets, and so on to others. Perhaps you just want an office suite for personal use at home. OpenOffice.org is a great option for home use because it's free and compatible with other office suites.

You can type letters to your friends and print and mail these letters. You can also send you letters via e-mail them to your friends. If your friends want a document in Microsoft Word format, for example, you can save it that way, and they can open it in Word. That's pretty flexible, isn't it?

If you take work home, you may have access to your company's intranet or database at home, e-mail documents to yourself as attachments, download documents from a company FTP site, or bring home floppy disks or burned CDs with the material that you need. In any event, you can access databases or open documents in a number of other formats, write and edit documents using OpenOffice.org, and then save the documents in the original format. No one will ever know that you didn't use Word, for example!

If the file you are importing has some advanced features listed later in this chapter, your document may open but look different than what you expect. Sometimes styles may change, or slight variations can occur which are easily fixed, or in the worst case, some information is lost or your files won't open at all — but that is very unlikely. (OpenOffice.org Calc, for example, has been reported to open Excel documents that even Excel couldn't read!)

In January 2003, ACM Queue (www.acmqueue.com) tested Microsoft Word, Excel, and PowerPoint files by opening them in other office suites. Out of 100 doc files collected at random from the internet, OpenOffice.org Writer opened 90 perfectly, 3 had minor differences, 4 had less minor but fixable differences, and 3 did not open at all — all were from older versions of Word. (Calc and Impress scored similarly). This test, however, was done using an earlier version of OpenOffice.org (version 1.0.1) and significant improvements have been made to the new version to improve its compatibility.

As a matter of fact, if you really want all your documents to be in Microsoft Word, Excel, and PowerPoint format, for example, you can set the default format of OpenOffice.org files to be the same as those that are used in Microsoft Office. That way, you never have to even think about multiple file formats.

Again, if you always work at home (lucky you!), you can open documents that people send you from other office suites and save documents in other formats that others can open.

In Chapter 3, we provide details about opening documents that were created in other formats, saving documents in other formats, and changing the default file format for OpenOffice.org.

Using OpenOffice.org at work

So you want to take the plunge and use OpenOffice.org at work. This may happen in one of the following situations:

- Your company lets you use whatever program you want (this is unlikely).
- You are the person that makes the software decisions for the entire company.

✔ Your board of directors has chosen to make OpenOffice.org the official
Office suite for your company.

✔ You *are* the company.

✔ You're the boss, and everyone has to do what you say.

Whatever the situation, you need everything to work properly and be compatible so that you don't drive your customers, suppliers, and employees
crazy. You also don't want to spend two hours writing a letter when you
could accomplish the task in one hour. You need advanced features such as
mail merge, graphics, tables, hyperlinks, and revision tracking.

As we explained in the previous section about using OpenOffice.org at home,
compatibility is a hallmark of this wonderful program. The techniques that we
described in that section, especially saving in another format, usually take care
of any problems.

Advanced features abound in OpenOffice.org. Word processing has been
around for a long time, and by now, programmers have a good idea of the features that people need. All the basics and most of the advanced features are
built right into OpenOffice.org. Sometimes you need to work a little differently, but that's what this book is for, after all — to explain how to use
OpenOffice.org.OpenOffice.org was created as a Microsoft Office clone, so
anyone migrating from Office will feel pretty comfortable right from the start.

As with any new software, if you are introducing OpenOffice.org to your
employees, some training is helpful and will be appreciated. You'll find many
small differences — sometimes they're improvements! — so people may need
some time to get up to speed.

Give employees this book to use as a reference.

Comparing OpenOffice.org to other office suites

Because interacting with other office suites is a fact of life and most people
have used another office suite before coming to OpenOffice.org, we often
need to compare OpenOffice.org to those office suites.

Such as comparison is useful for the following cases:

✔ Deciding whether you should make the switch

✔ Justifying a company switch, including preparing a cost/benefit analysis

✔ Understanding questions that you may have, such as why the mail
merge isn't working the way you expected it to

OpenOffice.org and Microsoft Office

Everyone knows that Microsoft Office is the heavy hitter among the office suites. Office boasts the vast majority of users and is the standard against which users usually compare another office suite. In the following tables, we compare OpenOffice.org with Microsoft Office XP.

The system requirements of OpenOffice.org compared to those of Microsoft Office XP are shown in Table 2-1.

Table 2-1	System Requirements	
Requirement	**OpenOffice.org**	**Microsoft Office XP**
Operating system	Windows 95 through XP, Linux, Solaris OE, Mac (with X11 installed)	Windows 98 through XP, Mac
RAM (memory)	64MB	128MB (varies with configuration)
Hard drive space	250–300MB	210MB (varies with configuration)

As you can see, OpenOffice.org gives you more operating system choices and requires less memory.

Even more important are the basic products that are included with OpenOffice.org, as shown in Table 2-2. In this table, we compare OpenOffice.org with Microsoft Office XP Professional, which includes the presentation program PowerPoint.

Table 2-2	Comparison of Products Included	
Product	**OpenOffice.org**	**Microsoft Office XP Professional**
Word processing	Yes	Yes
Spreadsheet	Yes	Yes
Presentation	Yes	Yes
Database	No	Yes (Access)
E-mail	No	Yes (Outlook)

Product	OpenOffice.org	Microsoft Office XP Professional
Calendar	No	Yes (Outlook)
Drawing	Yes	No
Image viewer	Yes	Yes
Formula creator	Yes	Yes
HTML editor	Yes	Professional Special Edition only

OpenOffice.org doesn't include a database program like Access or an e-mail/calendar program like Outlook. However, OpenOffice.org includes everything else that Office does. In fact, not all versions of Office include FrontPage, but OpenOffice.org has its own HTML editor. Also, OpenOffice.org has its own drawing program, unlike Microsoft Office.

We can't compare every possible feature or we wouldn't have any room left to tell you how to use the features — and which is more important? But Table 2-3 compares some important word processing features of OpenOffice.org Writer and Microsoft Word.

Table 2-3	Comparison of Word Processing Features	
Feature	Writer	Word
Customizable menus and toolbars	Yes	Yes
Shortcut keys	Yes	Yes
Tables	Yes	Yes
3-D effects	Yes	Yes
Revision tracking	Yes	Yes
Headers and footers	Yes	Yes
Tables of contents, indexes	Yes	Yes
Drawing tools	Yes	Yes
Mail merge	Yes	Yes
Macros	Yes (write only)	Yes (write and record)
Programmable	Yes	Yes

As you can see, the two programs are very comparable. We don't compare the spreadsheet features because they are both so similar. The presentation features are also very much alike, although OpenOffice.org has some different animation and transition effects, for example.

Although comparable programs in Microsoft Office and OpenOffice.org may be similar, many details are different. For example, Microsoft Office has AutoShapes, which are graphic objects that you can insert into your documents. OpenOffice.org has its own graphic shapes but doesn't specifically support Office's AutoShapes. Therefore, if you open an Office file that contains AutoShapes in OpenOffice.org, you may have trouble displaying these AutoShapes. In our AutoShapes test, we had good success opening and displaying Microsoft PowerPoint presentations in OpenOffice.org Impress, so you may not have any problems!

In most cases, you will have problems with compatibility between Office and OpenOffice.org only if the formatting is quite complex. Although, OpenOffice.org says that the following items may not appear or function correctly, we had excellent experience with most of these items:

- AutoShapes
- Revision marks
- OLE (embedded) objects
- Form fields
- Indexes
- Tables, frames, and columns
- Hyperlinks
- Bookmarks
- WordArt graphics
- Animated text
- PivotTables (Excel)

- New chart types
- Conditional formatting (Excel)
- Some functions and formulas (Excel)
- Background graphics (PowerPoint)
- Tab, line, and paragraph spacing
- Grouped objects
- Some multimedia effects (PowerPoint)

Microsoft Office and OpenOffice.org cannot run the same macros.

If you are ready to ditch Microsoft Office, use the OpenOffice.org Document Converter AutoPilot to convert all your Office files to OpenOffice.org files. Choose File➪AutoPilot➪Document Converter to open the Document Converter dialog box, as shown in Figure 2-1.

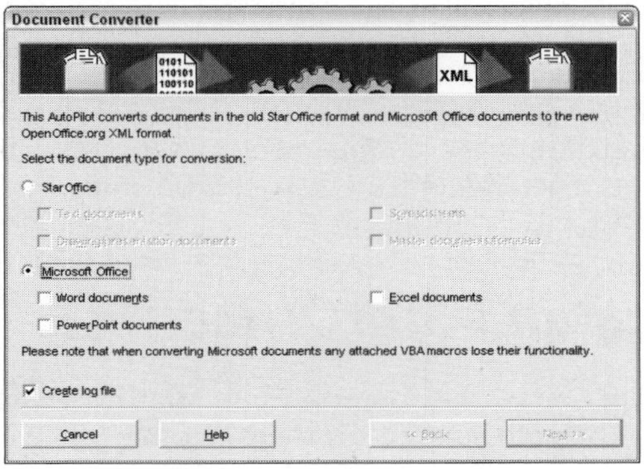

Figure 2-1:
The
Document
Converter is
an AutoPilot
(wizard) that
guides you
through the
process of
converting
your
Microsoft
Office
files to
OpenOffice.
org files.

Select the Microsoft Office option button and then choose which types of documents you want to convert. Then click Next. On the next screen, you can specify the folders that you want to include (you don't have to convert *all* your files) and where you want to save them. You can convert templates and regular application files.

You can specify the folder to be read and the folder where the converted files are to be saved. You can limit the conversion to specific file types, such as only Word files or only templates. You need to indicate the type of file and location for each of the Microsoft Office applications that you choose. The Document Converter confirms your choices. Click the Convert button to convert the files.

You may think that the Document Converter actually converts your Office files to OpenOffice.org files, but that's not true. Your original files remain as they are, and the Document Converter creates new files in the OpenOffice.org format. You don't have to worry about losing your original files!

Of course, you can open Microsoft Office documents in OpenOffice.org. However, converting documents first ensures a more perfect fit within OpenOffice.org.

OpenOffice.org and WordPerfect Office

How does OpenOffice.org compare to Corel WordPerfect Office? For the most part, because WordPerfect Office has so many features that are similar to

Microsoft Office, you can use the tables that we provided in the previous section. However, one important difference exists. As of this writing, you cannot open WordPerfect files in OpenOffice.org.

For word processing, you may find a workaround that exports WordPerfect files to XML or OpenOffice.org's `.sxw` format. Visit `http://libwpd.sourceforge.net/`, a Web site that contains resources for importing and exporting WordPerfect documents, and go to the Download page.

OpenOffice.org and StarOffice

StarOffice is an office suite that is distributed by Sun Microsystems. OpenOffice.org and StarOffice are sisters (brothers?). OpenOffice.org is the same program as StarOffice, with the following important differences:

- ✔ StarOffice costs $79.95, but OpenOffice.org can easily be obtained for free.

- ✔ OpenOffice.org is open source software. (We explain open source software in Chapter 1.) It is free software as defined by the Free Software Foundation in that users are free to run the program for any purpose, free to study and modify the program's source code, and free to redistribute modified or unmodified copies of the program, either gratis or for a fee, to anyone anywhere. Although StarOffice's code is mostly the same as OpenOffice.org's, the StarOffice code is not publicly available.

- ✔ Because OpenOffice.org is free software that can be widely redistributed for the public good, thousands of volunteers are attracted to developing it. StarOffice uses the code that's developed by these volunteers, but adds certain features using proprietary code that is not available in OpenOffice.org. Some of these features include a database program, additional Asian fonts, more templates and clip art, and more file filters. However, you can get some of these features by using third-party applications and resources. For more information on such OpenOffice.org resources, see Chapter 20.

Getting Help

If you have questions as you're using OpenOffice.org, the Help feature is always there for you. You can usually find what you're looking for with little difficulty. To start Help, choose Help➪Contents, as shown in Figure 2-2.

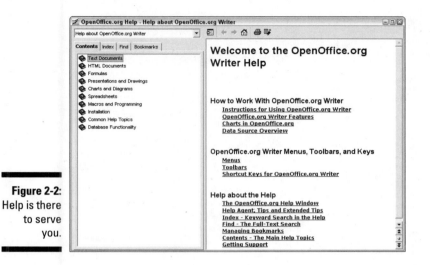

Figure 2-2:
Help is there
to serve
you.

The four tabs in the Help window help you find your answer easily. The Contents tab organizes help according to topics. The Index tab lists information alphabetically. Use the Find tab to search for keywords. When you find a page that you may want to refer to later, add it to the Bookmarks tab.

Using the Contents page

As you can see from Figure 2-2, you can use the Contents page to get help for any OpenOffice.org application. Once you decide which application you want, double-click the appropriate book icon on the left side of the page to display the list of topics for that application. Many topics have subtopics and sub-subtopics, so keep on double-clicking until you find what you want.

In Figure 2-3, you see the topic that discusses turning off the AutoCorrect function. You get to this topic by choosing the following path in the left side of the Contents page: Text Documents⇨Automatic Functions⇨Turning Off AutoFormat and AutoCorrect.

Just to confuse you, the Help system also contains another complete set of instructions. Choose the following path: Text Documents⇨General Information and User Interface Usage⇨Instructions for Using OpenOffice.org Writer. Here you see a long list of topics from which you can choose. You can probably find the answer you need from either set.

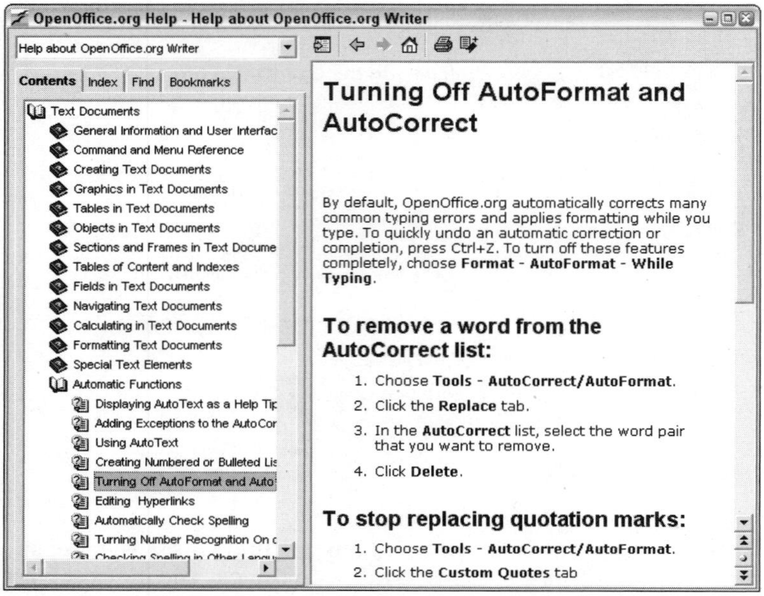

Figure 2-3:
This Help
page shows
you how to
toggle
AutoFormat
and
AutoCorrect
on and off.

At the bottom of many Help pages, you can find additional related topics that may be just what you are looking for, so always scroll down to the bottom of each page. You can also click on hyperlinked text for more information or to go to another Help page.

Finding information from the index

If you find it cumbersome to search through a list that's organized by topic, try using the Index tab. The index contains an alphabetical list of Help pages. Only the index items are actual topics. To get help on a particular topic, double-click the indented topic.

Searching

If you're really at a loss, try using the Find tab, where you can search for Help by entering keywords. Type a word or phrase in the Search Term text box, and press Enter. Double-click the topic that you want from the resulting list.

You cannot use Boolean search techniques that you use on the Web, such as AND or a plus sign.

Saving bookmarks

If you find a page that you think you may use again, bookmark it. From that point on, you can find the page quickly by clicking the Bookmarks tab, as shown in Figure 2-4.

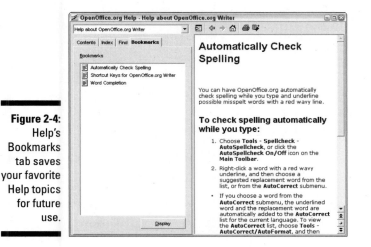

Figure 2-4:
Help's
Bookmarks
tab saves
your favorite
Help topics
for future
use.

To bookmark a topic, follow these steps:

1. **Display the topic.**

2. **Click the Add to Bookmarks button at the top of the Help page.**

   The Add to Bookmarks dialog box opens.

3. **To change the name of the bookmark to something that means more to you, type the new name in the Bookmark text box.**

4. **Click OK.**

When the Help topics can't answer your question, you can try visiting the OpenOffice.org Web site or asking a question on one of the discussion groups. For more information about online help, see Chapter 20.

Part II
Using Writer — The Word Processor

The 5th Wave

By Rich Tennant

"Unless there's a corrupt cell in our spreadsheet analysis concerning the importance of trunk space, this should be a big seller next year."

In this part . . .

Part II is all about processing — not food, but words. Writer doesn't mash up your words; instead it makes them look great. In any office suite, the word processor is the application that people use most, so you probably don't want to skip this part.

This part covers opening a document, entering and editing text, checking your spelling, printing, formatting, complex documents, and Web hyperlinks and HTML.

Chapter 3

Creating a Document

• •

• •

*W*riter is a full-featured word processor. It sounds like you're cooking something delicious — and in a way, you are. You can add ingredients (words) and then stir, whip, and flip them. Finally, you put them in the oven and out comes a fully printed document!

In this chapter, you find out how to create and edit Writer documents. All the basics are here, and everything else is like icing on the cake. If you've used another word processor, much of the material will be familiar. Skim through the chapter anyway. Writer has a few quirks and special features.

Opening a Document

You can't do anything in Writer until you have a *document* to work with. Writer files are called documents, because they document everything that you want to write. You can start with a spanking-new blank document, open a document that you have already created, or import a document.

Starting from scratch

When you open Writer, a new document awaits you automatically. You can simply start typing away without further ado. To create a new document while you're already in Writer, choose File➪New➪Text Document or click New on the Function Bar. This looks like a blank sheet of paper with a rectangle that represents your margins.

Writer formats new documents based on the default template. For more information on using templates to control the formatting of documents, see Chapter 4. Chapter 4 explains in detail how to format documents.

A vertical-line cursor is blinking patiently at you. This cursor represents the location where text appears when you start to type.

Using what you have

To open an existing document, choose File➪Open to display the Open dialog box, as shown in Figure 3-1. For faster access, click the Open button on the Function Bar or press Ctrl+O. In the Open dialog box, locate the file that you want and double-click it. The dialog box closes, and your document opens at its beginning. If necessary, use the scroll bars to move to another location. Later in this chapter, we explain how to quickly navigate through your document with ease and grace.

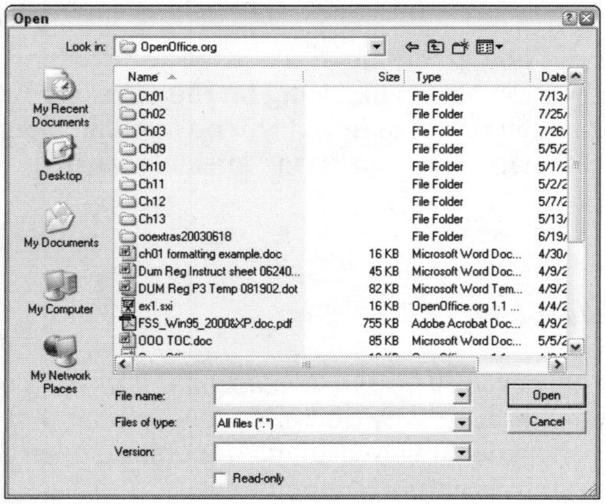

Figure 3-1:
Use the
Open dialog
box to open
existing
documents.

The discussion on the Open dialog box in this section is based on the Windows operating system. Other operating systems are either slightly or radically different! If you know your operating system fairly well, you won't have any trouble finding files in this dialog box.

You can use one of the buttons on the left side of the Open dialog box to help you find your file more easily. The Look in drop-down list displays the current folder or directory. Click this list to display all the folders (or directories) from the current folder back to the drive on which they are located. You can then choose another location to find your file.

The buttons at the top help you navigate as well. These buttons are as follows:

- ✔ **Back:** Click to return to the previous location (folder or directory). This button is only available after you first use some other method to navigate from one location to another.
- ✔ **Up One Level:** Moves you one folder or directory closer to the root directory of the drive.
- ✔ **Create New Folder:** Creates a new folder in the folder that's currently displayed in the Look in list box.
- ✔ **View Menu:** Choose a view from this drop-down list. You can choose to view a thumbnail image, tiles (large icons), icons (smaller than tiles), a simple list of filenames, or a detailed list of files.

Importing documents

You can open documents from any other format that OpenOffice.org accepts. Follow these steps to import a document:

1. **Choose File⇨Open (or use one of the shortcuts that was mentioned in the previous section).**
2. **In the Open dialog box, choose the format of the document from the Files of Type drop-down list.**
3. **Navigate to the file's location.**
4. **Double-click the file.**

Some of the more common formats that OpenOffice.org can import are as follows:

- ✔ Microsoft Word 97/2000/XP (.doc)
- ✔ Microsoft Word 97/2000/XP template (.dot)

✔ Rich Text Format (.rtf)

✔ Text/Text Encoded (.txt)

✔ HTML document (.html, .htm)

✔ DocBook (simplified) (.xml)

✔ Flat XML (.xml)

✔ Microsoft Word 2003 XML (.xml)

✔ StarWriter 1.0 (.sdw)

✔ StarWriter 2.0 (.sdw)

✔ StartWriter DOS (.txt)

If your format is not on the list, you may create one of these formats in your application. For example, maybe you can save your document in .txt, .rtf, or .html format and then import it. (You may lose some of the formatting. In .txt format, you lose all the formatting.)

When you install OpenOffice.org, you can choose whether you want OpenOffice.org to open various types of files. If you say yes, you can also double-click any appropriate file to open it in OpenOffice.org. For example, you can then double-click a .doc file, and that file opens in OpenOffice.org. However, if you said no, when you double-click a .doc file, Word opens (assuming that you still have Word on your computer). So in this case, you first need to open OpenOffice.org and then open the .doc file as described in the previous steps.

If you chose not to use OpenOffice.org to open .doc files when you installed OpenOffice.org, you can change this option by following these steps:

1. **Exit OpenOffice.org.**

2. **Start the OpenOffice.org Setup program, using the same procedure that you used originally. (The procedure depends on your operating system.)**

   The Setup window opens.

3. **Select the Modify option button, and click Next.**

4. **Select the Modify option button again.**

5. **Choose the file types that you want to open in OpenOffice.org.**

6. **Click OK.**

7. **Continue through the Setup program to finalize your changes.**

Laying Out the Page

Before typing too much of your word document, you should lay out the page. *Laying out* a page means setting its size, margins, and *orientation* (whether the page is oriented upright like a portrait or on its side like a landscape). You can also create headers and footers, and you can number pages. When you set up a page early in the game (isn't typing just a game?), you get an accurate idea of how the final document will look when printed.

Some types of layouts, such as tables, columns, and borders, are used only in more complex documents. We discuss these layout elements in Chapter 5.

Setting paper size, margins, and orientation

The paper size specifies the paper's size and type, of course. The margins decide how much white space you have around the edges of your text. The orientation determines whether the narrow or the wide edge of your paper is on top. To change paper size, margins, and orientation, choose Format⇨Page to open the Page Style dialog box, as shown in Figure 3-2 with the Page tab displayed.

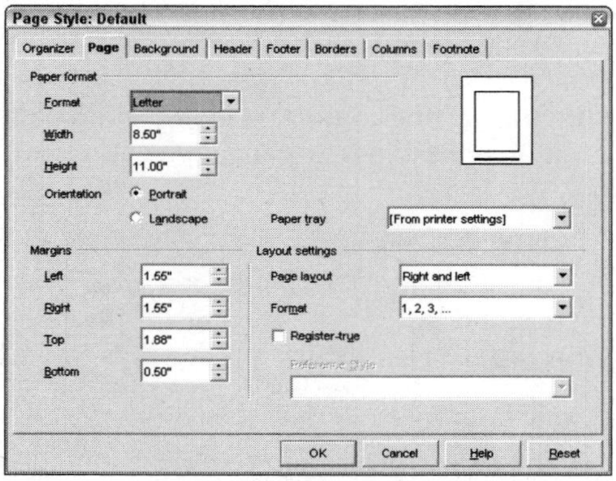

Figure 3-2: The Page Style dialog box offers many options for formatting your Writer pages.

The dialog box in Figure 3-2 is called Page Style: Default because the current page uses the default page style. Chapter 4 explains styles in more detail.

Paper size and orientation

Use the Paper Format panel of the Page Style dialog box to specify the page size and orientation. From the Format drop-down list, choose the paper type, which generally means the paper size, although you can also choose various envelope sizes. The default paper type is Letter, which is standard 8½×11-inch paper. When you choose a paper type, the dimensions automatically adjust.

Next, you define the exact paper size. The default is that same 8½×11-inch paper, so most of the time, you don't have to change anything. To change the paper size, type new dimensions in the Width and Height list boxes or click the arrow keys in the list boxes to change the dimensions.

You can create custom paper sizes. In fact, if you change the dimensions to something unusual, the paper type automatically changes to User. Don't forget to put your special paper in the printer. If you choose an envelope type, put the envelopes in your printer. Your printer usually comes with instructions to let you know the proper direction for inserting envelopes.

Choose Portrait (the narrow edge is on top) or Landscape (the wide edge is on top) to set the orientation. The image of the paper changes accordingly so that you can be sure that you made the right choice. You can also choose the paper tray that the printer uses, if your printer offers these options.

Margins

In the Margins panel of the Page Style dialog box, you set the left, right, top, and bottom margins. You can type a number or click the arrow keys in the list boxes to increase or decrease the current setting.

Specify whether to apply the formatting to odd pages, to even pages, or to both odd and even pages that use the current page style.

Layout settings

In the Layout Settings panel of the Page Style dialog box, you specify settings that determine how the page is laid out. These settings apply to all the other formatting settings and allow you to apply different settings to odd and even pages. In the Page Layout drop-down list box, you have the following options:

- **Right and left:** Applies the same formatting to both even and odd pages.

- **Mirrored:** Mirrors the formatting. For example, if you have a larger left margin on the first page to leave room for binding, the second page will have a larger right margin. The margin settings change from left and right to outer and inner.

- **Only right:** Applies the formatting only to odd pages.

- **Only left:** Applies the formatting only to even pages.

The Format drop-down list applies to page numbering, which we explain in later in this chapter.

Select the Register-true check box if you want to make sure that lines of text on each page are at the same vertical position on the page. You may use this feature if you want to create a two-page spread and you need text on both pages to line up. Then choose a paragraph style to specify the size of the text that OpenOffice.org uses to calculate the text line heights. Chapter 4 explains styles in detail.

When you're done specifying the settings for the Page Style dialog box, click OK to return to your document.

Creating headers and footers

You can create headers and footers for your pages. The most common use for headers and footers is to insert page numbers, which we explain in more detail in the next section. However, you can insert any text that you want.

To create a header or footer, follow these steps:

1. **Choose Format⇨Page to open the Page Style dialog box.**

2. **Click the Header tab or the Footer tab.**

   The Footer tab is shown in Figure 3-3. The Header and Footer tabs are sort of like Tweedledum and Tweedledee — they are identical except that one creates headers and the other creates footers.

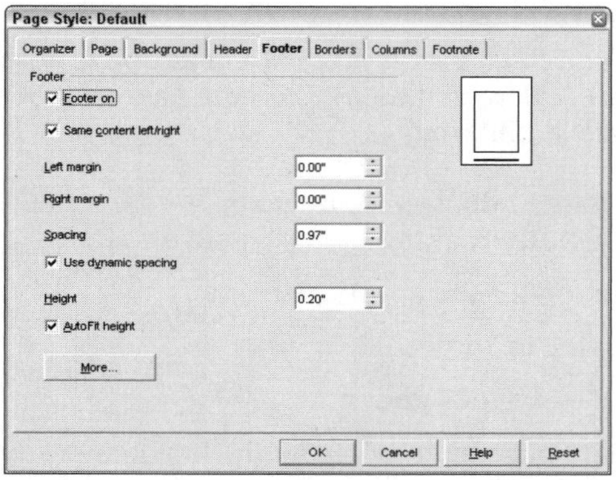

Figure 3-3:
Create headers and footers with the Headers tab and the Footers tab in the Page Style dialog box.

3. **Select the Header on check box or the Footer on check box.**

   To turn off a header or footer, deselect the check boxes.

4. **Specify the rest of the settings for the header or footer as follows:**

   - **Same content left/right:** Inserts the same header or footer content on both even and odd pages

   - **Left margin:** Sets the left margin between the page and the header or footer

   - **Right margin:** Sets the right margin between the page and the header or footer

   - **Spacing:** Sets the space between the top or bottom of the page text and the header or footer

   - **Use dynamic spacing:** Allows the header or footer to expand toward the text, overriding the spacing setting

   - **Height:** Sets the height of the header or footer

   - **AutoFit Height:** Adjusts the height of the header or footer according to the amount of text that the header or footer contains

5. **Click OK to return to your document.**

   You can now see the header or footer in your document.

6. **Click inside the header or footer, and enter the text that you want to place there.**

You can use headers and footers to insert automatically calculated fields, such as page numbers and today's date. See the next section for information on numbering pages. Chapter 5 explains how to insert other fields.

Numbering pages

The most common use for a header or footer is to insert page numbers. OpenOffice.org uses *fields* (calculated data) to create page numbers. Follow these steps to perfect page numbering:

1. **To place page numbers at the top of the page, create a header. For page numbers at the bottom of the page, create a footer.**

   See the previous section for the appropriate steps.

2. **Click inside the header or footer.**

3. **Choose Insert⇨Fields⇨Page Number.**

   OpenOffice.org inserts page numbers in all the headers or footers.

4. **To move the page number (left-align, right-align, or center it), select a page number.**

   Any page number will do. You don't have to (and can't) select them all.

5. **Choose the desired alignment on the Object Bar.**

   Choose Align Left for a left-aligned page number, Centered for a centered page number, or Align Right for a right-aligned page number.

You now have page numbers throughout your document. We explain more about aligning text in Chapter 4.

Entering and Editing Text

Once you have your page all laid out and set up, you are ready to start creating your document. If you've used other word processors before, this is child's play and you can just skim the next sections. If you're starting from scratch, read the next sections carefully.

Starting to say something

When you start a new document, you can just start typing. All text appears at the vertical blinking cursor. As you type, you may notice that the text automatically wraps to the next line when you reach the right margin. You don't need to press Enter unless you want to create a new paragraph.

Pressing Enter twice is a quick way to create a blank line between paragraphs. A cleaner way to work is to create a style that automatically crates this blank line when you press Enter once. See Chapter 4 for more information on styles. If you think your text looks boring, Chapter 4 also explains how to format your text so that it doesn't all look the same.

If you're in a hurry and make some mistakes, you may also see OpenOffice.org automatically correct the mistakes. We explain how this works later in this chapter. For now, enjoy the fact that OpenOffice.org is taking good care of you and trying to prevent you from making unnecessary errors.

Being selective

Without a doubt, before too long, you need to change something that you have typed. Editing is an integral part of the document-creation process. Before you can edit, you need to tell OpenOffice.org what to change; you do that by *selecting* the text. OpenOffice.org *highlights* selected text, as shown in Figure 3-4. Once you select text, you can make many changes to it — all you have to do is choose.

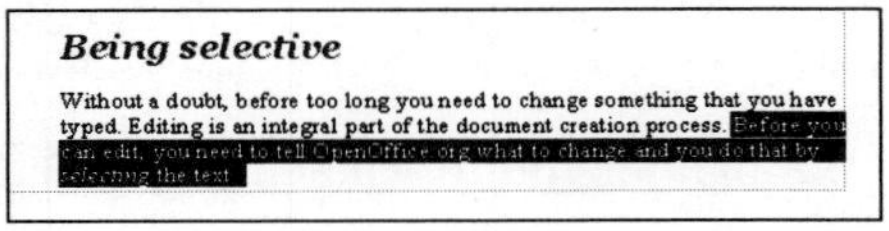

Figure 3-4:
Select the
text that you
want to edit,
and then
edit it.

> **Being selective**
>
> Without a doubt, before too long you need to change something that you have typed. Editing is an integral part of the document creation process. Before you can edit, you need to tell OpenOffice.org what to change and you do that by selecting the text.

Although you see the vertical cursor where typing appears, notice that another cursor, the *I-beam cursor,* shows you your mouse location. Move the mouse and you see the I-beam cursor move accordingly. The basic technique for selecting text is to use the mouse: Click where you want to start selecting and drag across the text. The I-beam cursor shows you where to start and stop dragging. If you drag to the left or right, you select along the same line of text. If you drag up or down, you add additional lines of text to the selection. Stop dragging when all the text that you want to change is highlighted.

To *drag* means to hold the mouse button down as you move the mouse.

The mouse shortcuts can make short work of selecting:

- **Select a word:** Double-click the word
- **Select a line of text:** Triple-click the line
- **Select the entire document:** Choose Edit⇨Select All (or press Ctrl+A)

If you like using the keyboard, use the following keyboard shortcuts to select text:

- **Select a word:** Press Shift+Ctrl+→
- **Select from the cursor to the end of the line:** Press Shift+End
- **Select from the cursor to the beginning of the line:** Press Shift+Home
- **Select from the cursor to one line up:** Press Shift+↑
- **Select from the cursor to one line down:** Press Shift+↓

When you have selected the text, you are ready to move it, copy it, and format it.

Modifying text

To change some text, select it and type the new text. Whatever you type replaces selected text. To insert text, you can also place the I-beam cursor where you want to add text and type. By default, the new text that you type appears at the cursor, and existing text politely moves over to the right. This behavior is called *Insert* mode because the new text is inserted in front of the existing text. If you instead want existing text to be overwritten, change to Overwrite mode. To change to Overwrite mode, press Insert or click the Insert button on the status bar. (If you don't see the status bar, choose View⇨Status Bar to make it appear.) The Insert key is used to toggle between Insert and Overwrite mode.

You should probably use Insert mode for most of your work. If you accidentally press Insert, you find that all your existing text is nuked as you try to insert text.

If you make a mistake, whether while typing or editing, you can undo your last action. Click the Undo button on the Function Bar, choose Edit⇨Undo, or press Ctrl+Z. To undo several previous actions, click the Undo button's down arrow and choose the actions that you want to undo. To redo an action you have undone, click the Redo button, choose Edit⇨Redo, or press Ctrl+Y.

Moving and copying text

If you think your logic isn't quite right, you can move some text to a different location. If you think you got a sentence just right, why not copy it and use it again somewhere else in the document? Moving and copying text are common tasks, so you need to know all about these capabilities.

You can move and copy text in the following two ways:

- ✔ **Drag and drop:** This method uses the mouse to move or copy text. To move text, select the text and drag it to a new location. To copy text, press Ctrl as you drag the text. Use drag and drop when you can see both the original location and the destination on-screen at the same time.

    From other word processing programs, you may expect an arrow cursor when you point to selected text. You won't find this cursor in OpenOffice.org. However, just click and drag in the same way that you're used to, and the text moves.

- ✔ **Cut, Copy, and Paste:** You use the clipboard to move or copy text. To move text, first select the text and choose Edit⇨Cut. To copy text, first choose Edit⇨Copy. To place the text, click at the desired location and choose Edit⇨Paste. Use this method when the original location and the destination are not both visible on-screen. You can also use this method to move or copy text from document to document or even across applications.

Cut, copy, and paste also have toolbar and keyboard shortcuts, as follows:

- **Cut:** Click the Cut button on the Function Bar or press Ctrl+X.
- **Copy:** Click the Copy button on the Function Bar or press Ctrl+C.
- **Paste:** Click the Paste button on the Function Bar or press Ctrl+V.

Finding and replacing text

Sometimes you need to change a certain word in many places. For example, you may want to reuse a document that you created for one client for another client by substituting the new client's name each time the name appears. Or, you may want to change a word but can't easily locate it. The Find and Replace feature comes to the rescue! You can simply find a word or use the Replace feature to automate changing the word. To find or replace text, choose Edit➪Find & Replace to open the Find & Replace dialog box, as shown in Figure 3-5.

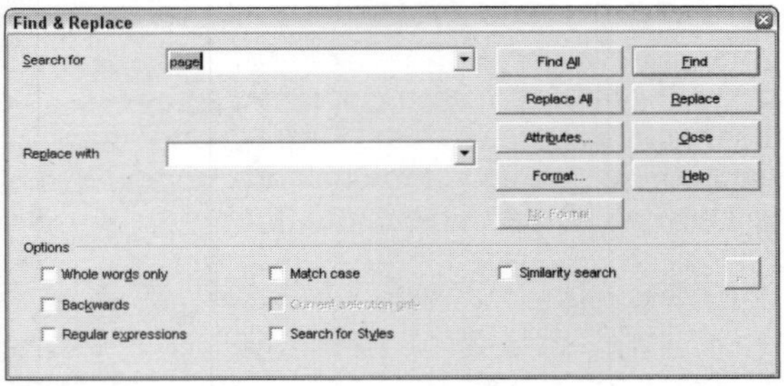

Figure 3-5:
The Find & Replace dialog box helps you find what you have lost.

Enter the text that you want to find in the Search for list box. To just find the next instance of the text, click the Find button. To select all the instances of the text, click the Find All button. You can then click the scroll bar and scroll through the entire document — each instance of the text is highlighted.

To replace text, enter the new text that you want in the Replace with list box. The careful way to work is to move to the next instance using the Find button and then click the Replace button to replace just that instance. If you're feeling sure of yourself, you can click the Replace All button to replace all instances of the text.

Use the Options panel of the dialog box to specify whole words (so that you don't get *band* if you only want *and*), to match the case (to find only *House* but not *house*), or to search backward. You can also select the Search for

Styles check box to search for text in a specific text style. (Chapter 4 explains text styles.) Click the Format button to search for text using specified formatting. For example, you can search for text in a particular font.

The Regular Expressions option enables you to fine-tune your search. For example, you can use wildcard characters, find only text at the beginning or end of a paragraph, and so on. Click the Help button in the Find & Replace dialog box, and look for the List of Regular Expressions link under the Regular Expressions heading.

When you have finished finding and replacing, click the Close button to return to your document.

Correcting mistakes automatically

For some sophisticated editing, try the AutoCorrect feature, which lets you correct commonly misspelled words automatically. You can also use AutoCorrect to create typing shortcuts. Do you think we typed **OpenOffice.org** each time it appears in this book? Certainly not! Instead, we created an AutoCorrect entry so that when we typed **ooo**, Writer instantly inserted OpenOffice.org. We saved countless seconds that way! You need to save seconds, too, so read on.

To create an AutoCorrect entry, follow these steps:

1. **Choose Tools⇨AutoCorrect/AutoFormat.**

   The AutoCorrect dialog box opens.

2. **Click the Replace tab, as shown in Figure 3-6.**

   You see two columns, Replace and With, including a long list of existing entries. Before adding an entry, check that it doesn't already exist.

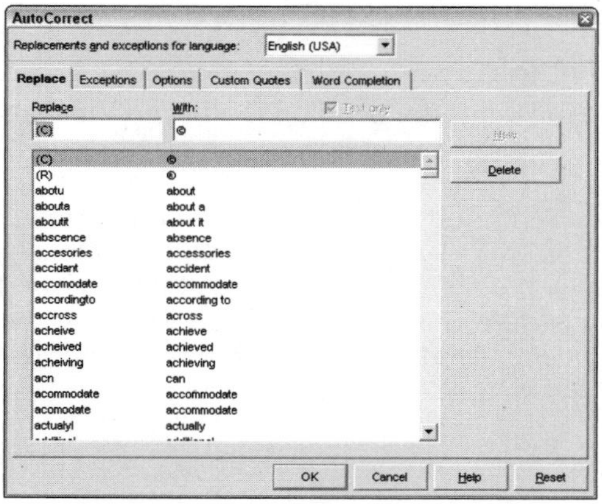

Figure 3-6: The AutoCorrect entries are on the Replace tab in the AutoCorrect dialog box.

3. To add an entry, enter the spelling to replace in the Replace text box.

If you clicked an existing entry, you see it in the Replace and With text boxes. You can simply select this entry and type your new one — this action doesn't delete the existing entry. Suppose that you often type **dialog** as **dilaog** (we're confessing). In this case, you would type **dilaog** in the Replace text box.

If you are using AutoCorrect to create a shortcut, make sure that you won't use the shortcut in another context, and keep it as short as possible. As we just mentioned, we type **ooo** to get OpenOffice.org. It's easy to type, and we won't use it for anything else. Perhaps we could have even used **oo**.

4. Enter the correct spelling in the With text box.

5. Click the New button.

To add another entry, repeat Steps 3 through 5.

6. When you're done, click OK to close the dialog box.

(Is the word *dialog* in the previous sentence misspelled? No. So AutoCorrect must have worked!)

As you type, OpenOffice.org automatically corrects incorrectly spelled items when you press the spacebar after the word or add a period.

Setting AutoCorrect options

Click the Options tab in the AutoCorrect dialog box to set a whole slew of options that change your text in one way or another. The first option relates to the Replace tab. If you deselect the Use Replacement Table check box, OpenOffice.org ignores the entries that are on the Replace tab.

The next two items on the Options tab correct two initial capital letters and capitalize the first letter of a sentence. Read the list and decide which options you want. Some are pretty annoying; you may find others helpful.

Making exceptions to the rule

You can make exceptions to two of the rules on the Exceptions tab in the AutoCorrect dialog box:

✔ **Abbreviations:** The rule on the Options tab that capitalizes the first letter of a sentence determines when a new sentence starts by the existence of a period. But what if you are typing an abbreviation (that ends with a period) in the middle of a sentence? The word after the abbreviation is automatically capitalized. You take care of this problem by listing common abbreviations so that OpenOffice.org knows not to start the next word with a capital letter. OpenOffice.org comes with a long list of common abbreviations. To add your own, enter the abbreviation and click the New button.

If you type an abbreviation that's not on the exceptions list and OpenOffice.org capitalizes the first letter of the next word, you can just select the capital letter and retype it as a lowercase letter.

✔ **Words with Two Initial Capitals:** The rule on the Options tab that corrects two initial capital letters in a word can be pretty frustrating if you use certain terms that are supposed to be that way. OpenOffice.org comes with a few examples, such as PCs and CDs. You can add your own terms so that OpenOffice.org doesn't correct what you don't want it to correct.

Using AutoText

The AutoText feature provides another way to create shortcuts to phrases that you use often. We prefer AutoCorrect because it is easier to use, but you can try both and judge for yourself.

One great advantage of AutoText is that you can use it to insert graphics, tables, and other objects.

To create AutoText, follow these steps:

1. **Type the full version of the text, and select it in your document.**

2. **Choose Edit⇨AutoText.**

   The AutoText dialog box opens.

3. **In the Name text box, enter a name for the shortcut.**

   This name can be anything that you can recognize if you read through the list of AutoText entries.

4. **In the Shortcut text box, enter your shortcut.**

   Notice that OpenOffice.org has suggested a shortcut for you. You can use that one or make up another one. Keep it short!

5. **Choose AutoText⇨New or AutoText⇨New (text only).**

   Use the Text Only option to ignore any selected graphics.

6. **Click the Close button to return to your document.**

To use AutoText, type the shortcut and then press F3 to change the shortcut to the longer version.

Putting words in your mouth with Word Completion

Did you notice that OpenOffice.org tries to complete your words as you type? Does this drive you crazy? One of the first things that we do when we install OpenOffice.org is to get rid of this feature. Being helpful can go too far.

To get rid of the Word Completion feature, follow these steps:

1. **Click the Word Completion tab in the AutoCorrect dialog box.**
2. **Deselect the Enable Word Completion check box.**
3. **Click the OK button.**

   Whew!

If you like Word Completion, you can refine it by limiting the number of words that it collects (remembers) or by telling OpenOffice.org not to collect words. You can also set the minimum word length.

Making it go away

Wrote too much? Deleting words is easy. Select the text and press Delete or Backspace. If you cut text to the clipboard, as explained earlier in this chapter, and never paste it, you effectively delete the text.

Navigating Through Your Document

We know that you have a lot to say, so your documents can get quite long. After a while, the typical scrolling method may get tedious. A few speedy navigation techniques would be helpful! We provide mouse and keyboard techniques and explain the Navigator panel, which is especially helpful for finding your way through long documents.

Hiking with your mouse

The most common way to navigate is with the mouse using the scroll bars. You may be surprised to know that the scroll bars have a few tricks and can be quite efficient. Use the following scroll bar items to increase your productivity:

✔ **Click the Up arrow:** Moves the display up one line.

✔ **Click the Down arrow:** Moves the display down one line.

✔ **Click the Double Up arrow:** Moves the display up one page, that is, to the top of the previous page.

✔ **Click the Double Down arrow:** Moves the display down one page, that is, to the top of the next page.

✔ **Click the space between the scroll box and the Up arrow:** Moves the display up one screen (displays the preceding screen of your document). You can quickly scan an entire document by using this method, and you won't miss a thing.

✔ **Click the space between the scroll box and the Down arrow:** Moves the display down one screen (displays the next screen of your document).

✔ **Drag the scroll box up or down:** Scrolls you through the document.

For longer documents, you can create *bookmarks.* A bookmark is simply a saved location in a document. You can then go to any bookmark. To create a bookmark, follow these steps:

1. **Place the cursor where you want the bookmark.**

2. **Choose Insert⇨Bookmark.**

   The Insert Bookmark dialog box opens, as shown in Figure 3-7.

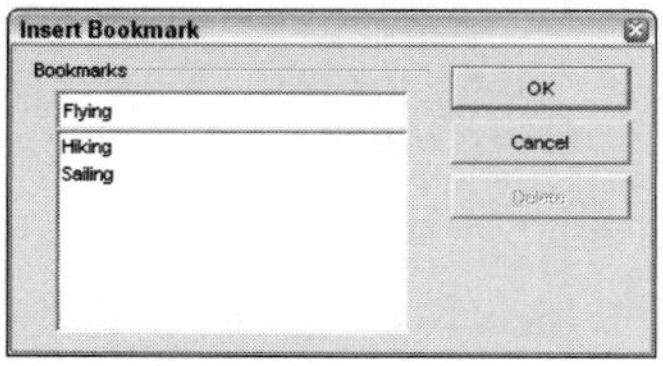

Figure 3-7:
Create bookmarks so that you can easily return to a place in your document.

3. **Type a name for the bookmark in the top text box.**

4. **Click OK.**

You cannot use the following characters in a bookmark name: / (slash), \ (backslash), @ (at sign), : (colon), * (asterisk), ? (question mark), " (double quotation mark), ; (semicolon) , (comma), . (period), and # (pound sign).

To use your bookmark, right-click the page listing at the left end of the status bar. All your bookmarks pop up. Click the one that you want. You can also use the Navigator and the Navigation floating toolbar to find bookmarks, as discussed later in this chapter.

Sailing with the keyboard

The keyboard offers a number of shortcuts for navigating through a document. These shortcuts are very useful and precise, and you don't need to leave them for the occasional emergency when your mouse isn't working. The shortcuts are as follows:

- **Left-/right-arrow key:** Moves the cursor one character to the left or right. Press Ctrl+→ or Ctrl+← to move one word to the left or right.

- **Up-/down-arrow key:** Moves the cursor one line up or down.

- **Home/End:** Moves the cursor to the beginning/end of the line. Press Ctrl+Home/End to move to the beginning/end of the document.

- **Page Up/Page Down:** Moves the cursor up or down one screen. The display changes only if necessary. Press Ctrl+Page Up or Ctrl+Page Down to move to the header or footer.

Try out these shortcuts, and you'll soon be moving around like a pro.

Flying with the Navigator

You can walk, you can run, and you can fly. The Navigator panel and Navigation floating toolbar help you fly through long documents. You can quickly go to any of the following items:

- Headings
- Tables
- Graphics
- OLE (embedded) objects
- Bookmarks
- Sections
- Hyperlinks

> ✔ References
> ✔ Indexes
> ✔ Notes
> ✔ Draw objects

The Navigator panel, shown in Figure 3-8, is larger and a little easier to use than the Navigation toolbar. To open the Navigator, choose Edit➪Navigator. You can also click the Navigator button on the Function Bar or press F5.

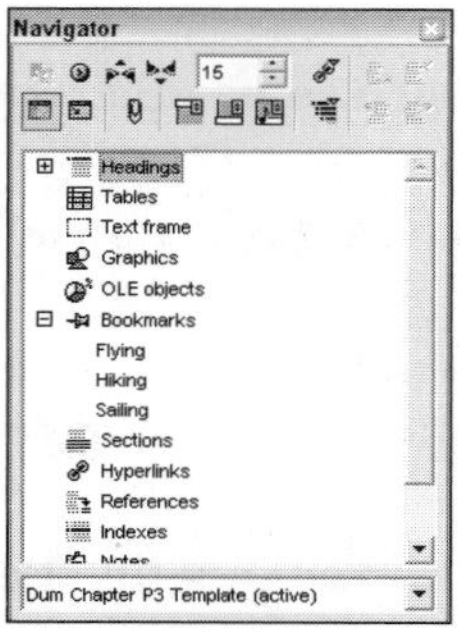

Figure 3-8: The Navigator flies you around the world — or at least through your document.

In Figure 3-8, you see a plus sign to the left of the Headings item; this indicates that headings are available. Click any plus sign to expand the list, and then double-click any item to go there. You can also see that the Bookmarks item is already expanded (it has a minus sign next to it), showing the three bookmarks in the document.

To go to any item, double-click the item.

You can dock the Navigator by pressing Ctrl and dragging to the left or right of your screen. You can also press Ctrl and double-click any empty gray space on the Navigator to alternately dock and undock it automatically.

To use the Navigation floating toolbar, click the Navigation button on the vertical scroll bar. The Navigation toolbar opens as shown in Figure 3-9. This toolbar has the same features as the Navigator, but in iconic form. Hover your mouse over any button, and a tooltip pops up to tell you what the button does.

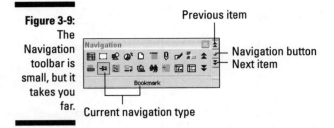

Figure 3-9:
The Navigation toolbar is small, but it takes you far.

To use the Navigation toolbar, follow these steps:

1. **Click the item that you want to look for, such as Headings or Bookmarks.**

2. **To find the next instance of that item, such as the next heading, click the Next item button.**

   This button changes its name according to the item that you have selected. If you choose Bookmarks, the button's tooltip says Next Bookmark.

3. **Continue to click the Next item button until you find the item that you want.**

As you can see, you can't choose a specific item as you can in the Navigator; you can only blindly go to the next item and hope that it's the one you want. (Eventually it will be.)

Viewing Your Words

If you find yourself squinting at the computer monitor, maybe your text is too small. On the other hand, if you text is too big, you may spend a lot of time scrolling around to see what's on the screen.

Zooming in and out

You can change the size of the display of your text. This feature is called *zooming;* you can zoom in to make text look bigger or zoom out to make it look smaller. Zooming doesn't change the actual size of your text as it will print. (If you want to do that, see Chapter 4, where we explain how to change font size.)

The easiest way to change the zoom is to use the Zoom button on the status bar. Right-click, and choose an option from the shortcut menu that appears. You can choose from several zoom factors (50%, 75%, 100%, 150%, and 200%), Optimal (which doesn't look very optimal to us), Page Width (to display the entire width of the document), or Entire Page (to show the entire page, did you guess?).

For more control, double-click the Zoom button or choose View⇨Zoom to open the Zoom dialog box. Choose Variable, and enter the zoom that you want.

You can change the default zoom for an OpenOffice.org document. See the bonus chapter on the CD-ROM, "Writer: "Fine Tuning Your Preferences," for more information.

Viewing full-screen

If you really want to see the maximum information on your screen, you can hide all the menus and toolbars. You probably don't want to do this for all your work, but it could certainly help when you have a complex structure that you want to see all at once.

To view your document full-screen (without menus or toolbars), choose View⇨Full Screen. A Full Screen On/Off button appears, which you can click to go back to your menus and toolbars.

In full-screen mode, you can still access menus using keyboard shortcuts. For example, you can press Alt plus the underlined letter of any menu (such as *f* for the File menu) to display that menu. You can use all your favorite keyboard shortcuts — such as Ctrl+C to copy selected text to the clipboard.

Seeing secret characters

Sometimes you can get frustrated trying to get your text just right. Your word processor seems to know something that you don't know, and you want in on the secret. OpenOffice.org can display characters that don't print, such as hard returns (to move text to the next line) and spaces between words. You can use these characters to help you troubleshoot — we don't want you to be frustrated for long.

To display these nonprinting characters, click the Nonprinting Characters On/Off button on the Main toolbar or choose View⇨Nonprinting Characters. The keyboard shortcut is Ctrl+F10. Nonprinting characters clutter up your text mightily, so you'll probably want to turn them off, using the same procedure, when you've figured out what the problem was.

Spelling It Correctly

Misspelled words look unprofessional in your document, so take the time to check the spelling. These days, you don't have to find the dictionary to check your words; your word processor has its own dictionary.

To check any word, select it and choose Tools⇔Spellcheck⇔Check or press F7. If the word is not misspelled, OpenOffice.org informs you that the Spellcheck is complete. Click OK to return to your document.

Using the Spellcheck dialog box

To check the entire document, use the procedure described in the previous section but don't select any text. If you are not at the beginning of the document, OpenOffice.org asks you whether you want to start at the beginning of the document. Click Yes to start at the beginning. Either way, the Spellcheck dialog box opens, as shown in Figure 3-10. (Strangely enough, if you type **Spellcheck** in a document, it comes up as a misspelled word — and rightly so. So why name a spell-checking dialog this way?)

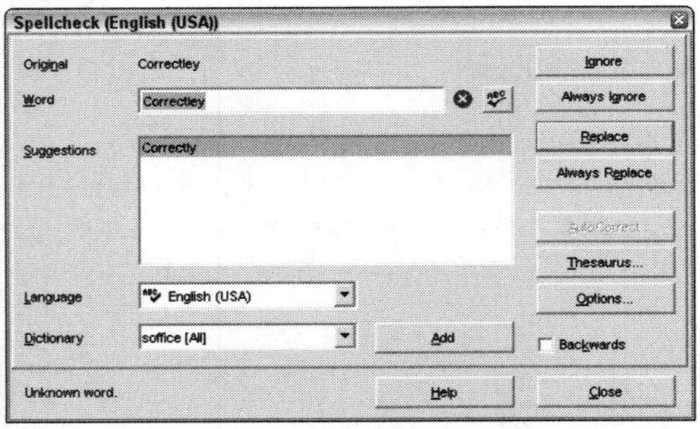

Figure 3-10:
Use the Spellcheck dialog box to clean up any spelling errors.

The Spellcheck dialog box displays the misspelled word (if Spellcheck finds any) at the top, along with a list of suggested words with similar spellings. To use one of the suggested words, select it and click the Replace button.

- ✔ To always replace the misspelled word this way in this document, click the Always Replace button.

- ✔ To always replace the misspelled word in every document, click the AutoCorrect button to add an AutoCorrect entry. (AutoCorrect is explained in the section "Correcting mistakes automatically," earlier in this chapter.)

✔ If you think the word is fine as it is (you're the boss), click the Ignore button.

✔ To ignore this word throughout the document, click the Always Ignore button.

✔ To add the word to the current dictionary (see the Dictionary drop-down list), click the Add button. The word will never appear as being misspelled again.

If you're not sure which word to choose, try one and click the Thesaurus button to get a list of synonyms. You can choose a different language from the Language drop-down list. Click the Options button to specify how spell-checking works. For more information on setting language and spelling options, see the bonus chapter on the CD-ROM, "Writer: "Fine Tuning Your Preferences."

If you're checking the entire document, when you choose an option for a mis-spelled word, OpenOffice.org automatically goes to the next word, until the spell-check is complete. At any time, you can click the Close button to close the dialog box and return to your document.

Checking spelling as you type

To correct spelling as you type, turn on Auto Spellcheck. Click the AutoSpellcheck button on the Main toolbar, or choose Tools⇨Spellcheck⇨AutoSpellcheck. When AutoSpellCheck is on, OpenOffice.org places wavy red lines under misspelled words. When you see a wavy red line, right-click and choose one of the suggested words from pop-up list that appears. You can also choose one of the following:

✔ **Spellcheck:** Opens the Spellcheck dialog box

✔ **Add:** Opens a submenu of dictionaries to which you can add the word

✔ **Ignore All:** Ignores all instances of the word in the document

✔ **AutoCorrect:** Creates an AutoCorrect entry for one of the suggested words

If you don't mind the wavy red lines, AutoSpellCheck is a nice feature and enables you to quickly correct words as you work.

Saving Your Opus

You've created your document, edited it, and now you should save it. In fact, you should save it often. Don't wait until you're finished working on it. You can save in OpenOffice.org format or in another format. You can also export your document to PDF and other graphic formats. In this section, we explain all you need to know about saving and exporting.

Saving for OpenOffice.org

To save a document, choose File⇨Save, click the Save button on the Function Bar, or press Ctrl+S. The first time you save, the Save As dialog box opens, because the document does not yet have a name or location. From the Save in drop-down list, navigate to the desired location. You can use the buttons on the left side to go to specific locations, such as the My Documents folder or a network location.

The Save As dialog box is similar to the Open dialog box, which was discussed at the beginning on this chapter. (See Figure 3-1.) It has the same buttons at the top that can help you navigate and change the views in the dialog box.

In the File Name list box, type a name for the document. Click the Save button. The OpenOffice.org format adds an .sxw extension to the filename.

Once you have saved the document one time, subsequent saves happen invisibly. You can know if you have unsaved changes by looking at the Document Modified section of the status bar. When you make a change, a tiny asterisk (*) appears to let you know that you haven't saved. As soon as you save, the asterisk disappears. Add so much as a space, and the asterisk reappears to nag you until you save again.

If you tend to forget about saving, set the AutoSave feature to save every 5 minutes or so. For more information, see the bonus chapter on the CD-ROM, "Writer: "Fine Tuning Your Preferences."

If you save in OpenOffice.org's native .sxw format, you can protect the document with a password. Select the Save with Password check box. In the Enter Password dialog box, enter the password twice and click OK. If you give the document to someone, be sure to include the password. And don't forget the password!

Saving in other formats

Let's face it. The whole world doesn't use OpenOffice.org — at least not yet. So you sometimes have to give your documents to people who don't have OpenOffice.org. You can easily share your documents with others by saving the documents in another format.

To save your document in another format, choose File⇨Save As. In the Save As Type drop-down list, choose a file type. If you have already saved your document in OpenOffice.org format, you now have two copies of your document. Of course, if you make further changes, the two documents become different.

If you are saving in another format only for the purpose of sending it to another person, complete the document first and then save it in the new format. Otherwise, you may have two different versions of the document and get confused about which is the final version.

You can also choose to always save your documents in another format. For example, you can set the default file type to be Microsoft Word's .doc format.

You can save in the following formats:

- ✔ Microsoft Word 97/2000/XP (.doc).
- ✔ OpenOffice.org 1.0 Text Document (.sxw), OpenOffice.org's native format.
- ✔ OpenOffice.org 1.0 Text Document Template (.stw), OpenOffice.org's template format. For more information on using templates, see Chapter 4.
- ✔ Microsoft Word 95 (.doc).
- ✔ Microsoft Word 6.0 (.doc).
- ✔ Rich Text Format (.rtf).
- ✔ StarWriter 5.0 (.sdw).
- ✔ StarWriter 5.0 Template (.vor).
- ✔ StarWriter 4.0 (.sdw).
- ✔ StarWriter 4.0 Template (.vor).
- ✔ StarWriter 3.0 (.sdw).
- ✔ StarWriter 3.0 Template (.vor).
- ✔ Text (.txt).
- ✔ Text Encoded (.txt).
- ✔ HTML document (OpenOffice.org Writer) (.html, .htm).
- ✔ DocBook (simplified) (.xml).
- ✔ Flat XML (.xml).

As you can see, you have lots of options. So save away!

Exporting to other formats

When you export an OpenOffice.org document, you save it in a format that isn't really a text format anymore. For example, you can save to Adobe Acrobat PDF format, which is a graphic file format. To export a file, follow these steps:

1. **Choose File⇨Export to open the Export dialog box.**

   This dialog box looks just like the Save As dialog box.

2. **In the Save as Type drop-down list, choose one of the following options:**

   - **PDF - Portable Document Format (.pdf):** A graphic format that can be viewed with the free Adobe Reader
   - **XHTML (.xhtml):** An XML markup language that's designed for display on the Web, or HTML that is written in XML

   For quicker access, click the Export Directly as PDF button on the Function Bar or choose File⇨Export to PDF.

3. **In the File Name text box, enter a filename.**

4. **Click the Save button.**

If you choose the PDF option, the PDF Options dialog box opens. If you have selected part of your document, you can choose the Selection option. Otherwise, select the All option button or the Range option button. You can enter a range of pages, such as 1-3 or 7;9;11-13. You can also choose a compression option, depending on the intended use of the PDF (printing or viewing). Click the Export button to create the file.

Printing

In most cases, the final product of your work is a printed document. Some variations may exist based on your operating system and printer, but the basic process is the same.

Previewing your work and saving a tree

Before you commit to paper, preview the document to see what it will look like. You can avoid wasting paper this way. To preview a document, choose File⇨Page Preview. The Object Bar changes to provide you with the tools that are appropriate to the Page Preview mode, as shown in Figure 3-11.

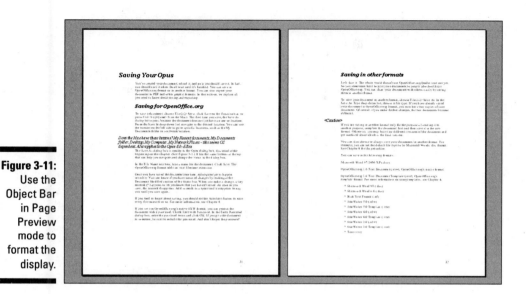

Figure 3-11:
Use the
Object Bar
in Page
Preview
mode to
format the
display.

If you like what you see, click the Print Page View button and print away.
Otherwise, click the Close Preview button and make any changes that you
want before printing. You just saved a tree.

Getting the words on paper

Printing is very simple, and you are no doubt familiar with the process from
other programs. Use one of the following options to print your document:

 ✔ Choose File⇨Print to open the Print dialog box if you want to make any
   adjustments in your printer settings. For example, you can change the
   number of copies that you print or choose to print only a portion of the
   document. You can also click the Options button to fine-tune which
   types of objects you want to print.

 ✔ Click the Print button on the Function Bar to immediately print your
   document using the settings in the Print dialog box.

Sending your document as an e-mail attachment

You can quickly send your document as an e-mail attachment using your
default e-mail program. (This doesn't work if you have a Web-based e-mail
program, such as Yahoo! or Hotmail. Some OS X and open source e-mail don't

work with this feature.) Follow these steps to send your document as an e-mail attachment:

1. **Choose File➪Send➪Document as E-mail.**

   Your default e-mail program opens, with the document already inserted as an attachment.

2. **Enter the recipient, the subject, and a message.**

3. **Click the Send button to send the e-mail.**

You can also send your document as a PDF attachment. For more information about the PDF format, see the section "Exporting to other formats," earlier in this chapter. Choose File➪Send➪Document as PDF Attachment. The PDF Options dialog box opens, as explained in that earlier section. Then follow the steps that precede this paragraph.

Chapter 4

Formatting to Perfection

. . . .

. . . .

*T*yping and editing is not enough — you want your document to look good, too. OpenOffice.org has excellent tools to help you format your document so that it looks professional and is easy to read. You can keep it simple and just choose the right font and paragraph alignment. Or you can streamline your work using templates and styles. Either way, OpenOffice.org makes it easy to get the results that you want.

Molding the New Document

Well done is half begun. If you start your document out right, the entire process is smoother. You can use *AutoPilot,* which guides you through the creation of documents automatically, or you can use a template to structure the look of the fonts and possibly include some of the text.

Creating new documents with AutoPilot

AutoPilot is a set of screens that guides you through the process of creating a document. You may have worked with *wizards* in other word processing programs — the concept is the same. When you use AutoPilot, you end up with a document that includes fonts and some of the text. You just fill in the details.

Okay, you fill in most of the document. AutoPilot can just give you the basics. The nice thing about AutoPilot is that it creates a template that you can then use repeatedly. (See the next section of this chapter for the lowdown on templates.) You can create AutoPilot documents for the following items:

- ✔ Letters
- ✔ Faxes
- ✔ Memos
- ✔ Agendas

To create one of the preceding documents, choose File⇨AutoPilot and choose the type of document that you want to create from the submenu that opens. AutoPilot opens. The choices vary according to your choice, but in all cases, you complete the information on each screen and then click the Next button. For example, to create a memo, follow these steps:

1. **Choose File⇨AutoPilot⇨Memo.**

   The first screen appears.

2. **Choose the layout that you want: Modern, Classic, or Decorative.**

   Unfortunately, the preview doesn't change to show you how your choices change the layout.

3. **Choose whether you want the title of your memo to be text or a graphic.**

   If you choose text, enter the title of your memo (such as Memorandum). If you choose a graphic, click the Select Graphics button and choose a graphic. Click Next.

   OpenOffice.org doesn't come with any graphics for you to use. You need to find or create your own. For information on creating your own graphics, see Part V of this book.

 Save graphics that you may want to use for this purpose in the folder where you keep your templates. To find your templates, choose Tools⇨Options. Click the OpenOffice.org option to expand it (if necessary), and then click Paths. Look for the Templates item in the list. Click OK to close the Options dialog box.

4. **Choose the elements that you want your memo to contain, and then click Next.**

   Include such items as the date (choose the desired date format from the drop-down list), the To and From lines, and so on. Click Next.

5. **Choose items that you want to see in the headers of continuation pages (if any) and in the footers. Click Next.**

6. **You can specify Doc information, whether to automatically assign a filename, and how to name the template.**

   Doc information refers to properties that appear when you choose File⇨Properties. Choose the source of the title and subject from the drop-down lists. Click Next.

7. **Click the Create button to create the document.**

   The new document opens, as shown in Figure 4-1.

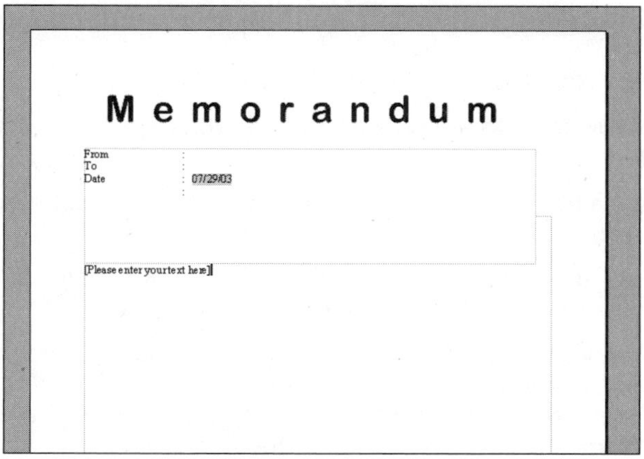

Figure 4-1:
Our first memo, which was created using AutoPilot. We're so proud! We used a graphic to create the word *Memo-randum.*

After you create your document by using AutoPilot, you can reuse the template that it creates to create more documents. See the next section of this chapter for instructions on creating a document from a template.

Starting out with a template

A *template* contains formatting and perhaps text. You use a template as a basis for a new document. The template and the document are separate files; the template just functions to structure the formatting of the document. When you create a new document based on a template, the template is never changed, although you make changes in the document. By default, documents open with the Default template.

A template is a great way to ensure consistency in your documents. If you create memos or letters on letterhead, you can start with the same template, and the repeated content (such as a logo) and the font formatting are always the same. Templates also save a lot of time. You don't have to change the formatting each time you create a document. Instead, you format once, save a template, and then create documents from the template, knowing that your formatting is already there for you.

Unfortunately, OpenOffice.org doesn't come with much of a supply of templates for Writer. You can find a few templates at `http://ooextras.sourceforge.net/`. Click the link for your language. In the section "Creating your own templates," later in this chapter, we explain how to create your own templates.

To create a new document based on a template, follow these steps:

1. **Choose File⇨New⇨Templates and Documents.**

2. **The Templates and Documents dialog box opens, with the Templates option selected.**

   You may see a list of folders or a list of templates, depending on what you displayed the last time you used this dialog box.

3. **If you see a list of folders, double-click the Default folder to display the templates in that folder, as shown in Figure 4-2.**

   If you have saved templates in another location, navigate to that location. To find the default location for templates, choose Tools⇨Options. Click the OpenOffice.org option to expand it (if necessary) and click Paths. Look for the Templates item in the list.

Up one folder   Document properties

Back | Print   Preview

Figure 4-2:
Use the Templates and Documents dialog box to create a new document based on a template.

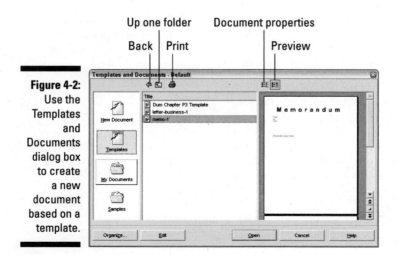

4. **Choose the template that you want to use.**

5. **To see a preview of the template, click the Preview button.**

6. **Click the Open button.**

A new document opens. You can now use the document. Don't forget to save it!

Refining a template

You can modify any template by editing it as you would edit any document. OpenOffice.org templates have a filename extension of .stw. You open STW files in the same way that you open Writer documents. (See Chapter 3 if you need instructions.)

If the template contains text, you can format the text any way you want. See the rest of this chapter for information on formatting text. You can place the following items in templates:

✔ **Styles:** Styles are sets of formatting for text, paragraphs, and pages. See the section "Styling with the Stylist" later in this chapter for more information. Styles are the most common formatting that is used in templates.

✔ **Graphics:** You can add a logo or any other graphic. See Chapter 5 for the lowdown on inserting graphics in documents. The same steps apply to templates. Also see Part V of this book for information on creating your own graphics.

✔ **Tables:** You can set up a table but leave the content blank so that you can easily complete the table.

✔ **Columns:** Perhaps you create a newsletter each month. You can set up the banner heading and the columns. Then all you have to do is add the text for the columns.

Creating your own templates

To create the template when you finish refining it, you need to save the template. Follow these steps to save a template:

1. **Choose File⇨Templates⇨Save.**

The Templates dialog box opens, as shown in Figure 4-3.

2. **In the New Template text box, type a name for the template.**

3. **In the Categories box, choose Default.**

4. **Click OK.**

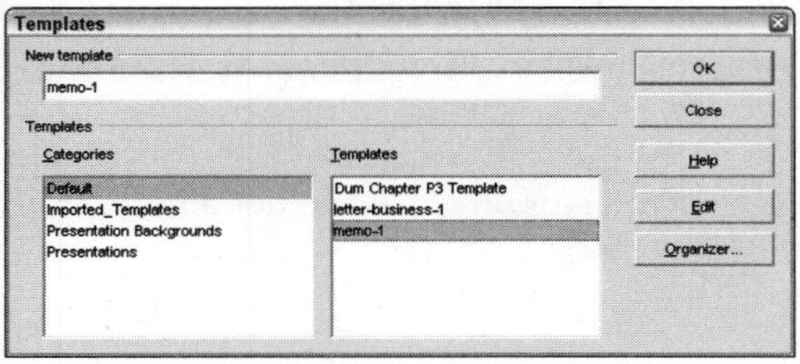

Figure 4-3:
Use the
Templates
dialog box
to save
your own
templates.

What do you do if you don't want to start with an existing template? You start from a document. If you have created the perfect newsletter, you can save it as a template. Delete the text or leave it in — it's up to you. Saving it as a template ensures that you'll always have the right starting point for your new newsletter.

When the document has the text and formatting that you want, follow the previous steps to save it as a template.

To use a template that you created as the default template, you can change the default by following these steps:

1. **Choose File⇨Templates⇨Organize.**

   The Template Management dialog box opens.

2. **In the Category list, double-click the Default folder.**

   The list of templates appears.

3. **Right-click the template that you want to use, and choose Set as Default Template from the shortcut menu that appears.**

4. **Click the Close button.**

Importing templates

You can use templates from Microsoft Word and use them as the basis for documents in OpenOffice.org. Follow these steps to import a template from Microsoft Word:

1. **Choose File⇨Templates⇨Organize.**

   The Template Management dialog box opens.

2. **Click the Imported Templates folder.**

3. **Choose Commands⇨Import Template.**

   The Open dialog box opens.

4. **In the Files of Type drop-down list, choose All Files.**

5. **Navigate to the template, select it, and click the Open button.**

   You are returned to the Template Management dialog box.

6. **Click the Close button.**

Fiddling with Fonts

Most of your document is probably text, so you want the text to look good. *Fonts* define the shapes of the letters. You can choose from all the fonts that you have on your computer, make them any size, make them boldface or italic, underline them, and generally have a good time with them.

Choosing a font

You can choose a font before or after you type. To choose a font before you type, follow these steps:

1. **Choose Format⇨Character.**

   The Character dialog box opens.

2. **Click the Font tab, as shown in Figure 4-4.**

3. **From the Font list, choose a font.**

   You can immediately see what the font looks like in the Preview box at the bottom of the dialog box.

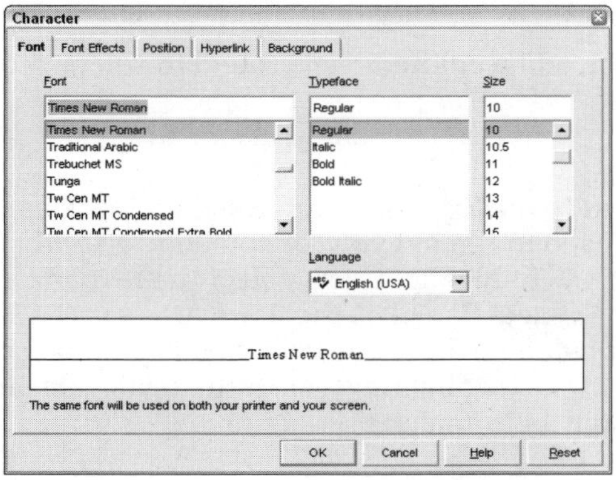

Figure 4-4:
The Font tab in the Character dialog box is the place to choose your fonts.

4. **From the Typeface list, choose Regular, Italic, Bold, or Bold Italic.**

   You can also make text bold, italic, or underlined by clicking the appropriate button on the Object Bar.

5. **From the Size list, choose a font size.**

   Font sizes are measured in *points*. A point is $\frac{1}{72}$ of an inch. The most common point sizes for paragraph text are 12 and 10. Headings are usually larger.

6. **Click OK.**

7. **Start typing.**

To apply a font to existing text, first select the text. Then, follow Steps 1 through 6.

Adding character to your characters

If you think that the plain old fonts are boring, you can add some font effects to your text. Don't overdo it, though — make sure that people can still read what you write! To add font effects, use the various tabs of the Character dialog box, as follows:

- ✔ **Font Effects:** You can add several kinds of underlining, use strikethrough text, change text color, make small capitals, add an embossing or engraving effect, add a shadow, add outlining, and add blinking (please don't!). You can also change the font color by clicking the Font Color button on the Object Bar.

- ✔ **Position:** You can create superscript or subscript text, rotate text, scale the width of text, and expand or condense text.

- ✔ **Hyperlink:** You can attach a hyperlink to text. For details, see Chapter 6.

- ✔ **Background:** You can add a colored background to selected text.

When you're done making your text look fancy, click OK.

You can also highlight text to make it stand out. Highlighting is usually a temporary effect that is used to remind you (or someone else) that some text needs further attention. To highlight text, select the text and click the Highlighting button on the Object Bar. Click the down arrow in the Highlighting button to display a color palette, where you can choose your favorite highlighting color. To get rid of the highlighting, select the text again and choose No Fill from the Highlighting color palette.

Planning Your Paragraphs

Part of document layout involves aligning paragraphs and setting line spacing. These tasks are easy in OpenOffice.org.

Aligning paragraphs

Do you want your paragraphs to be lined up on the left or right side of the page or centered on the page? Or are you a control freak who likes both sides to be perfectly aligned? You can choose any of these options.

You can set paragraph alignment before or after you type. To set the alignment after you type, select the text first. The easiest way to set paragraph alignment is to use the following buttons on the Object Bar:

- ✔ **Align Left:** Aligns the text along the left margin of the page.

- ✔ **Centered:** Centers a line of a text on the page. This option is not normally used for long paragraphs. Paragraphs look weird when the Centered option is chosen.

- ✔ **Align Right:** Aligns the text along the right margin of the page.

- ✔ **Justified:** Makes each line of text reach the left and the right margin of the page.

You can also use the ruler to set margins, tabs, and indentation. If the ruler is not visible, choose View⇨Ruler to make it appear. You can use the ruler, shown in Figure 4-5, to perform the following tasks:

- ✔ **Change margins:** Drag the border of the gray areas at the left and right.

- ✔ **Insert or delete tabs:** To insert a tab, click in the paragraph that you want to change and click the ruler where you want to add the tab. To delete a tab, click in the paragraph and drag the tab off the ruler.

  You can set the type of tab by clicking the Tab button at the left end of the horizontal ruler. You can set left, right, centered, and decimal tabs.

- ✔ **Set indentation:** Click in the paragraph that you want to change. Drag the left indent marker to change the left indentation. Drag the right indent marker to change the right indentation. Drag the first-line indent marker to change the indentation of the first line of the paragraph.

Figure 4-5:
Use the
ruler to
quickly set
margins,
tabs, and
indentation
without
opening a
dialog box.

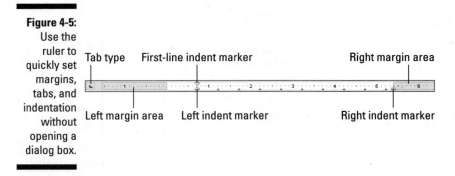

Tab type   First-line indent marker   Right margin area

Left margin area   Left indent marker   Right indent marker

To create a hanging indent, where the first-line margin is to the left of the margin for the rest of the paragraph — such as for numbered items — drag the first-line indent marker to the left of the left indent marker. To indent the first line of a paragraph, drag the first-line indent marker to the right of the left indent marker.

For more control, choose Format⇨Paragraph to open the Paragraph dialog box. Use the tabs to set the indents, spacing, alignment, text flow, numbering, tabs, drop caps, borders, and background.

Spacing your lines

Remember double-spacing your book reports in school to make them look longer? You can still do that. In fact, double-spacing is actually preferred for academic papers. (And you thought you were getting away with something!)

You can set line spacing before or after you type. If you have already typed your text, select the text first. The easiest way to set line spacing is to use the buttons on the Object Bar, but they are not displayed by default. To display these buttons, right-click the Object Bar and choose Visible Buttons from the shortcut menu that appears. From the list, click one or more of the three line-spacing buttons (1, 1.5, and 2).

You can also select text, right-click it, and choose Line Spacing from the shortcut menu that appears. Then, choose one of the line-spacing options from the submenu.

Making Lists

Everyone makes lists these days. You're probably tired of lists, but you can't get away from them, either. For the times when you need to make lists, OpenOffice.org can help.

Bulleting lists

Use bulleted lists when the items in the list don't have a sequential order. Most bullets look like little dots, but you can create other types of bullets. (The bullets in this book look like check marks.)

You can set your bullets before you start typing or change regular text to bulleted text. OpenOffice.org adds a bullet for each paragraph, which means that each time your press Enter, you get another bullet. To bullet existing text, select the text first.

 To create bulleted text, click the Bullets On/Off button on the Object Bar. Do the same to get rid of bullets for selected text.

To change the way that your bullets look, choose Format⇨Numbering/Bullets. Choose the type of bullets that you want from the examples, and click OK.

Still bored? OpenOffice.org has the most amazing collection of picture bullets. You can create bullets of balls, stars, or diamonds, or use your own graphic file. How about bullets made from a photo of yourself? (Not vain enough?) Okay, just because you *can* do it doesn't mean you *should* do it.

To add pizzazz to your bullets, choose Format⇨Numbering/Bullets and click the Graphics tab. Choose one of the graphical bullets, and click OK. To choose your own graphic, follow these steps:

1. **Choose Format⇨Numbering/Bullets.**
2. **Click the Options tab.**
3. **From the Numbering drop-down list, choose Graphics.**
4. **From the Graphics drop-down list, choose From File.**

    You can also choose Gallery to see the same bullets that you see on the Graphics tab. If you choose From File, the Link dialog box opens.

5. **Choose a graphic file, and click the Open button.**

   You return to the Numbering/Bullets dialog box. You probably need to change the size of the graphic to make it fit next to a line of text.

6. **Change the size of the image by using the Width and Height text boxes.**

   To keep the image's proportions the same, select the Keep Ratio check box.

7. **If you want, set the alignment of the bullet in relation to the line of text.**

8. **Click OK.**

Numbering lists

Create numbered lists when you want the items in the list in a certain order. You can set your numbers before you start typing or change regular text to numbered text. OpenOffice.org adds a number for each paragraph, which means that each time your press Enter, you get another number. To number existing text, select the text first.

 To create numbered text, click the Numbering On/Off button on the Object Bar. Do the same to get rid of numbering for selected text.

To specify how your numbers look, choose Format➪ Numbering/Bullets and click the Numbering Type tab. Choose one of the numbering types, and click OK.

 When you number text, you see a gray box around each of the numbers. You can ignore this box — it doesn't show up when you print.

Styling with the Stylist

Styles are collections of font or paragraph settings that define how your text looks. You can ignore styles for short documents, but they are indispensable for longer documents, especially ones with repeated features such as headings. Styles make sure that all your headings look the same. They also help you make global changes if you need to do so. Imagine a 30-page school paper with lots of headings. You hand it in, and your teacher says that the headings need to look different. Do you really want to individually format each heading? Probably not!

If you created the headings with a style, you can just redefine the style, and presto, they all now look just the way your teacher wants them to. You get an A+.

Understanding styles

In the previous sections, we covered just the basics of formatting, but with styles, you can manage many more types of formatting. For example, you can specify how much space comes after each paragraph. If you specify spacing equal to the size of your font, you don't need to press Enter twice to create a paragraph. Just press Enter (Return) once, and the style creates the space between the paragraphs. You can also create complex formatting for a paragraph, such as borders and background fills. (For more information on borders and fills, see Chapter 5.)

OpenOffice.org offers the following kinds of styles:

- **Paragraph:** Formats entire paragraphs. This is the most common style type. In fact, it may be the only type that you need.
- **Character:** Formats one or more characters.

  Use character styles when you need to vary the formatting of characters within a paragraph.
- **Frame:** Formats text frames and frames for graphics. (Chapter 5 explains these concepts in more detail.)
- **Page:** Formats the structure of a document, including such features as page numbers and margins.

  Page styles are great for long, complex documents with varying types of page layouts.
- **Numbering:** Formats numbers and bullets for lists.

Using a style

OpenOffice.org comes with many styles already set up for you, so you can just start creating a basic document without any preliminary setup.

Refer to the section, "Creating a style," later in this chapter to find out how to create custom styles.

The most efficient method of selecting a style depends on how much of your document has been created, as follows:

- The Apply Style drop-down list on the Object Bar accesses styles that are already used in the document. It's not a good place to start, but it's most convenient after you apply a number of styles.
- The Stylist panel accesses all styles or a selected set of styles.

Drop-down list

The Apply Style drop-down list is found on the Object Bar. This list, as shown in Figure 4-6, only includes styles that you have already used in your document.

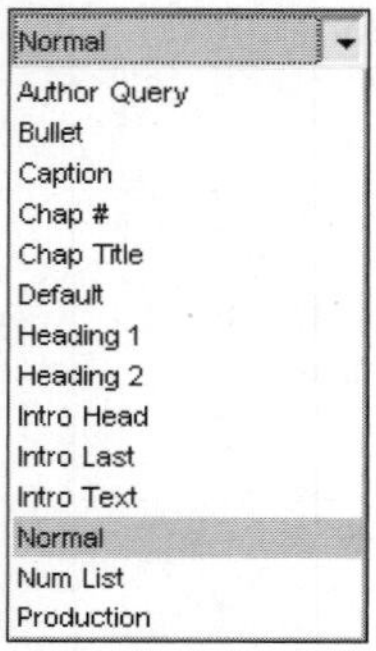

Figure 4-6:
The Apply Style drop-down list on the Object Bar offers quick access to styles that you have already applied in your document.

Normal ▼
Author Query
Bullet
Caption
Chap #
Chap Title
Default
Heading 1
Heading 2
Intro Head
Intro Last
Intro Text
Normal
Num List
Production

To apply a style from the Apply Style drop-down list, select the text and choose the style you want from the list.

Stylist panel

The Stylist panel is devoted to styles. You can open the Stylist panel with any of the following actions:

✔ Choose Stylist On/Off on the Function Bar.

✔ Press F11.

✔ Choose Format➪Stylist.

The Stylist panel opens, as shown in Figure 4-7.

You can dock the Stylist panel so that it doesn't cover your document. Press Ctrl, and drag the panel to the right side of your screen.

A drop-down list at the bottom of the Stylist panel specifies which kinds of styles you see, as follows:

✔ **Automatic:** Displays the styles that OpenOffice.org thinks are appropriate for the current use. (How does OpenOffice.org know?) This is the default.

✔ **All Styles:** Gives you access to every available style.

You can limit the Stylist panel to specific sets of styles, such as the following:

✔ Custom styles that you have created

✔ List styles for creating numbered or bulleted lists

To apply a style from the Stylist, select some text and double-click a style in the Stylist panel.

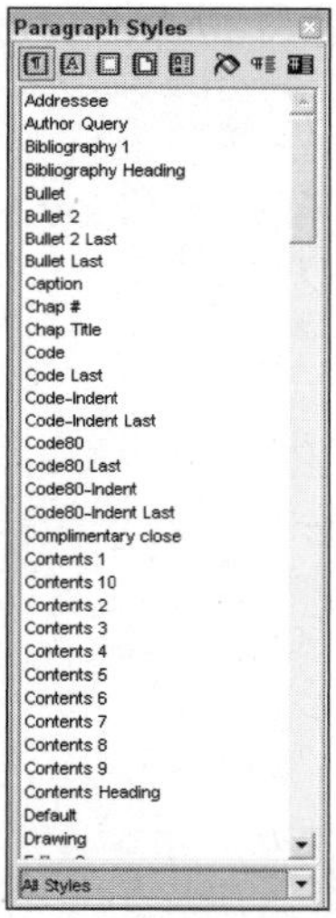

Figure 4-7:
Use the
Stylist panel
for easy
access to all
styles.

Creating a style

You don't have to use the styles that are included in OpenOffice.org. In fact, most people design their own styles. You can define a style by using one of the following methods:

✔ Formatting some text and using that text as an example

✔ Specifying the style settings

Create a style by example

When you create a style by example, you format some text first. You can use the ruler, the buttons on the Object Bar, and the options on the Format menu to format the example text. When the text is picture-perfect, follow these steps to create a style:

1. **Open the Stylist panel (press F11).**

2. **Click the type of style that you want to create.**

   The icons for the style types are along the top of the Stylist panel. For example, to create a paragraph style, click the Paragraph icon. If the Paragraph icon is already selected, you don't need to do anything for this step.

3. **Either click in the text that you formatted (for example, in the paragraph) or select one character or object that you formatted. (For page and frame styles, just select one object in the page or frame.)**

4. **If you clicked in the text, click the New Style from Selection button in the Stylist panel. If you selected text or an object, drag the text or object into the Stylist panel.**

   The Create Style dialog box opens.

5. **Type a name in the Style Name text box.**

6. **Click OK.**

You can now use your style for other text.

Create a style by specifying settings

If you want to be very precise about your settings, you may want to start by naming a style and then specifying all its settings. You have more control over the settings by using this method. Follow these steps to create a style by specifying settings:

1. **Choose Format⇨Styles⇨Catalog.**

   The Style Catalog dialog box opens.

2. **From the drop-down list at the top of the dialog box, choose the type of style that you want to create.**

3. **Click the New button.**

   The dialog box that opens is named according to the type of style that you chose from the drop-down list. For example, if you chose Paragraph styles, the Paragraph Style dialog box opens. The settings that are available in each dialog box are appropriate for each type of style. The Organizer tab is displayed, as shown in Figure 4-8.

4. **In the Name text box, type a name for the new style.**

5. **From the Next Style drop-down list, choose which style should come after the new style.**

   OpenOffice.org applies the next style when you press Enter after typing a paragraph using this style. This setting applies to paragraph and page styles only.

6. **From the Linked With drop-down list, choose a style to use as a basis for your new style.**

   If you think that your new style resembles an existing style, choose it here. Then, when you specify your settings, many of them are already set for you on the various tabs. This means that you have to make fewer changes, and you can finish more quickly. To start from scratch (the settings for the Default style), choose None.

7. **From the Category drop-down list, choose a category.**

   Choose a category to help you find the style more easily in the Stylist panel. If you usually work with the Applied Styles list and plan to apply the style (otherwise, why create it?), the category is not very important.

8. **Go through each tab, and specify the settings for your style.**

   For example, if you are creating a paragraph style, you have Indents & Spacing, Alignment, Text Flow, Font, Font Effects, Position, Numbering, Tabs, Drop Caps, Background, Borders, and Condition tabs. Whew! That's a lot of settings. If you have questions on any tab, click the Help button to see a description of the functions on that tab.

9. **Click OK.**

   You return to the Style Catalog dialog box. Your new style appears on the list.

10. **Click the Close button to return to your document.**

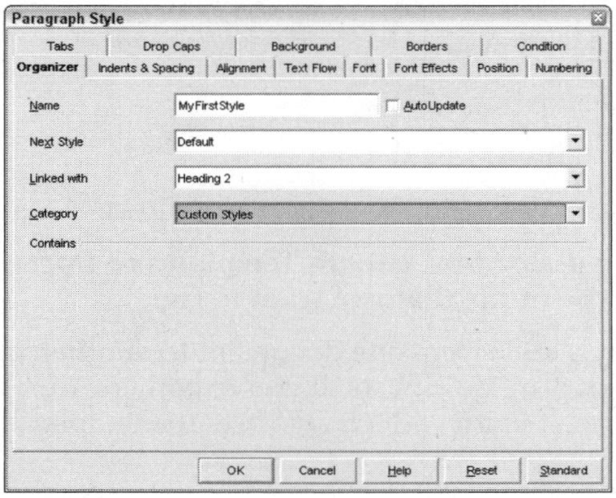

Figure 4-8:
Use the Paragraph Style dialog box to name and format a new paragraph style.

Changing and organizing styles

You can modify an existing style, and all text using that style is automatically updated. This feature is one of the great advantages of styles. You can also copy styles from another template or document.

To modify an existing style, follow these steps:

1. **Choose Format➪Styles➪Catalog.**

   The Styles Catalog dialog box opens.

2. **Choose the style that you want to modify.**

3. **Click the Modify button.**

   The dialog box that opens depends on the type of style that you chose and the style's name. Each dialog box has the settings that you need for that style.

4. **Go through the tabs and change any settings that you want to.**

5. **Click OK to change the style.**

6. **Click the Close button to close the Styles Catalog dialog box and return to your document.**

Suppose that you have a very nice style in another document or template that you want to use in your current document or template. Why re-create the wheel? Instead, you use the Style Manager. Follow these steps to copy a style:

1. **Open the documents that you want to use.**

   For example, if you want to copy a style from one document to another, both documents should be open.

2. **Display the document that is to receive the style.**

3. **Choose Format➪Styles➪Catalog.**

   The Styles Catalog dialog box opens.

4. **Click the Organizer button.**

   The Template Management dialog box opens, as shown in Figure 4-9.

5. **At the bottom of the dialog box, choose Templates or Documents, depending on the type of file that you want to use.**

   For example, to copy a style from one document to another, choose Documents from both drop-down lists. If you're copying from a template to a document, it doesn't matter which side lists the templates and which side lists the documents. If you chose Documents on either side, you see a list of open documents. If you chose Templates on either side, you see the template folders.

6. **If you're copying from a template, double-click the appropriate template folder and choose the template that has the style that you want. If you're copying from a document, choose the document that has the style that you want.**

7. **Double-click the template or document name to display the word *Styles*.**

8. **Double-click the word *Styles* to display the list of all the styles.**

When the styles are displayed, choose Commands⇨Print to print a list of all the styles and their settings for the selected document or template. This is a great way to troubleshoot and analyze styles.

9. **On the other side of the dialog box, display the template or document that is to receive the style.**

10. **Choose the style that you want to copy.**

11. **Press Ctrl and drag the style to the other side of the dialog box. When you see a horizontal line below the file or template, release the mouse button.**

If you just drag, you move the style. This means that the style is removed from its original source. You rarely want to do this, so be sure to press Ctrl as you drag!

12. **Click the Close button to return to the Style Catalog dialog box.**

13. **Click OK to return to your document.**

Try out your new style. You should find it in the Stylist panel.

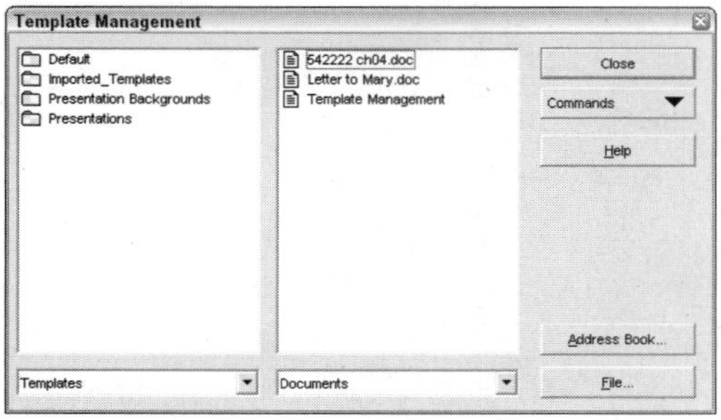

Figure 4-9:
Use the
Template
Manage-
ment dialog
box to copy
styles from
one doc-
ument or
template to
another.

Chapter 5

Designing Complex Documents

· ·

In This Chapter

▶ Creating tables and columns

▶ Using borders

▶ Adding graphics

▶ Working with long documents

▶ Creating personalized documents

· ·

Sometimes your work gets complicated. You need to add graphics, create a newsletter, or insert a table. You may be writing your thesis and need to add a table of contents and an index. Or perhaps you want to send out letters (or invoices) to your customers. OpenOffice.org is up to all these tasks, and in this chapter, we explain how to do them.

Dividing Text into Tables and Columns

After a while, plain paragraph text can get boring. And if you're working with lots of numbers, you may need to organize the numbers into a neat, orderly table. When writing a newsletter, you may want to split up the page into columns. Laying out the page into a table or into columns is a common task for many people.

Tabling the issue

A *table* is a grid of rows and columns that creates cells where you can place text or numbers. Tables are an easy way to make complex data clear, and they are easy to create in OpenOffice.org Writer.

To create a table, follow these steps:

1. **Choose Insert⇨Table.**

   The Insert Table dialog box opens, as shown in Figure 5-1.

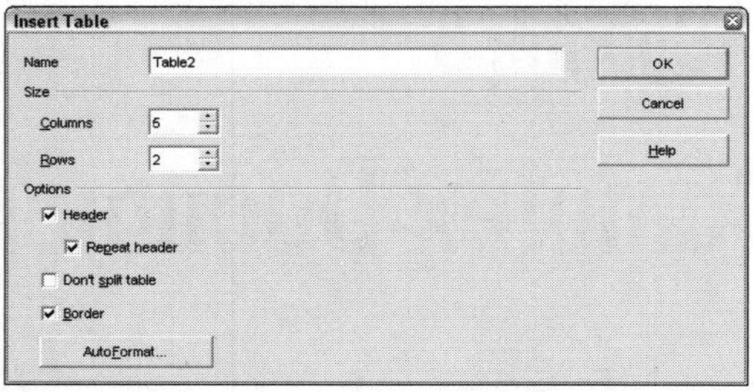

Figure 5-1:
Use the
Insert Table
dialog box
to set up
a table.

Insert Table dialog box showing Name "Table2", Size section with Columns 6 and Rows 2, Options section with Header, Repeat header, Don't split table, Border checkboxes, and AutoFormat button. OK, Cancel, Help buttons on the right.

2. **In the Size section, set the number of columns and rows in the Columns and Rows text boxes.**

3. **In the Options section, set the basic options for the table, as follows:**

   • **Header:** Creates a header row at the top of the table. The header text is centered, italic, and boldface.

   • **Repeat Header:** Repeats the header text on the next page if the table continues to the next page.

   • **Don't Split Table:** Prevents the table from being split onto more than one page.

   • **Border:** Creates a border around the table. (If you deselect this check box, the table is invisible, which makes it difficult to work with. You can always turn off the border when you're finished.)

   • **AutoFormat:** Opens the AutoFormat dialog box, where you can choose one of the preset table formats. Click OK after you choose a format.

4. **Click OK.**

 To quickly create a table with the default settings, choose Insert➪Insert Table. You see a small grid. Drag across the grid to specify the number of rows and columns.

To enter data in the table, click in the upper-left cell and type. Press Tab to go to the next cell to the right. Continue in this way throughout the entire table.

Formatting the table

To format the table, you can use the Object Bar, which has an entirely new set of buttons when the cursor is inside the table, as shown in Figure 5-2.

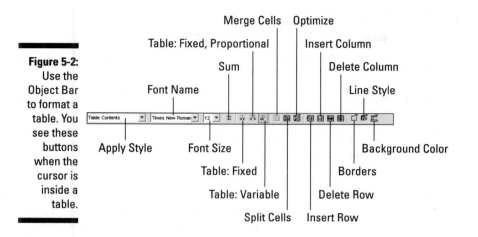

Figure 5-2:
Use the
Object Bar
to format a
table. You
see these
buttons
when the
cursor is
inside a
table.

Most of these items are self-explanatory, but a couple require some explanation, as follows:

✔ The table display mode specifies what happens to the entire table when you adjust the number or size of a row or column, as follows:

  • **Fixed:** The width of the table remains the same. Changes to a cell affect only the adjacent cell.

  • **Fixed proportional:** The width of the table remains the same, but changes affect the entire table, so changes affect adjacent cells proportionally.

  • **Variable:** Changes affect the size of the entire table.

✔ The Optimization setting has four options that automatically set the spacing of the rows and columns, as follows:

  • **Space columns equally:** Makes all the columns the same width.

  • **Space columns equally:** Makes all the rows the same height.

  • **Optimal row height:** Sets the row height so that it's just high enough for the contents.

  • **Optimal column width:** Sets the column width so that it's just wide enough for the contents.

Another way to format a table is to choose Format⇨Table. This opens the Table Format dialog box. Use the tabs in this dialog box to finesse your table. When you're done, click OK. Many of the settings are also on the Object Bar, but some settings have more options in the dialog box.

Writing in columns

Columns are ideal for newsletters and whenever you have a long list of short items and want to save space. Follow these steps to perfect columns:

1. **Choose Format⇨Columns.**

   The Columns dialog box opens, as shown in Figure 5-3.

2. **Choose the number of columns that you want in the Columns list box (or use the up and down arrows), or click the type of columns that you want in the sample boxes.**

   You see the result in the Preview box.

3. **To make additional adjustments, use the Width and Spacing section to individually set the width of each column and the spacing between the columns.**

4. **To add a separator line between the columns, use the Separator Line section to specify a line type, height, and position.**

5. **If you have created page styles, specify the page style that you want in the Apply to list box.**

6. **Click OK.**

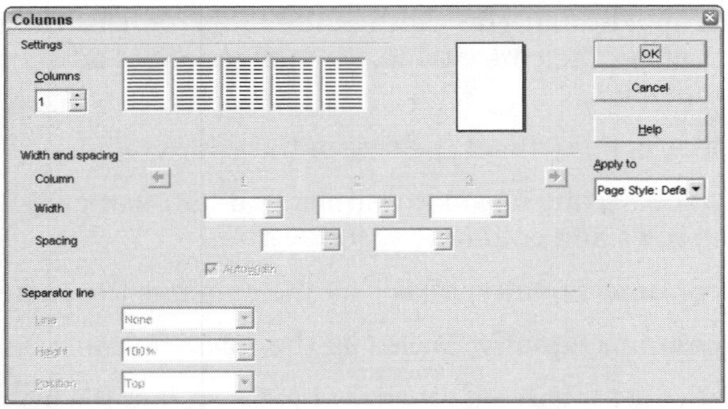

Figure 5-3:
The Columns dialog box splits your page into columns.

Working with sections

What do you do if you want one part of your document to have one column and another part to have two columns? You use *sections*. Sections divide your text. You can use sections to vary the numbers of columns.

Another way to lay out columns for part of a document is to put the text in a frame. We explain frames in the section, "Framing text," later in this chapter.

To insert a section, follow these steps:

1. **Click where you want to insert a section. You can also select existing text to convert it to a section.**

   The text must be one or more complete paragraphs.

2. **Choose Insert⇨Section.**

   The New Section dialog box opens.

3. **In the New Section text box, enter a name for the section.**

   You can link a section to another file so that the section is automatically updated when that file changes; you can write-protect the section so that no one else can change it (with or without a password); and you can hide the section.

4. **Click the Columns tab and set the columns, as described in the previous section.**

5. **Click the Insert button.**

You now have a new section, shown by two horizontal lines. If you selected text before inserting the section, the lines are around the text. If you are creating a spanking new section, be sure to place the cursor inside the section before you type.

You can also modify a section. Choose Format⇨Sections, and make any adjustments that you want. Click the Options button to find the settings for columns. Click OK when you're done.

Creating Long, Long Documents

Okay, you have a lot to say. Maybe you're writing a novel or your Ph.D. thesis. In any case, you need some hard-core tools to help you out. You may need to divide your book into chapters, create a table of contents, or index the book. In this section, we explain how to format your magnum opus.

When you need to create long documents with many parts, you can create a *master document*. A master document is a holder for other documents, such as the chapters of a book. Working with one very long document can get unwieldy, so you can create separate documents for each chapter and then pour all the smaller documents into your master document. Finally, you can add page numbers as well as create a table of contents and index for the whole shebang.

The master document contains only its own text and links to the subdocuments. You make changes to your subdocuments directly and then update the master document so that it is always current. Master documents have their own filename extension, .sxg.

Heading up your text

Usually, you start by creating all your subdocuments (for example, your chapters). When the subdocuments are all ready, you create a new master document. However, you can also turn an existing document into a master document.

Creating a new master document

If you already have all your subdocuments, choose File⇨New⇨Master Document. The Navigator automatically opens. (See Chapter 3 for more about the Navigator.) However, you have a special toolbar for working with master documents.

The Navigator starts by showing one item, Text. To add other files, follow these steps:

1. **Choose Insert⇨File from the Navigator toolbar.**

   The Insert dialog box opens.

2. **Choose the file that you want to insert.**

3. **Click the Insert button.**

Figure 5-4 shows a master document with some text and two subdocuments.

To reorder the contents of a master document, select a subdocument or any text in the Navigator and drag it up or down. You can also select any item and use the Move Up or Move Down button.

To insert text into the master document, place the cursor in the section below where you want the text and choose Insert⇨Text from the Navigator toolbar.

If you move a subdocument, right-click the subdocument in the Navigator and choose Edit Link from the shortcut menu that appears. You can then specify a new location for the subdocument.

To delete a subdocument, right-click it in the Navigator and choose Delete from the shortcut menu that appears.

Turn an existing document into a master document

If you have an existing document, you can convert it to a master document. OpenOffice.org creates a new subdocument at each Heading 1 style. Use this method if you thought you were creating a short story but things got out of hand and you now have a full-fledged novel. You can also insert documents. This method also works well if you want to use a document that was created from your own template and turn it into a master document.

Save Contents as Well (embeds subdocuments within master document)

Insert (documents or files)

Update (links and indexes)

Edit (opens subdocument for editing)

Move Up

Toggle (between master document and regular display)

Move Down

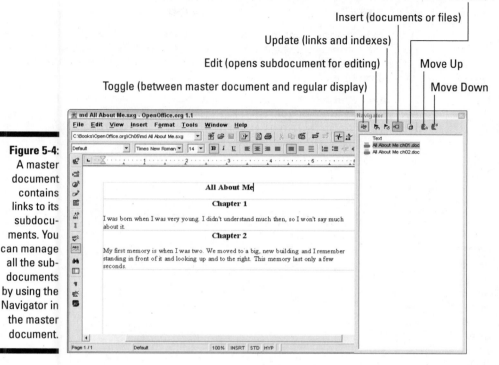

Figure 5-4:
A master
document
contains
links to its
subdocu-
ments. You
can manage
all the sub-
documents
by using the
Navigator in
the master
document.

Choose File➪Send➪Create Master Document. Name the document, and click the Save button. Don't worry, OpenOffice.org doesn't delete your original document.

Creating a table of contents

The easiest way to create a table of contents is to use the heading styles that come with OpenOffice.org; these are Heading 1, Heading 2, and so on. You can redefine these headings to look the way you want (as explained in Chapter 4) and save the result as a template (also discussed in Chapter 4). Then use the template to create your document. To create the table of contents, follow these steps:

1. **Click where you want to create the table of contents.**

   Usually you create the table of contents near the beginning of your document.

2. **Choose Insert➪Indexes and Tables➪Indexes and Tables.**

   The Insert Index/Table dialog box opens.

3. **Click the Index/Table tab, as shown in Figure 5-5.**

4. **From the Type drop-down list, choose Table of Contents.**

5. **In the Create Index/Table section, choose whether you want to create a table of contents for the entire document or for just one chapter. Also, in the Evaluate Up to Level list box, choose what level of heading you want to include.**

   If you have four levels of headings, you may only want to include two levels in your table of contents. In that case, you would evaluate up to level 2.

6. **Click OK.**

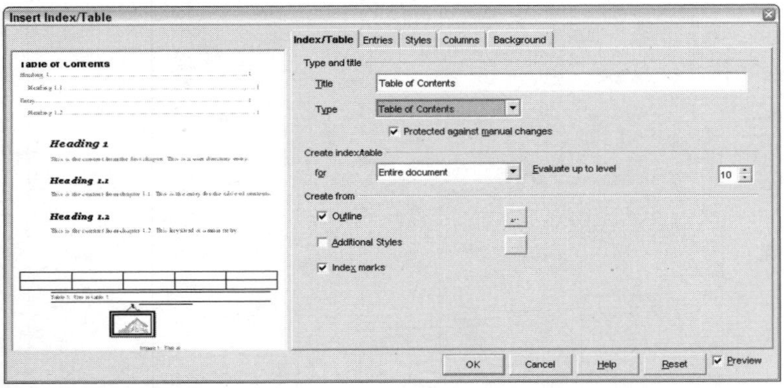

Figure 5-5:
Define a
table of
contents in
the Insert
Index/Table
dialog box.

If you don't want to use the preset heading names, you can use other styles for your headings. In the Create From section of the Insert Index/Table dialog box, select the Additional Styles check box and then click the adjacent ellipsis button. In the Assign Styles dialog box, choose a style and use the double-left and -right arrow buttons to assign a level to the style. For example, if you have MainHeading and SubHeading styles, move MainHeading to level 1 and move SubHeading to level 2. Click OK to finish assigning your styles to levels.

Although you should create your table of contents when your document is finished, is a document ever finished? If your document changes yet one more time, you need to update the table of contents. Just right-click in the table of contents, and choose Update Index/Table from the shortcut menu that appears.

If you find that you cannot place your cursor in the table of contents, choose Tools⇨Options⇨Text Document⇨Formatting Aids. Then select the Enable check box in the Cursor in Protected Areas section.

To modify the table of contents setting, right-click in the table of contents and choose Edit Index/Table from the shortcut menu that appears. The Insert Index/Table dialog box opens, where you can modify your settings.

To delete a table of contents, right-click in the table of contents and choose Delete Index/Table from the shortcut menu that appears.

Indexing your book

Indexing is a little different from creating a table of contents because you cannot use standard headings. Instead, you have to specify each place that you want to use as an index entry.

Inserting an index entry

To create an index entry, follow these steps:

1. **Select the text that you want to put in the index, or click in front of a word that you want to put in the index.**

2. **Choose Insert⇨Indexes and Tables⇨Entry.**

   The Insert Index Entry dialog box opens, as shown in Figure 5-6.

 You can insert an index entry from the Main toolbar. Long-click the Insert button until the floating toolbar remains open. Place your cursor or select your text, and click the Insert Index Marker button.

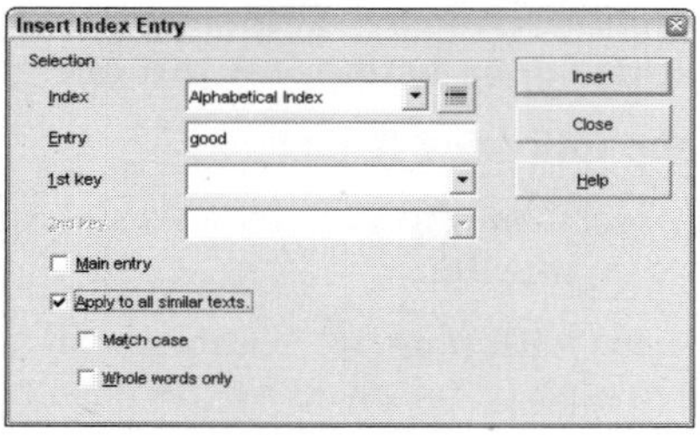

Figure 5-6:
Define an index entry in the Insert Index Entry dialog box.

Insert Index Entry	
Selection	
Index	Alphabetical Index
Entry	good
1st key	
2nd key	
☐ Main entry	
☑ Apply to all similar texts	
☐ Match case	
☐ Whole words only	

(buttons: Insert, Close, Help)

3. **If you want the word to be a subentry to a main entry, type the main entry word in the 1st Key list box.**

   You can even create a sub-subentry. Place the main entry in the 1st Key list box and the subentry in the 2nd Key list box.

4. **Select the Apply to All Similar Texts check box to insert an index entry to the same text where it occurs elsewhere in your document.**

   To use this feature, you must have selected the text before you started. Select the Match Case check box to insert an index entry only if the text matches the case of the current entry. Select the Whole Words Only check box to mark only whole words that match the current entry.

5. **Click the Insert button to insert the index entry.**

   The dialog box stays open so that you can enter other index entries if you want. You can select words while the dialog box is open.

6. **Click the Close button to close the Insert Index Entry dialog box.**

To edit an index entry, place the cursor in front of the entry and choose Edit➪Index Entry. The Edit Index Entry dialog box opens, which is just like the Insert Index dialog box. Make your changes, and click OK.

Creating the index

When all your index entries are ready, it's time to create the index. Follow these steps to do so:

1. **Click where you want to insert the index; this is usually at the end of the document.**

2. **Choose Insert➪Indexes and Tables➪Indexes and Tables.**

3. **Click the Index/Table tab.**

4. **From the Type drop-down list, choose Alphabetical Index.**

5. **In the Create Index/Table section, choose whether you want to create a table of contents for the entire document or for just one chapter.**

6. **In the Options section, set the following items:**

   • **Combine identical entries:** Combines all instances of an entry and lists the pages numbers on one line.

   • **Combine identical entries with p or pp:** Combines all instances of an entry that occur on one page, followed by the page number and the letter *p* (for example, Mars 3p). Combines all instances of an entry that occur on consecutive pages, followed by the first of the consecutive pages and the letters *pp* (for example, Mars 3pp, if *Mars* occurs on pages 3 and 4).

   • **Combine with -:** Combines all instances of an entry on consecutive pages with a hyphen, as in Mars 3-4.

   • **Case sensitive:** Distinguishes between uppercase and lowercase words.

   • **AutoCapitalize entries:** Capitalizes the first letter of each entry.

- **Keys as separate entries:** Keys are used to create subentries. This option places the subentries on a separate line, indented below the main entries.

- **Concordance file:** Lets you create a separate file that contains index entries. Then choose File➪New to create the file. (To modify the file, choose File➪Edit.) The Edit Concordance File dialog box opens, where you can create the concordance file by using a preset grid.

7. **Click OK to create the index.**

To update an index, right-click in the index and choose Update Index/Table from the shortcut menu that appears. You can also delete or edit the index from the shortcut menu that appears when you right-click (or Control+click) the index.

Creating Personalized Form Letters

Sometimes you just want to get personal. If you're sending out the same letter to many people, it's nice to address each letter (and envelope) individually. The process of combining a letter with a list of names and addresses (or any other set of data) is called *mail merge,* and the letter that you create is called a *form letter.*

To create personalized letters, follow these steps:

1. **Create the form letter.**

2. **Create or register a data source.**

   A *data source* is a database that contains the data that you use to personalize the letters. The data source often contains names and addresses but could contain any information that you want. To *register* a data source means to let OpenOffice.org know the location and format of the data.

3. **Drag fields from the data source into the form letter.**

   A *field* is a column name in the database. For example, FirstName and Address are typical fields.

   The term *field* in OpenOffice.org also means any calculated information that you insert into a document. For example, you use a field to insert a page number or today's date.

4. **Output the form letter to your printer or individual documents. Outputting the form letter also merges the individual rows of data with the form letter.**

Creating the form letter

You create the form letter from any document. At first, don't worry about where the personalized information will go. Just type the letter (or invoice or other document). When you're done, save the letter.

Creating and registering a data source

This step is a little more complex, because you can use many types of databases. We begin with a simple example. Suppose that you want to maintain a simple text database of your friends. Follow these steps to create the database:

1. **Type in your headings, tabbing between each heading. Press Enter, and add your names and addresses. Place tabs between each column. Save the document in** .txt **format.**

   For example, your headings could be FirstName, LastName, Address, City, State, and ZipCode. To save a document in .txt format, choose File⇨Save As and choose Text (.txt) from the Files of Type drop-down list. Click the Save button.

2. **Choose File⇨AutoPilot⇨Address Data Source.**

   The Address Data Source AutoPilot opens.

3. **To choose the type of data source, choose one of the options. In our example, choose Other External Data Source. Click Next.**

4. **On the next screen, click the Settings button to open the Create Data Source dialog box.**

5. **In the Name text box, type the name of the data source file.**

   Use the filename of the database.

6. **From the Database Type drop-down list, choose a type. In our example, choose Text.**

   If you have your data in a spreadsheet, such as Calc (see Part III of this book), choose Spreadsheet as the type of database.

7. **To the right of the Data Source URL, click the ellipsis button to browse for your database file. Find the folder (directory), and click OK.**

   Your screen should appear similar to Figure 5-7.

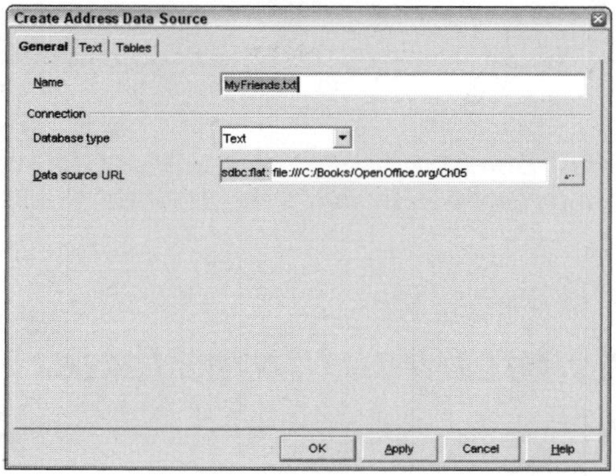

Figure 5-7:
In the Create
Address
Data Source
dialog box,
you specify
the name
and type of
the file that
contains
your data
source.

8. **Click the Text tab, and specify the row and file format. In our example, the fields are separated by tabs (the other separators don't matter) and the file is in** `.txt` **format. Click OK.**

   You are returned to the Address Data Source AutoPilot.

9. **Click the Field Assignment button to assign field names to specific types of preset fields.**

10. **In the Address Data - Field Assignment dialog box, choose each type of field that you use and then choose your actual field (column) names from the field's drop-down lists, as shown in Figure 5-8.**

    Scroll down to the bottom of this screen, to find four user fields that you can use as necessary. For example, if you have an Address2 field for apartment or suite numbers, you can use one of these user fields.

11. **Click OK.**

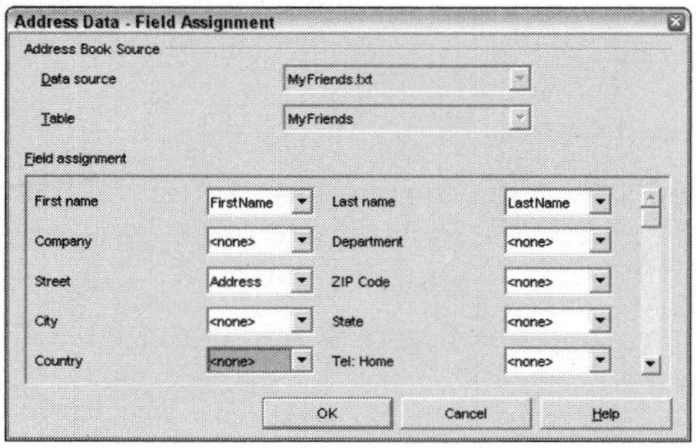

Figure 5-8:
Use the
Address
Data - Field
Assignment
dialog box
to assign
field names
to standard
fields.

12. **Click the Create button.**

13. **Click OK, and accept the message tells you that you can now access this address data.**

The steps and screens differ somewhat for different types of databases. For example, you can use an address book from Microsoft Outlook and other types of address book data.

Inserting fields into your form letter

You are now ready to add the fields in your data source to your form letter. Follow these steps to do so:

1. **Display your form letter.**

2. **Choose View⊅Data Sources, or press F4.**

   The Data Sources window opens at the top of your document. At the left, you see your registered data sources.

3. **Double-click the data source that you want to use to expand it. If necessary, double-click the Tables item until you see a table listed, as shown in Figure 5-9.**

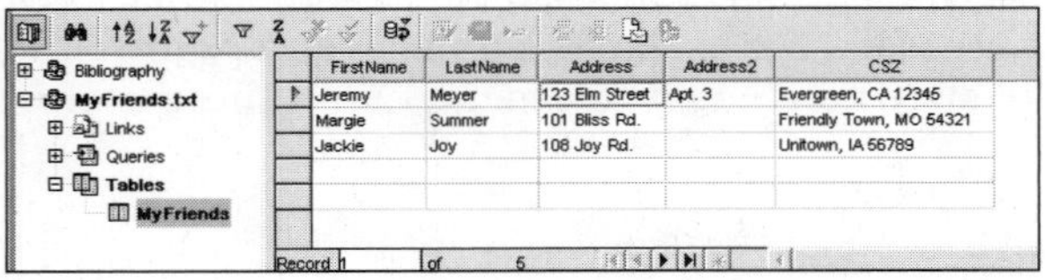

Figure 5-9:
The Data
Sources
window
displays
your
database.

	FirstName	LastName	Address	Address2	CSZ
⊞ 🕮 Bibliography					
⊟ 🕮 MyFriends.txt	Jeremy	Meyer	123 Elm Street	Apt. 3	Evergreen, CA 12345
⊞ 🗒 Links	Margie	Summer	101 Bliss Rd.		Friendly Town, MO 54321
⊞ 🗒 Queries	Jackie	Joy	108 Joy Rd.		Unitown, IA 56789
⊟ 🕮 Tables					
🕮 **MyFriends**					

Record 1 of 5

4. **Double-click the table to display it.**

   The data in that table displays in the right side of the Data Sources window, as shown in Figure 5-9. This window has its own toolbar that lets you sort and filter the data in your database.

   You can double-click any field heading to widen it so that you can see all the data in that column.

5. **If necessary, scroll through your form letter so that you can see the area where you want to insert the fields. Then drag the field name (that is, the column head) of the first field to the desired location in your form letter.**

6. **Continue to drag field names into your form letter. Be sure to add spaces where necessary, such as between a first name and a last name.**

   Your letter should look something like what is shown Figure 5-10.

Creating the output

You're ready to print your letters! You can also save them to a file. The rows in your database will be merged with your form letter at the same time. Follow these steps to create personalized form letters:

1. **Choose Tools⇨Mail Merge.**

   The Mail Merge dialog box opens.

2. **Choose the From This Document option, and click OK.**

   If you created a template from your form letter, choose From a Template. The Mail Merge dialog box opens. (Okay, there are two Mail Merge dialog boxes. This is the big one.)

3. **To sort or filter the records, use the toolbar in the dialog box. Otherwise, choose the records that you want to include in the Records section. (The default is All.)**

4. **In the Output section, choose the Printer or File option.**

   If you choose File, click the adjacent ellipsis button to choose a location for the files. (OpenOffice.org creates a separate file for each row and numbers the files sequentially.) Choose to name the file according to one of the database fields (which you can choose from the drop-down list) or manually (you get to name the file).

5. **Click OK.**

   If the Save As dialog box opens, choose the location and filename again and click the Save button. Your letters are either printed or saved.

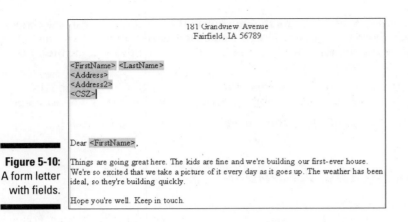

Figure 5-10:
A form letter
with fields.

Using Borders and Frames

You've written enough. Now it's time to liven up your documents a little. One simple way is to put a border around text and graphics. You can also add colored backgrounds.

Boxing text

Boxing text is a great way to make it stand out. You can also place lines above and below the text — or on any side, for that matter. To add a box, use the border feature. Usually, you add a border to an entire paragraph. Follow these steps to box a paragraph:

1. **Select the paragraph.**

2. **Choose Format⇨Paragraph and click the Borders tab, as shown in Figure 5-11.**

   The Borders tab of the Paragraph dialog box displays.

3. **In the Line Arrangement section of the dialog box, click the border arrangement that you want from the small boxes near the top of the section.**

You see the result in the Preview pane in the User-Defined area. Use the left, blank box near the top of the panel to delete all borders. (This box is selected in Figure 5-11.)

4. **From the Style list in the Line section, choose the width and style of the line.**

5. **From the Color drop-down list, choose a border line color.**

6. **Use the Shadow Style section to create a shadow effect, if you want one.**

7. **In the Spacing to Contents section, specify the distance between the border line and the text (or other contents).**

8. **Click OK.**

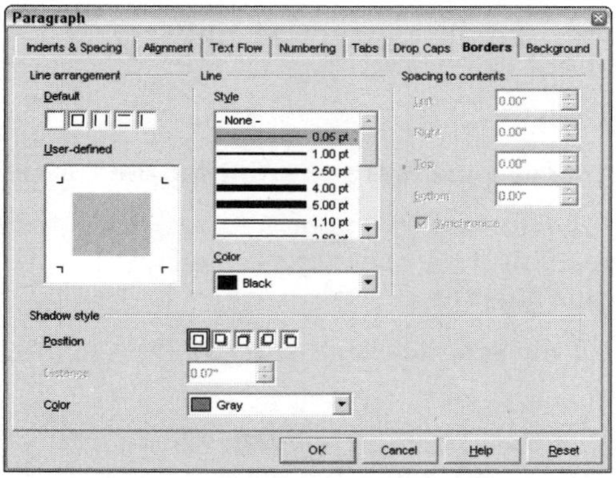

Figure 5-11:
Use the
Borders
tab of the
Paragraph
dialog box
to place
boxes
around
your text.

You can click individual sides of the border in the User-Defined area and set different settings for each side.

To give your box a colored background, click the Background tab of the Paragraph dialog box. Choose Color from the As drop-down list, and choose a color. To create a background of an image, choose Graphic from the As drop-down list and browse for the graphic file that you want to use.

Framing text

When you add a border to text, the text stays in the confines of the page's alignment and column settings. But suppose that you want to move a box of text anywhere on your page? For example, if you create a two-column news-letter, you may want a box of text that straddles the middle of the page. This type of text is called a *callout* or a *sidebar.* You use frames to create a movable box of text. Framed text acts like a graphic — you can drag a frame anywhere, resize it, and so on.

To frame text, follow these steps:

1. **Select the text that you want in the frame.**

   To create an empty frame, skip this step.

2. **From the Main toolbar, long-click the Insert button and click the Insert Frame Manually button.**

   You see a preview of columns.

3. **Choose the number of columns that you want for the framed text.**

   Using a frame is one way to specify columns for part of a document. The other way is to use sections. Using sections is explained in "Working with sections," earlier in this chapter.

4. **Click at one corner of the selected text, and drag to the diagonally opposite corner.**

   The text appears with a box and eight *handles,* which are small boxes that you can use to resize the frame. To create an empty frame, drag across an empty area of your page.

5. **Click anywhere outside the frame to deselect the frame.**

You can manipulate a frame in the following ways:

- **Move it:** Click the frame to select it. Move the cursor so that you see a four-headed arrow, and drag in any direction.
- **Resize it:** Click the frame. Drag any of the handles.
- **Delete it:** Click the frame and press Delete.
- **Edit the text:** Click inside the frame and edit the text as you would any other text.

For more options, right-click any frame and choose one of the formatting options from the shortcut menu that appears.

Linking text frames

You can link text frames so that the text flows from one frame to another. This is a cool desktop publishing trick and looks great in a newsletter, as long as the frames are not too far apart. Follow these steps to link text frames:

1. **Create some framed text, following the steps that we describe in the previous section.**

2. **Create an empty frame, also using the previous steps.**

3. **Click the edge of the first frame.**

 4. **Click the Link Frames button on the Object Bar.**

   This button only appears when you have selected a frame that does not already have a next link.

5. **Click the edge of the second frame.**

   OpenOffice.org draws a line from the first frame to the second frame.

6. **Type more text in the first frame.**

   When the first frame is full, it spills into the second frame. Cool!

To unlink frames, select a frame and choose the Unlink Frames button from the Object Bar.

Inserting Graphics

A picture is worth a thousand words, they say, and you would rather add one graphic than type those thousand words. Why waste time? OpenOffice.org offers lots of features for adding graphics.

Clipping art

The easiest way to insert art is to find some and insert it. Why create it yourself? Of course, don't use copyrighted art without permission. But you can find lots of art that is available for anyone to use — often for free. To insert an image, follow these steps:

 1. **Click in your document where you want the graphic to appear.**

2. **Choose Insert⇨Graphics⇨From File. Or, long-click the Insert button on the Main toolbar and choose Insert Graphics.**

3. **In the Insert Graphics dialog box, locate and click the graphic file that you want.**

4. **Click the Open button.**

The graphic appears with eight square handles that show you that the graphic is selected. Click outside the graphic to deselect it.

Editing graphics

When you select a graphic, you can do the following things:

- **Move it:** Point to the graphic so that you see a four-headed arrow cursor. Drag the graphic to a new location.
- **Resize it:** Click one of the eight handles and drag inward (to make the graphic smaller) or outward (to make it bigger).
- **Delete it:** Press Delete.

When you select a graphic, the Object Bar changes to provide tools for editing the graphic. You can make the following edits:

- **Filter:** Adds special effects. You have to try the different filters to see what they do.
- **Graphics mode:** Changes a graphic from its default to grayscale, black and white, or a *watermark* (a faint image that's often used as a background).
- **Red, green, and blue:** Changes the coloring of the graphic.
- **Brightness:** Makes the graphic lighter or darker.
- **Contrast:** Increases or decreases the contrast.
- **Gamma:** Increases or decreases the gamma, which determines contrast in dark areas of a graphic.
- **Transparency:** Sets the percentage of transparency.
- **Flip horizontally or vertically:** Mirrors the graphic along a horizontal or vertical axis.
- **Graphic properties:** Opens the Graphic dialog box, where you can set even more properties.

Using the Gallery

The Gallery is a place to hold graphics for later use. OpenOffice.org comes with a selection of 3-D shapes, bullets, and other graphics, but no clip art. If you have clip art that you may want to reuse, you can add it to the Gallery.

To use the Gallery, follow these steps:

1. **Choose Tools➪Gallery.**

   The Gallery appears at the top of your screen, as shown in Figure 5-12.

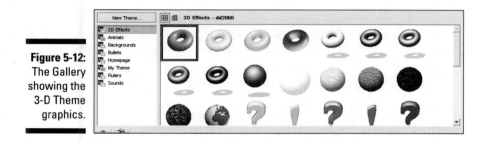

Figure 5-12:
The Gallery
showing the
3-D Theme
graphics.

2. **Choose one of the themes in the Gallery.**
3. **Drag a graphic into your document.**

You can create your own themes, which are just categories of graphics. Then you can add graphics files to the themes. Follow these steps to create a new theme:

1. **Choose Tools➪Gallery.**
2. **Choose New Theme.**

   The Properties of New Theme dialog box opens.

3. **Click the General tab, and enter a name for the theme.**
4. **Click the Files tab.**
5. **Click the Add button. Locate and file, select it, and click the Open button to add that file to the Gallery.**
6. **Click OK.**

Adding shapes

OpenOffice.org has an excellent supply of tools for creating your own shapes. You can fill the shapes with all sorts of cool fills and otherwise manipulate them as you want.

If you want to create your own graphics, the Draw program offers the most options, including 3-D effects. See Part V of this book for more details on the Draw program. You can create a drawing in Draw and then copy and paste it into your Writer document.

Creating shapes

When you start to draw, you should display the Draw Functions toolbar for easy access to all the tools. Long-click the Show Draw Functions button on the Main toolbar. Then drag the Draw Functions toolbar to a new location so that it stays open, as shown in Figure 5-13.

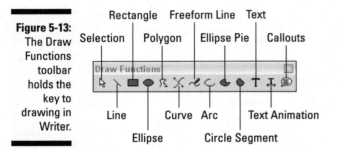

Figure 5-13: The Draw Functions toolbar holds the key to drawing in Writer.

The Draw Functions toolbar offers the following tools:

- **Selection:** Click to select all objects within a rectangular boundary. Drag from one corner to the diagonally opposite corner of the boundary. Then you can move all the selected objects by placing the cursor inside the boundary and dragging. You can also resize all the objects at once by dragging on any of the square handles.

  You can press and hold Shift and click to select additional objects.

- **Line:** Click, drag in the desired direction, and release the mouse button where you want the line to end. To constrain lines to 45-degree angles, press and hold Shift as you drag.

- **Rectangle:** Click and drag from one corner to the diagonally opposite corner. To create a perfect square, press and hold Shift as you drag.

- **Ellipse:** Click and drag from one corner to the diagonally opposite corner. Ellipses don't have corners, but try it and you'll get the idea. To create a perfect circle, press and hold Shift as you drag.

- **Polygon:** Click at the start point and drag; then release the mouse button at the next point. To continue, click at the next point and keep clicking away. Double-click to end the polygon.

✔ **Curve:** Click and drag at the start point; then release the mouse button where you want to start defining the curve. Move the cursor to the curve's endpoint and click. Continue this process to create more curves. You can simply click at a new point to create a straight segment. Double-click to end the curve. You have to try this a few times to get used to how it works.

✔ **Freeform Line:** Click and drag wherever you want. Just scribble. It's fun! Release the mouse button to stop scribbling.

✔ **Arc:** Follow the instructions to draw an ellipse or circle. When you stop, you see a radius line. Click where you want the arc to start; then move counterclockwise and click where you want the arc to end.

✔ **Ellipse Pie:** This works just like the arc, but you get a closed shape that looks like a slice of pie. That is, the closed shape is bounded by the arc (a line from the arc's center to the start point and a line from the arc's center to the endpoint).

✔ **Circle Segment:** This works like the ellipse pie, but the closed shape is bounded by the arc and a line from the start point to the endpoint of the arc.

✔ **Text Frame:** Drag diagonally to define the text frame, and then type your text inside. To modify the frame's properties, right-click and choose from the options on the shortcut menu that appears.

✔ **Text Animation:** This inserts text that scrolls horizontally, like a ticker tape.

✔ **Callouts:** This creates a callout with a line that points to something and a rectangular box. Double-click inside the callout to type your text. You can change the box to a circle by dragging inward on the largest corner handle when the cursor becomes a hand.

Editing shapes

You can edit shapes like graphics. Click shapes to select them, and follow the instructions that we present in the section "Editing graphics," earlier in this chapter.

When you select a graphic, the Object Bar changes to provide tools for editing the graphic. You can do the following with the Object Bar:

✔ **Edit Points:** Some types of shapes display points when you click this button so that you can individually drag each point to modify the shape.

✔ **Line:** Opens the Line dialog box, where you can change the line style, color, and width.

✔ **Line Style:** Offers a choice of line styles, such as dashed and dotted.

✔ **Line Width:** Offers a choice of line widths.

✔ **Line Color:** Lets you choose the line color.

✔ **Area Style/Filling:** Lets you choose the type of fill for closed shapes. You can choose invisible, color, gradient, hatching, or bitmap. For more options, right-click any filled shape and choose Area from the shortcut menu that appears to open the Area dialog box. Use this dialog box to define the fill. You'll find lots of options here!

✔ **Area Style/Filling 2:** This drop-down list lets you choose the specific fill based on the type of fill that you chose in the first Area Style/Filling drop-down list. For more options, use the Area dialog box, as explained in the previous item.

✔ **Object rotation mode:** Select a shape, click this button, and then drag one of the corner handles to rotate a shape.

✔ **Change anchor:** Changes the connection of the shape to a paragraph or page, or places it as a character.

✔ **To Foreground:** Moves the selected shape in front of text.

✔ **To Background:** Moves the selected shape behind text.

✔ **Bring to Front:** Places the selected shape in front of other shapes.

✔ **Send to Back:** Places the selected shape behind other shapes.

✔ **Arrange Object:** If you select more than one object (press and hold Shift and click to select additional objects), this tool aligns the objects vertically or horizontally for a nice, neat look.

Chapter 6

Keeping Control of Your Documents

*Y*our documents do not live on an isolated island. Instead, they have connections with other documents, Web pages, Calc spreadsheets, and all sorts of other files. Managing all these relationships can be tricky, but hyperlinking is one way to make your documents friendly with all their relations.

If you're the type that edits, re-edits, and then edits again, you may want to keep track of all your changes. Also, people who work on documents in a collaborative environment often need to know who is changing what. In this chapter, we explain two techniques for keeping control of your documents and their relationships with the outside world.

Linking to the World

A *hyperlink* is a connection to another file. You may want to tell your readers where they can find more information or learn about something new. Either way, you can link text to any other file, whether that file is on your hard drive, on a network or intranet, or on the World Wide Web. Readers who are looking at your document on a computer (as opposed to on paper) can click the hyperlink and immediately view the other file.

Creating a hyperlink

Hyperlinks are easy to create. Follow these steps to create a hyperlink:

1. **Select the text that you want to hyperlink.**

2. **Choose Insert⇨Hyperlink, or click the Hyperlink Dialog button on the Function Bar.**

   The Hyperlink dialog box opens, as shown in Figure 6-1.

   If you prefer, you can also use the Hyperlink Bar. Choose View⇨Toolbars⇨ Hyperlink Bar. It's quicker for creating several hyperlinks, but you have to type in the URLs or filenames.

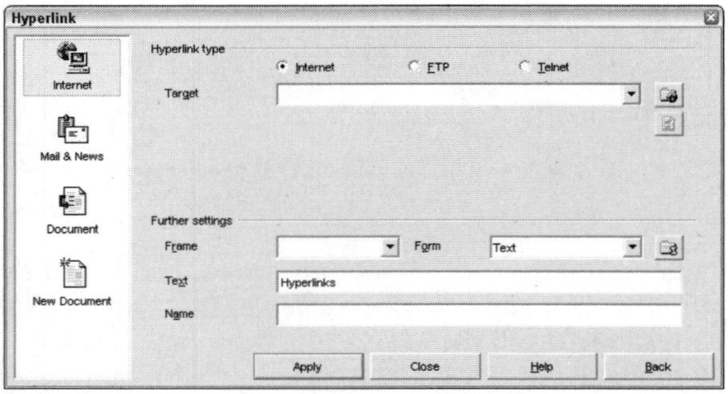

Figure 6-1:
The Hyperlink dialog box leads you anywhere in the world.

3. **In the left side of the dialog box, choose the type of link that you want to create — to the Internet, to an e-mail address or newsgroup, to a document, or to a new (as yet uncreated) document.**

   The Hyperlink dialog box changes according to your choice.

4. **Specify the location of the Web page, document, or whatever you choose.**

   You can browse to find the document, so you don't have to remember its location by heart. If you hyperlink to a document, you can specify a bookmark in the document. For more information on creating bookmarks, see Chapter 3.

5. **If you want, change the text that the hyperlink displays by entering the desired text in the Text box.**

6. **From the Form drop-down list, choose to add the hyperlink to the selected text or to create a cute little button next to the text.**

   As of this writing, a bug keeps buttons in Design mode after you first create them — and they don't work! To turn off Design mode, select the button that you just created. The Object Bar becomes the Control Bar and now contains different buttons. From the Control Bar, choose the

Design Mode On/Off button. Now your button works. Future buttons that you create in that document will also work.

7. **Click the Apply button.**

8. **Click the Close button.**

To use a hyperlink, click it. When the cursor is over the hyperlink, the cursor becomes a hand.

Editing a hyperlink

You can edit hyperlinks to change their address or the text that they display. Editing a text hyperlink is somewhat different from editing a button hyperlink.

Editing text hyperlinks

Text hyperlinks are easy to edit. To edit the hyperlink, follow these steps:

1. **Select the hyperlink by pressing and holding Alt and then clicking the hyperlink. (This avoids activating the hyperlink.)**

   You can also click the HYP box on the status bar (the box display changes from HYP to SEL) so that you can select a hyperlink.

2. **Choose Insert⇨Hyperlink.**

   The Hyperlink dialog box opens.

3. **Make any changes that you want in the Hyperlink dialog box.**

   See the instructions in the previous section for information on using the Hyperlink dialog box.

4. **Click the Apply button.**

5. **Click the Close button.**

Editing button hyperlinks

Editing button hyperlinks is slightly more involved than editing text hyperlinks, because the button is a *form,* a structure that is used to create interfaces that help you work with your computer software. Follow these steps to edit a button hyperlink:

1. **On the Main toolbar, long-click the Show Form Functions button so that the Form Functions floating toolbar remains open.**

2. **Click the Design Mode On/Off button.**

   You can now select the buttons in your document.

3. **Click the button hyperlink that you want to edit.**

4. **Right-click and choose Control from the shortcut menu that appears to open the Properties: Button dialog box, as shown in Figure 6-2.**

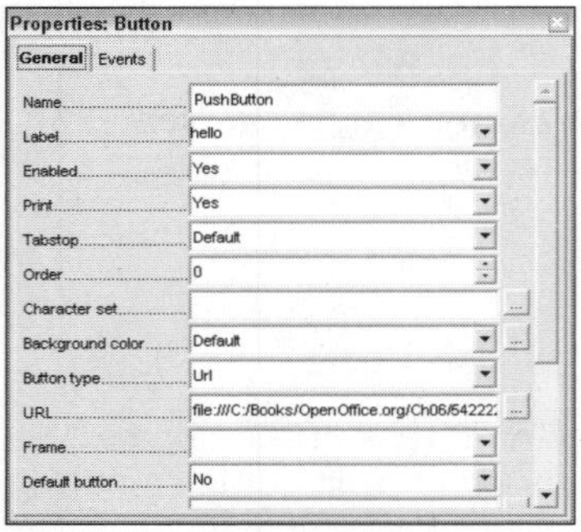

Figure 6-2:
Use the
Properties:
Button
dialog box
to edit
hyperlink
buttons.

5. **Use the URL text box to change the URL, and use the Label text box to change the text that appears on the button.**

6. **Click the Close button in the Properties: Button dialog box.**

7. **To activate the hyperlink button again, choose the Design Mode On/Off button from the Control Bar.**

Tracking Changes in Documents

You may want to keep track of changes that you or another person makes to a document. Perhaps you are not sure that you want to keep the changes and want a way to easily undo them. You may need to show the changes to your boss and get approval before finalizing them. Or maybe you are suggesting changes to a subordinate or colleague but want that person to clearly see what has been changed and then respond to your suggestions. If many people are collaborating on a document, wouldn't you like to know who is suggesting which changes? You have many reasons to want to know exactly what has changed in a document.

The Record Changes feature of OpenOffice.org Writer enables you to mark each change that was made in a document and distinguish the author of all changes. When a document has changes marked, you can easily

✔ See exactly what has changed and how.

✔ Know who made the change.

✔ Accept or reject any change.

✔ Enter a comment for a change — perhaps to explain it to yourself later.

✔ Merge changes into the original document.

Displaying changes

To start displaying changes in your document, choose Edit⇨Changes⇨Record.

✔ Any subsequent additions that you make are underlined and have a different color that depends on the author of the change.

✔ Deletions have a horizontal line through them.

✔ Lines that contain changes show a vertical line in the left margin, as shown in Figure 6-3.

To stop marking changes, choose Edit⇨Changes⇨Record again.

You can specify how changes are marked. Choose Tools⇨Options⇨Text Document⇨Changes. On the right side of the Options dialog box, use the drop-down boxes to change how insertions, deletions, and changed attributes are displayed.

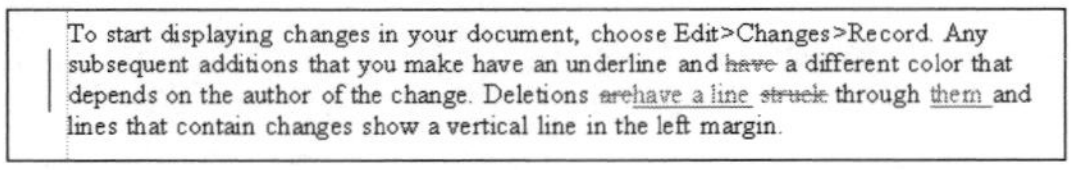

Figure 6-3:
A paragraph shows some additions and deletions.

> To start displaying changes in your document, choose Edit>Changes>Record. Any subsequent additions that you make have have an underline and have a different color that depends on the author of the change. Deletions arehave a line struck through them and lines that contain changes show a vertical line in the left margin.

Working with changes

When you start recording changes, you simply edit your document as you normally would and you see the changes automatically. However, you may want to add a comment to explain why you made a change. To add a comment, follow these steps:

1. **Select the change.**

2. **Choose Edit⇨Changes⇨Comment.**

   The Comment dialog box opens.

3. **In the Text box, enter the comment.**

4. **Click OK.**

When you create a comment, the comment appears in the Accept or Reject Changes dialog box, which is discussed next and shown in Figure 6-4. If you have Extended Tips turned on (choose Help⇨Extended Tips), the comment also appears when you place the cursor over the change.

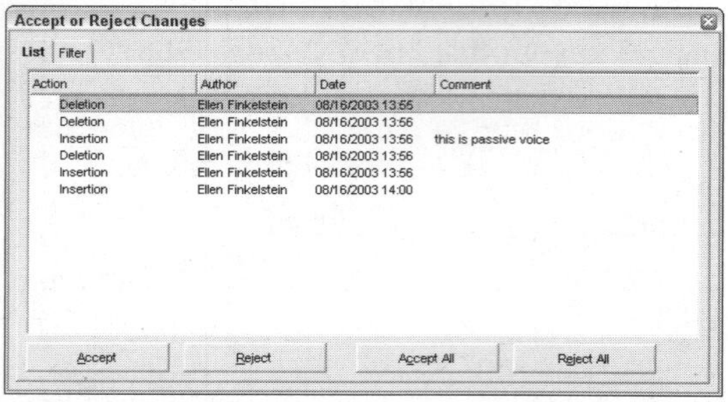

Figure 6-4:
Use the
Accept
or Reject
Changes
dialog box
to decide
the fate of
marked
changes
in your
document.

The most common task that you need to accomplish with a document that marks changes is to accept or reject the changes. (You can follow a simple rule — accept those that you make and reject those that others suggest!) To accept or reject changes, follow these steps:

1. **Choose Edit⇨Changes⇨Accept or Reject.**

   The Accept or Reject Changes dialog box, shown in Figure 6-4, opens, with the List tab displayed.

2. **On the List tab, click the first item.**

   OpenOffice.org highlights the insertion or deletion in your document.

3. **Click the Reject button or the Accept button to reject or accept the change.**

   Click the Reject All button or the Accept All button to process all the changes at once.

4. **Click the Close button in the Accept or Reject Changes dialog box.**

Click the Filter tab to filter the list of changes. You can filter changes by date, author, action (insertion or deletion), or comment.

Suppose that you want to make sure that no one makes changes without marking them. You can password-protect the Record Changes feature so that no one can turn it off or accept or reject changes. You want complete and final control!

To password-protect the Record Changes feature, choose Edit⇨Changes⇨ Protect Records. Enter a password (and confirm it), and click OK. Repeat this process to turn off password protection.

In the section "Password-Protecting Documents," later in this chapter, we explain how to password-protect an OpenOffice.org document so that only authorized people can open it.

Comparing and merging documents

If you forget to use the Record Changes feature and send a document to others for editing, you need a way to find their changes. Proofreading the two documents side-by-side would take forever! OpenOffice.org comes to the rescue with its Compare Documents feature, which essentially creates the addition and deletion markings for you. You can then decide whether to incorporate the changes into your original document. Follow these steps to compare and merge two documents:

1. **Open your original document.**

   We'll call the original document Document 1.

2. **Choose Edit⇨Compare Document.**

   The Insert dialog box opens.

3. **In the Insert dialog box, choose the document that contains the changes and click the Insert button.**

   We'll call this changed document Document 2. You now see, in Document 1, markings that show all the differences between the two documents.

   Read carefully now. Text that's in Document 1 but not in Document 2 (text that someone else deleted in Document 2) appears as inserted text (with an underline) in Document 1. Text that's in Document 2 but not in Document 1 (text that someone else added in Document 2) appears as deleted text in Document 1. (This is the opposite of what we expected.)

4. **To accept or reject changes, choose Edit⇨Changes⇨Accept or Reject.**

   You can find further instructions on using this feature in the previous section of this chapter.

5. **To accept the changes that the other person made in Document 2, you reject the insertions and deletions. To keep Document 1 in its original form, accept the insertions and deletions.**

Managing Versions

Sometimes you need to keep several versions of a document so that you can quickly go back to an earlier version if necessary. Version management keeps track of successive states of a document within one file. If you want, you can eventually merge your versions.

The Versions feature only works if you save your files in OpenOffice.org's native .sxw format.

To save versions of a document, follow these steps:

1. **Create and save a document. Name it** `Letter to Joanne`, **for example. Then make further changes to it so that you have an original document and a version of the document that differs from the original.**

2. **Choose File⇨Versions.**

   The Versions of Letter to Joanne dialog box opens, as shown in Figure 6-5.

   Your actual file name appears in the title bar of the dialog box.

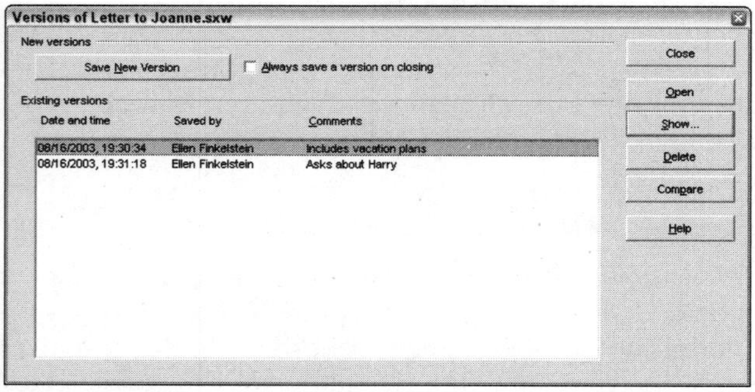

Figure 6-5: When saving versions of a document, OpenOffice.org keeps track of your changes within one file.

Versions of Letter to Joanne.sxw	
New versions	Close
Save New Version ☐ Always save a version on closing	Open
Existing versions	Show...
Date and time · Saved by · Comments	
08/16/2003, 19:30:34 · Ellen Finkelstein · Includes vacation plans	Delete
08/16/2003, 19:31:18 · Ellen Finkelstein · Asks about Harry	Compare
	Help

3. **Click the Save New Version button to save a new version of the document.**

   The Insert Version Comment dialog box opens.

4. **In the Insert Version Comment dialog box, enter a comment that explains what you have added or deleted and click OK.**

   OpenOffice.org automatically includes the date and time of the version as well as the name of the person who saves the version.

5. **To be sure that you always save a version for this document, select the Always Save a Version on Closing check box.**

6. **To save the version and return to your document, click the Close button.**

You can manage your versions in the following ways:

✔ To revert to one of the previous versions, select the version and click the Open button. OpenOffice.org opens the version as a read-only file. Choose File⇨Save As to save the version as a separate file.

✔ To display a long comment that doesn't fit in the Versions of [filename] dialog box, click the Show button to open the Insert Version Comment dialog box.

✔ To delete a version, select the version and click the Delete button.

✔ To compare versions, click the Compare button. OpenOffice.org marks the changes in your document so that you can see what you have added or deleted, as compared to previous versions. In the Accept or Reject Changes dialog box, accept or reject the changes, as explained in the section "Tracking Changes in Documents," earlier in this chapter.

Accepting changes does not delete your versions, so you can still revert to a previous version.

If you use the File⇨Save As command to save a copy of a file, OpenOffice.org does not save version information.

Inserting Notes

If you need to remind yourself about a task that you need to complete (I need to complete this chapter!) or if you want to leave a note for a colleague who will read the document, you can insert a note. A *note* is a place to store comments that shouldn't go in the text of the document itself. A note shows up as a small yellow rectangle, so you can easily see where the notes are.

To insert a note, follow these steps:

1. **Place the cursor where you want the note to appear.**

2. **Choose Insert⇨Note.**

   The Insert Note dialog box opens.

3. **Type the text for the note. If you want to add the author's name, the date, and the time, click the Author button.**

4. **Click OK.**

A thin yellow rectangle appears where you placed the cursor.

To read the note, place the cursor over the rectangle. The note expands to display the entire text of the note. To edit the note, double-click the note and make any changes that you want in the Edit Note dialog box. If you have more than one note in a document, you can use the left and right arrow buttons to navigate from note to note.

Password-Protecting Documents

For the ultimate in protection, you can make sure that only people who have your special, secret password can open your documents.

You can only password-protect documents that you save in OpenOffice.org's native .sxw format.

To password-protect a document, follow these steps:

1. **Choose File⇨Save As.**

The Save As dialog box opens.

2. **Select the Save with Password check box.**

3. **Click the Save button.**

If you have already saved the document once and want to resave it with a password but without changing its name or location, confirm that you want to replace the original file. The Enter Password dialog box opens.

4. **Enter the password twice, once in the Password text box and again in the Confirm text box.**

5. **Click OK.**

The next time that you or someone else tries to open the document, the Enter Password dialog box opens. Enter the password and click OK to open the document.

When you password-protect a document, you obviously can't open it without the password. So — don't forget the password!

To remove the password protection, choose File⇨Save As and deselect the Save with Password check box.

Chapter 7

Creating Web Pages

*O*penOffice.org Writer allows you to create great-looking Web pages with astonishing ease. Generate your own Web pages for business or pleasure, and make your presence known in the virtual reality of the World Wide Web.

Plunging Into HTML Land

With just a few steps, you too can be in HTML land, viewing your own Web page on your browser.

Creating a new HTML document

To create a simple Web page, choose File⇨New⇨HTML Document. Then create your Web page by typing what you want and inserting any graphics you like. Insert graphics by choosing, oddly enough, Insert⇨Graphics.

To create a simple Web page, you could also choose View⇨Online Layout, or click the Online Layout button on the Main toolbar, but we do not recommend this, because this method does not change the Main toolbar to include Web-related buttons, such as the HTML Source button and Text Animation button. Also, it does not always import graphics as well as using File⇨New⇨HTML Document.

Before you can view your Web page on a Web browser, you need to save it. To save your Web page, do the following:

1. **Choose File⇨Save.**

   The Save As dialog box appears.

    2. **Browse through your folders to the desired location and click the Create New Directory button (Linux and Macintosh) or Create New Folder button (Windows).**

   A dialog box appears for creating a new folder or directory.

   You almost always want to create a new folder when you create a new Web page because Writer creates gif or jpeg files for any graphics that you paste into your Web page and saves them into the same folder that contains the Web page document. If this is a unique folder, your life is much simpler. When you upload your Web page onto your server, you can simply upload the entire folder.

3. **Type in the folder's name and click OK.**

4. **Type in the file name and choose HTML Document (Linux or Windows) or Web Page (Macintosh) from the File type list box.**

   HTML Document or Web Page are the default file types if you chose File⇨New⇨HTML Document to create your document.

5. **Click OK.**

   OpenOffice.org automatically generates the HTML code that Web browsers require to display Web pages. HTML is short for HyperText Markup Language, which is the standard language of the World Wide Web.

You can now view your Web page with a browser. When you do this, notice that Writer automatically lines up your graphics vertically and left-justifies them. Also, your text all gets lined up and is left-justified automatically.

You probably want a more detailed layout than just the simplest Web page. Fortunately, OpenOffice.org's Writer allows you to create sophisticated-looking Web sites quickly and easily — without a B.S. in computer science! See the section "Setting the Table" later in this chapter for more details.

Converting your text document into a Web site

If you have a text document that you want to convert into a Web page, Writer has a nifty feature for doing that. Writer can automatically break up your document into a series of separate Web pages and create a Home page with links to each Web page. Writer does this simply by generating a new Web page each time it encounters a style that you specify, such as Heading 1. The Heading 1s, for example, then become links on the home page of your Web site.

To convert your text document into a Web site with more than one Web page, do the following:

1. **Choose File⇨Send⇨Create HTML Document.**

   The Name and Path of the HTML Document dialog box appears.

2. **Browse through your folders to the desired location and click the Create New Directory button (Linux or Macintosh) or Create New Folder button (Windows) and fill in the name of your new folder. (Linux and Macintosh users click OK, too.)**

   You always want your Web page or Web site to reside in a folder of its own.

3. **Type in your file name.**

4. **Select a Style from the Styles list box that you want new Web pages to occur.**

   If you have no styles other than default, then your Web page consists of a single Web page.

   If you choose a style such as Heading 1, then your document transforms into a Web site, breaking into a new Web page each time it encounters a Heading 1. And the first page of your Web site, or your home page, consists of any text up to the first Heading 1 in your document and a list with each Heading 1 style appearing as links.

5. **Be sure that the Automatic File Name Extension check box is selected, (Otherwise, you need to type the extension .html to the end of your filename.) Click Save.**

   Your new Web site (or Web page) is available for viewing on a Web browser.

Converting your text document into a Web page

If you want to save your text document as a single Web page, Writer offers a simple solution. Just do the following steps:

1. **Choose File⇨Save As.**

2. **Browse through your folders to the desired location and click the Create New Directory button (Linux or Mac) or Create New Folder button (Windows) and fill in the name of your new folder. (Linux and Mac users click OK, too.)**

3. **Choose HTML document (Windows & Linux) or Web Page (Mac) from the File Type list box.**

4. **Click Save.**

Creating Web pages using the AutoPilot

Writer offers a wide choice of Web page templates, each with a choice of backgrounds and layouts. To create a Web page template by using the AutoPilot, do the following:

1. **Choose File⇨AutoPilot⇨Web Page to bring up the AutoPilot Web Page dialog box.**

2. **Choose a template from the Which Template Should Be Used? list box.**

   You can move the AutoPilot Web Page dialog box and see behind it to view the form.

3. **Choose the layout for your template from the Which Layout Should Be Used? list box. Choose either the Tiled or Scaled Background Image options, if available.**

   Writer offers layouts ranging from sophisticated to cute. The Scaled background image gives a larger and sometimes more fuzzy image than the tiled option. Most often, you will probably want the Tiled option.

4. **Click Create.**

   The new Web page appears and is ready for customization.

To customize the text in your new Web page, just click in the text, write in your own text, and then delete the existing text. To customize graphics, see the section "Changing your graphics." To customize the hyperlinks, see the section "Creating Lots of Links."

The Contact Form and Customer Form, as well as the other forms available in the AutoPilot Web Page dialog box, require special programming on your Web server for any kind of practical use. This is beyond the scope of our book.

Setting the Table

In order to lay out a Web page in the most appealing way, HTML likes to use tables — that's right, the same kind of tables that are in a spreadsheet. But with HTML, you don't need as many cells as you have in a spreadsheet, and you can merge cells and split cells so that your table can have a different number of cells in each row. For example, Figure 7-1 has three cells on the first row, six cells on the second row, and then three cells in each of the remaining rows. In a Writer table, unlike a spreadsheet table, your text always wraps in the cell, and when you press return you can start a new paragraph in the same cell of your table. So any cell in an HTML table can hold as many rows of text as you wish. That is why Figure 7-1 has only a total of 12 cells. Neat, huh?

Figure 7-1:
An easy-to-
create Web
page that
uses a table.

Inserting a table

The first thing that you typically do to create a Web page is to create a table, unless all you want to do is just upload some pictures of your kids so that your mother can see them. In the latter case, you can skip the table. But to create a professional-looking Web site to impress your boss, client, customers — or even your mother — you need to use a table.

To create a table, perform the following steps:

1. **Click in the HTML Document so that a cursor appears and choose Insert⇨Table.**

   The Insert Table dialog box appears. (This is the same Insert Table dialog box that's shown in Figure 5-1.)

2. **Choose a name for your table, if you want, or just use the name that Writer inserts.**

3. **Enter the number of columns and rows into the list boxes.**

   In Figure 7-1, we chose three rows and three columns. We choose one row for the title, one row for the buttons, and one row for the body of the Web page. Then we inserted three more columns into the middle cell, and added one row to the cell in the lower right-hand corner. You can always create more cells or merge cells in any row, and you can always add rows or columns later. Or you can insert another table below this table later on.

4. **Select or deselect the Header check box and the Repeat Header check box.**

   You'll probably want a header for each Web page. A header automatically chooses the table heading style in the first row of boxes and allows you to repeat the header at the top of every page (if your table is more than one page and if you select the Repeat Header check box).

5. **Select the Border check box, if you want a border.**

   This is a personal preference. You can always put borders in or take them out later. We always select the Border check box because we like to see exactly where our cells are.

6. **To AutoFormat your table, click the AutoFormat button, choose a style from the Format list box in the AutoFormat dialog box, and click OK.**

   Unless you have lots of columns and rows, like a spreadsheet, you probably don't want to AutoFormat your table.

7. **Click OK.**

   If you do not select the Borders check box in Step 5, you don't see much change in your page. The only difference is that the ruler now has settings for your cells.

   If you select the Borders check box in Step 6, you see your table with borders. Don't be surprised by how small your table is. Remember, as you type text and insert graphics into your cell, the cell (and the entire row) expands vertically to hold it all. That's how just a few cells can become an entire Web page — even a whole Web site.

Formatting a table

Tables with no formatting are like grids. And unadorned grids are not always very aesthetically interesting. So, Writer offers ways to format your table. You can change the column width if you want a small column for links on one side of the page and a much larger column for the body of your Web page. Also, with the ease of clicking the mouse, Writer lets you merge cells together or split cells apart. In Figure 7-1, the cells in the second row, which contains the buttons, were split several times.

You may want to insert or delete rows or columns, you may want to display some nicely aligned graphics. To do this, you may need to equalize some column widths and/or row widths. Writer can do all that for you and more.

Resizing columns

Pass your mouse over the border between two columns (even if it is invisible), and when your mouse pointer changes to a double-headed arrow, click and drag to resize the column.

Getting the right look for your table

Your Table Object Bar provides easy access to those many useful table features, such as splitting cells, merging cells, adding or deleting rows or columns, spacing rows and columns equally, and so on.

If your Table Object Bar does not already appear, click the small triangle that's on the right side of the Object Bar. If that does not produce the Table Object Bar, click in a cell of the table, making sure that you do not select a graphic. This may make the Table Object Bar appear; if not, click the small triangle again.

You can get the right look for your table by following these tips:

✔ To split a cell, click inside the cell and click the Split Cell button on the Table Object Bar. In the Split Cells dialog box, enter the number of cells that you want to split your cell into, and click the Horizontally or Vertically box. Then click OK. Your cell is split into the number of parts you specified.

✔ To merge two cells, select the cells that you want to merge and click the Merge Cell button on the Table Object Bar.

✔ To insert a row, select a cell in the row above the row that you want to insert and click the Insert Row button on the Table Object Bar.

✔ To insert a column, select a cell in the column to the left of the column that you want to insert and click the Insert Column button on the Table Object Bar.

✔ To space rows or columns equally or optimize your column or row widths or heights, select your column or row, and long-click the Optimize button on the Table Object Bar to view the Optimizing toolbar. Then click one of the following:

- **Space Columns Equally:** Makes all selected columns the same width as the widest selected column.

- **Space Rows Equally:** Makes all selected rows the same height as the widest selected row.

- **Optimal Row Height:** Shrinks row heights to fit the largest entry.

- **Optimal Column Width:** Shrinks the column to fit the largest entry.

✔ To delete a row or column, click in a cell of the row or column that you want to delete. Be careful, of course, not to select a graphic. Then click the Delete Row button or the Delete Column button on the Table Object Bar.

Selecting your cells

To select more than one cell, click in a corner cell of the range of cells that you want to select. Hold the mouse button down so that a cursor appears, and without releasing the button, drag to select the entire range of cells.

To select a single cell, click in the cell that you want to select. Hold the mouse button down so that a cursor appears, and without releasing the button, drag to an adjacent cell and then drag back to the original cell.

Adding and modifying borders and colored backgrounds

Borders and backgrounds add flair to your Web page. You can also use a border to help you begin designing your Web page and then delete the border.

You can use the buttons on the Table Object Bar to select your background, background color, and so on, but using the Table Format dialog box gives you more detailed options.

To insert, delete, or modify borders, perform the following steps:

1. **Select the cell or cells for which you want to insert, delete, or modify a border. Or, click in any cell to modify the entire table.**

2. **Choose Format⇨Table, and click the Borders tab.**

   The Table Format dialog box appears, with the Borders tab displayed.

3. **Choose an arrangement from one of the Line Arrangement boxes, or click a line in the pane below the Line Arrangement boxes to define your own border. Then choose your line style from the Line list box, and choose a color from the Color list box. You can even adjust the spacing between the lines and the cell contents by choosing new values in the Left, Right, Top and Bottom list boxes in the Spacing to Contents pane (or you can keep the defaults).**

4. **Click OK.**

   Your new border appears, or if you chose a line arrangement with no lines or the line style None, your border disappears.

To fill your table cell or cells with a background color, perform the following steps:

1. **Click in the cell, row, or table that you want to fill with a background color.**

2. **Choose Format⇨Table, and click the Background tab.**

   The Table Format dialog box appears, with the Background tab displayed.

3. **To apply the background to the entire row or entire table, choose Row or Table from the For list box. Otherwise, choose the default of Cell.**

4. **Choose Color from the As list box and click the color that you want for your background, or click the No Fill button.**

5. **Click OK.**

   The background color fills your cell. Save your document, and check it out in your browser. Like it?

Keeping your Web browser window open all the time gives you instant feedback about what your page looks like in a browser window. Just save your HTML document each time you want to take a look at it, and reload the page in your browser to view it.

Getting Your Web-Safe Colors

Some computers out in Web land are still showing only 256 colors instead of millions of colors. If you don't mind your colors changing a bit to accommodate the browsers in these computers, you can skip this section. But, if you want all users to see the same colors that you see, you need to change your color palette to Web-safe colors. The Web-safe colors are 216 colors that display the same on all computer systems when the monitor is set to 256 colors. (Forty of the 256 colors do not display exactly the same on both Mac and Windows.)

To change your color palette to Web-safe colors, perform the following steps:

1. **Click the Text Animation button on the Main toolbar.**

   This makes the Draw Object Bar appear; you need this Draw Object Bar to change your colors. (It has nothing to do with animating text. For information on animating text check out Chapter 14.)

2. **Click the Paint Can button on the Draw Object Bar. Or choose Format⇨ Area.**

   The Area dialog box appears.

3. **Click the Colors tab. (Don't click the Colors button; click the tab at the top of the dialog box.)**

   The Colors tab appears.

4. **Click the Load Color List button.**

   The Open dialog box appears and displays a list of files with the `.soc` extension.

5. **Choose** `web.soc`**, and click the Open button.**

   The Open dialog box closes, and the colors on the Colors tab in the Area dialog box now show the Web-safe colors. You can tell these are Web safe colors because when you click any color, the color's name appears in the Name box, and it is a set of numbers. For example, bright yellow is 255 255 0, turquoise blue is 0 255 255, and olive green is 153 204 0.

6. **Click OK.**

   The Area dialog box closes. Now, whenever the color palette appears, it offers only Web-safe colors.

Dealing with Text

Writer allows you to toggle back and forth between the Text Object Bar and the Table Object Bar by clicking the button with the triangle on the right side of the Object Bar. Select the text and use the Text Object Bar to change the color of your text, change the justification, or change the type size. Refer to Chapter 4 for the scoop on formatting text.

HTML styles

When you create your HTML document, Writer automatically fills the Apply Styles list box with styles such as Heading 1, Horizontal Line, and Table contents. These styles use font types and font sizes appropriate to Web pages. Also, when using tables, Writer automatically applies the Table Heading style when you click in the first row of a table. This style is centered, boldface, and uses Bitstream Vera Serif font. The lower rows of a table all have Table Contents style — left-justified, not boldface, the same font.

You can change any of these styles, of course, by clicking anywhere in a paragraph and choosing a different style from the Apply Style list box on the Object Bar. You can also add new styles, as you like. (See Chapter 4 for details.) You might not want to get too fancy with customized styles in your Web page, because the browser viewing your Web page may not have the same font that you specify. For this reason, sticking to the styles that Writer offers is usually best.

Aligning text

Aligning text horizontally is easy — just use the Align buttons on the Text Object Bar. But sometimes you also want to center your text vertically, especially when your cell's row height is large enough to hold more than one line of text. Or you may want to align it to the top or the bottom of the cell. To adjust your text vertically in the cell, do the following:

1. **Click the cell in which you want to align your text vertically.**

   A cursor appears. If it doesn't, you may have accidentally selected a graphic. Click again — not on the graphic this time.

2. **Choose Format⇨Table.**

   The Table Format dialog box appears.

3. **Click the Text Flow tab.**

4. **Select either Top, Centered, or Bottom from the Vertical Alignment option buttons, and click OK.**

   Your text aligns vertically in the cell, according to the option that you chose, but you need to save your document and check it out in a browser to really see the effect.

Creating great-looking titles

Browsers often change fonts, so don't get attached to any beautiful lettering. If you want your text to look in other people's Web browsers exactly how you create it, you need to open a Draw document, type in your text, and then export the document to a GIF file into the same folder as your HTML document. Then return to your HTML document, choose Insert⇨Graphics, and insert your GIF file into your cell. Having some of your text as GIF files looks nicer, but your browser takes longer to load the GIF files than the text in the HTML document, so GIF files may not be practical for your whole Web page. Just a few titles here and there are usually enough to give your page the right touch. In Figure 7-1 (earlier in this chapter), the title Fabulous Flowers is a GIF file.

Check out your finished Web page on as many browsers as you can to make sure that it looks good on all of them. Include the Internet Explorer, Netscape, and Safari browsers. Sometimes something that works perfectly in one browser doesn't work in another. For example, the vertical alignment of text does not work in the Konquerer browser. This is not Writer's fault. This happens because perfect compliance with evolving HTML standards does not exist in the World Wide Web. Some things may always appear different in different browsers. Webmasters spend much of their time inserting code into HTML documents to adjust for these irregularities.

Adding Pretty Pictures

Pictures are a huge part of Web pages today. Web designers used to need to keep pictures to a minimum in order for Web pages to load quickly, but now many people have DSL or faster connections, and even videos can be downloaded. So, if you want pictures, go ahead and add them. Place your pictures where you want by inserting them or copying and pasting them from a Draw document or by dragging them in from the Gallery. You can also use pictures as links or backgrounds for your cells. In Figure 7-1 (earlier in this chapter), the flowers are imported from the Gallery as backgrounds.

To import a graphic into your Web page, perform the following steps:

1. **Copy the graphic file to the folder that contains your HTML document (if they're not already in the same folder).**

   - You can do this in Windows by right-clicking a file in Windows Explorer, dragging the file from one folder to the other, and then choosing Copy Here from the shortcut menu that appears.

   - On the Mac, you can do this by Option+clicking the file in the Finder and dragging the file from one folder to another.

   - The way to copy a file in Linux varies depending on your particular window manager, but the procedure is usually similar to either the Windows or Mac approach.

   If you have lots of graphics for your Web page, you may want to create a separate folder for them within the folder containing your HTML Document. Doing this is okay, just be sure you move your graphic files into the folder *before* you import the graphics into your document. Also, graphic files that Writer automatically generates from pasted graphics should remain in the same folder as the HTML Document unless you want to change their paths in the HTML code — which you probably don't want to do.

2. **Click in the document where you want to import the graphic to.**

   A cursor appears.

3. **Choose Insert⇨Graphics.**

   The Insert Graphics dialog box appears.

4. **Browse through your files to the folder that contains your HTML document, and select the image file that you placed there in Step 1.**

5. **Click the Open button.**

   The image appears. If the image is in a cell, the image fills the cell and is selected, and it may even expand the cell's size vertically. The Frame Object Bar/Web Bar replaces the Text Object Bar or Table Object Bar.

6. **Resize the image by clicking and dragging the green handles around the edges of the image.**

   The image resizes.

7. **If the image is in a cell or on a page that also contains text, you may choose one of these alternatives:**

   - To wrap your text around the image on the left, select your image, click the Align Right button on the Frame Object Bar, and then click the Wrap Left button.

   - To wrap your text around your image on the right, select your image, click the Align Left button, and then click the Wrap Right button.

The image moves to the left or the right, and the text flows around it. If you want greater control over the placement of your image, see the section "Fine-tuning your graphic's size, position, anchor, and text wrapping."

8. **Add borders to your graphic by clicking the Borders button and choosing your border style. Then refine your border by clicking the Line Style button or the Line Color of Border button or the Background Color button.**

That's it!

You can also copy and paste an image into your document, such as an image from Draw. Just copy the object, and then click in your HTML document where you want the image to appear. Make sure that a cursor appears, and then press Ctrl+V to paste the image. Your object appears. Now you can perform Steps 6 through 8 to resize your image, align it, or add a border to it.

To insert a Gallery item, open the Gallery by choosing Tools⇨Gallery. If the Gallery is already open, click the Show triangle on the far left immediately above the Object Bar. Then drag any item into a cell in the table, and perform Steps 6 through 8.

Keep track of how your graphics look with different Web browsers. Some irregularities may be lurking out there.

Fine-tuning your graphic's size, position, anchor, and text wrapping

To get the greatest control over the size and position of your graphic and to anchor your graphic in various ways, do the following:

1. **Select your graphic.**

2. **Click the Graphics Properties button on the Object Bar and choose the Type tab to bring up the Type section of the Graphics dialog box, as shown in Figure 7-2.**

3. **To change the size of your graphic, do one of the following:**

    • Select a new Width or Height from the list boxes.

    • Type in a new Width or Height in the list boxes.

    • Select the Relative check box and choose a new Width or Height from the list boxes as a percentage of your graphic's original size.

    • Select the Relative check box and type in a new Width or Height into the list boxes as a percentage of your graphic's original size.

    • Select the Original Size box to return your graphic to its original size.

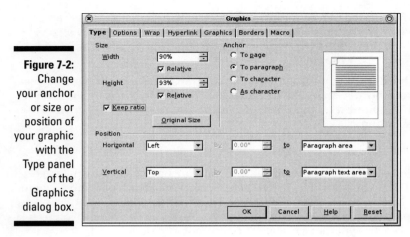

Figure 7-2:
Change
your anchor
or size or
position of
your graphic
with the
Type panel
of the
Graphics
dialog box.

4. **To change the anchor, choose one of the following from the option boxes and notice how the change affects the diagram in the Preview window:**

   - **To Page:** Anchors your graphic to the page. Whatever text is inserted into the page, the graphic stays put wherever you position it on the page.

   - **To Paragraph:** Anchors your graphic to the current paragraph. If paragraphs are inserted above the paragraph your graphic is anchored to, your graphic adjusts its position on the page as the paragraph adjusts its position.

   - **To Character:** Anchors your graphic to a specific character and moves in the page according to the position of the character.

   - **As Character:** The row that your graphic resides on is enlarged to the height of your graphic.

5. **To change the position of your graphic, do one of the following and notice how the diagram in the Preview window adjusts:**

   - Choose a position from the Horizontal and/or Vertical list boxes (for example, Left or Right).

   - Select values from the To list boxes.

   - Select values from the By list boxes (if they are active).

6. **To fine-tune the position of your graphic even further or to wrap text around your graphic, click the Wrap tab.**

7. **To position your graphic left or right, choose a spacing value from the Spacing Left or Right list boxes. To position your graphic up or down, choose a value from the Top or Bottom list boxes.**

   Notice that the Left and Right list boxes each change to the same value. Writer measures from the side that the graphic is aligned to. (The same is true of the Top and Bottom list boxes.) Feel free to type a value into the list boxes for more precision.

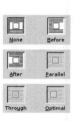

8. **To wrap text around your graphic, choose the appropriate button:**

   - **None:** No text wrapping.
   - **Before:** Text wraps to the right of an image aligned to the left.
   - **After:** Text wraps to the left of an image aligned to the right.
   - **Parallel**: (This is not usually an active button.)
   - **Through:** Text wraps through an image. (Also, click the In Background button in the Options section to send your image behind the text.)
   - **Optimal:** (This is not usually an active button.)

9. **Click OK.**

   Your image appears in its new size, position, and text wrap as you specified.

Changing your graphics

Sometimes you just want to replace a graphic that already exists in a Web page. To do that, follow these steps:

1. **Copy the new graphic files to the folder that contains your HTML document (or sub-folder of it).**

   - You can do this in Windows by right-clicking a file in Windows Explorer, dragging the file from one folder to the other, and then choosing Copy Here from the shortcut menu that appears.
   - On the Mac, Option+click the file in the Finder and dragging the file from one folder to another.
   - The way to copy a file in Linux varies depending on your particular window manager, but the procedure is usually similar to either the Windows or Mac.

2. **In your document, select the graphic that you want to change to a new graphic.**

3. **Choose Insert⇨Graphics to open the Graphics dialog box, and then click the Graphics tab if it is not already selected.**

   The Graphics section appears, showing the selected graphic and its file name.

4. **Click the button in the Link section beside the file name.**

   The Link dialog box appears.

5. **Browse through your folders to the folder containing your HTML document and if necessary, open the sub-folder containing your graphic. Select the graphic that you want to replace the current graphic, and click Open.**

   The graphic appears in the Preview window of the Graphics dialog box.

6. **If you want to flip the graphic vertically or horizontally on all pages or just the left or right pages, click in the appropriate option buttons.**

7. **Click Ok.**

Using graphics as backgrounds

To create a background in your cell, row, or table by using an image from a file or from the gallery, perform the following steps:

1. **Copy the graphic file to the folder that contains your HTML document (if they're not already in the same folder).**

   - You can do this in Windows by right-clicking a file in Windows Explorer, dragging the file from one folder to the other, and then choosing Copy Here from the shortcut menu that appears.

   - On the Mac, Option+click the file in the Finder and dragging the file from one folder to another.

   - The way to copy a file in Linux varies depending on your particular window manager, but the procedure is usually similar to either the Windows or Mac.

   The path to the gallery files in Windows and Linux is OpenOffice.org1.1/share/gallery/www-back. On the Mac, the path is OpenOffice.org1.03/share/gallery/www-back.

2. **Click the cell in which you want to create your background.**

3. **Choose Format⇨Table, and click the Background tab.**

4. **Choose Cell from the For list box if you want the background to appear in just the selected cell, choose Row to have the background appear in a row, or choose Table if you want the background to appear in the whole table.**

5. **Choose Graphic from the As list box.**

The grid of colors closes and a new set of panes appears in the tab.

6. Click Browse to select the file that you want to import.

The Find Graphics dialog box appears.

7. Select the file that you want to import. (This is the file that you moved into the same folder as your HTML document in Step 1.)

If the Preview check box in the dialog box is selected, the image appears in the Preview area at the far right of the dialog box.

8. Click the Open button.

The Find Graphics dialog box closes, and the image appears in the Preview area of the Table Format dialog box. (If it does not, select the Preview check box.)

9. You usually tile a background, so select the Tile check box. If you don't want to tile it, select the Position check box and click in one of the nine circles to specify where it should be in the cell.

10. Click OK.

Your background now fills your cell, row, or table, depending on what you specified in Step 3.

Creating Lots of Links

Links are one of the most dazzling features of Web design, yet they are also one of the simplest features to add. You can use graphics for links or you can use text — whichever suits your fancy. You can link to the Internet, FTP, Telnet, or your own Web pages. You can also bring up a new e-mail message with your e-mail address entered to allow the user to contact you easily. Also, OpenOffice.org has very advanced features that can send information from customer reply forms so that your server can decode it — but to make use of that feature requires knowledge of programming and is beyond the scope of this book.

Transforming text or graphics into links

Here's how to create links to your own Web pages, or an Internet, FTP or Telnet address, or bring up an e-mail message with your subject and address. Follow these steps to create a link:

1. If you are not sure of the precise URL for your Internet, FTP, or Telnet link, open your Web browser and browse to find the Web page that you want to link to. Then copy the entire URL.

This URL can be from your own files or from the Internet.

2. **Select the text or graphic that you want to transform into a link.**

3. **Choose Insert⫐Hyperlink. Or, click the Hyperlink Dialog button on the Function Bar.**

   The Hyperlink dialog box appears, as shown in Figure 7-3. The selected text appears in the Text input box.

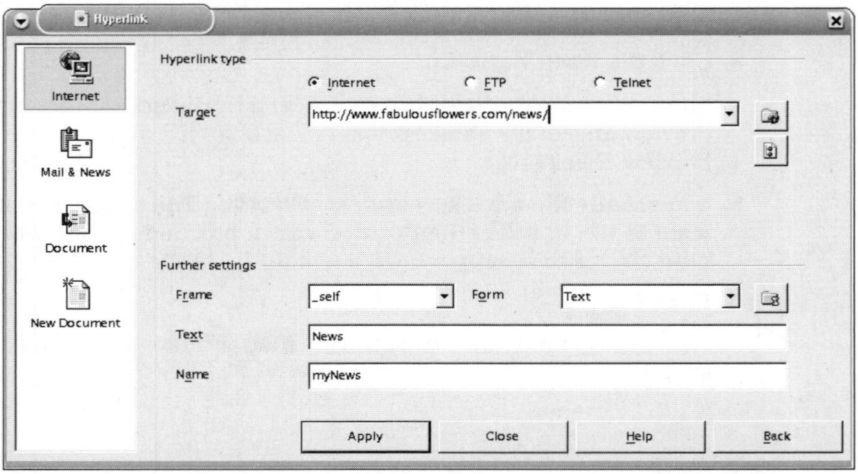

Figure 7-3:
Creating
links
with the
Hyperlink
dialog box.

4. **Select one of the following:**

   Internet: Click this button if your link is on the Internet, FTP, or Telnet.

   Document: Click this button if you are linking to a new page in your Web site and your link resides in the same folder or sub-folder as your Web site. (If it doesn't, then move it there.) Then go to Step 6.

   Mail & News: Click this button to bring up a blank e-mail; then go to Step 7.

5. **If you chose the Internet option, do the following:**

   • Choose one of the following option buttons: Internet, FTP, or Telnet.

   • Paste in the URL in the Target input box from Step 1 or type in the URL. (Don't press the Browse button because it doesn't always work, depending on your computer.)

   • If you choose FTP, you also need to type the name and password.

   Skip to Step 8.

6. If you chose Document in Step 4, do the following:

- Type the URL into the Document Path input box. Alternatively, click the Browse button, select your file name, and click Open. (This Browse button works just fine.)

- Feel free to click the Target in Document button and select a table or other object for your window to open to.

Skip to Step 8.

REMEMBER

Put all your graphics and Web pages in the same folder so that they can be easily uploaded to the Web. Having sub-folders is fine — just be sure to move your graphics or Web pages into sub-folders before they are inserted into your documents.

7. If you chose Mail and News in Step 4, then choose the Email option button and fill in the address and subject for the e-mail.

8. From the Frame list box, choose _blank to open a new window with your link. Or, choose _self to open the link in the same browser window.

The commands parent and top are useful only when using frames. (Frames are HTML documents that can be displayed together in a single Web page so that the browser appears to contain a single document, when it actually contains more than one document. And these frames can link to other frames. So part of your Web page can change when someone clicks a link, and the rest can stay the same.)

9. Type a unique name into the Name box.

HTML needs a name for the link. Any name will do; just be sure that it's different from the name of any other link.

TIP

Always choose Text and never choose Button from the Form list box. The only practical way to use Form buttons for Internet links and Document links is to use them with special server-side programming, which we do not cover in this book. You could use a button to send e-mail, but it requires several more steps to make it work and is much simpler to use a graphic or text link instead.

10. Click the Apply button.

If you selected text, the text that you selected is now underlined and is now active in your HTML document. Don't try selecting your text or graphic link again, unless you want to follow the hyperlink.

11. Click the Close button to close the Hyperlink dialog box.

Editing your links

To modify a hyperlink, click the HYP box on the status bar. (If the status bar is not visible, choose View⇨Status Bar to make it appear.) Clicking the HYP box toggles between hyperlink (HYP) and select (SEL) modes. The SEL mode allows you to select and edit a hyperlink without activating it. Be sure that this box displays SEL, and then you can resize or move your graphic or text. Or if you want to change the hyperlink address, return to Step 3 in the previous section.

Seeing Your HTML Code

The question is, "Do you really want to see your HTML code?" If you do, click the HTML Source button on the Main toolbar. Your HTML code appears. (This method works for documents created by choosing File⇨New⇨HTML Document, but it doesn't work for documents created by choosing File⇨New⇨Text Document.) Scroll down to get a good look. Like it? If so, you may want to consider a career in computer programming. The typical reaction is to close the window again as soon as possible.

Actually, some reasons to fiddle with the code do exist. One reason is if the paths of the graphic files change, you could change their locations in the HTML code. (Although, deleting the graphics and re-inserting them may just be as easy.) Also, sometimes a specific item in the Web page is not displaying well on a lone browser, and a Web site creator can modify the code to work for that specific browser. Other reasons exist, as well, but detailed instructions for changing the HTML code are beyond the scope of this book.

Part III
Using Calc — The Spreadsheet

The 5th Wave   By Rich Tennant

"I can tell a lot from your résumé. You're well educated, detail oriented and own a really tiny printer."

In this part . . .

Spreadsheets are a nifty tool for organizing data. They are perfect for keeping track of money, information, all kinds of things. Anything that requires a list is a good candidate for putting into a spreadsheet.

Not only does your spreadsheet store your data, but it can also do wonderful, almost magical things with it. Want to see a pie chart of how you spend your money? Or to figure out your monthly payments on a new home you want to purchase? It's easy in a spreadsheet. How about storing a mailing list for your business and printing out labels in Zip code order? And while you're at it, why not automatically keep track of your inventory, accounts receivable, accounts payable, budgets, payroll, financial statements, and more!

And if your business uses a database program, such as dBase, MySQL, or many other types, you can link to your database using Calc to find the information you need or to create the reports and charts. The number of things that can be done using this program is amazing.

In this part, you experience the awesome power of Calc.

Chapter 8

Creating a Spreadsheet

In This Chapter

▶ Creating your spreadsheet

▶ Moving around in your spreadsheet

▶ Editing your data

▶ Saving your spreadsheet

*I*n this chapter, you find out how to create a spreadsheet in Calc and navigate around your document. We show you how to easily input and edit your data, and how to add, delete, or hide your columns and rows. And, most importantly, you read about how to save your handiwork.

Getting the Basics Down

A spreadsheet is a grid of boxes. Each box is called a *cell*. Each cell is located in a particular row and column in the grid, as you can see in Figure 8-1. Your spreadsheet's ability to store numbers (and text) is enormous. The spreadsheet can contain 32,000 rows and 255 columns. If each row were about ¼ inch tall, Calc could produce a single sheet in your spreadsheet as tall as a 40-story skyscraper!

Each cell is available to store data. You can store a single number in a cell or an entire book (although that is rare). Or, the cell can be empty. Whatever use you make of your cells is up to you.

More than one cell is called a *range* of cells. You can select a range of cells and move them, copy them, format them, and so on as easily as a single cell.

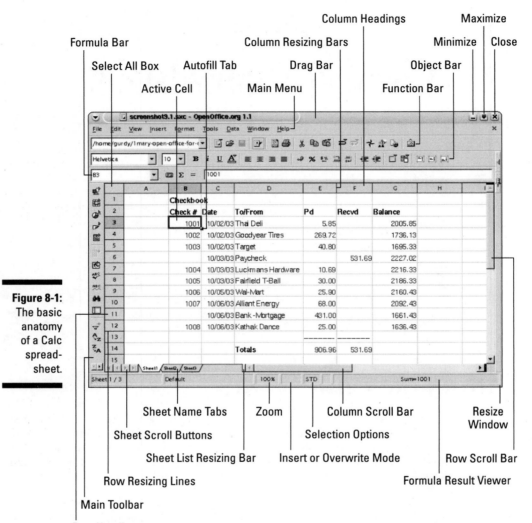

Figure 8-1:
The basic
anatomy
of a Calc
spread-
sheet.

Usually, you use spreadsheets to store a table or groups of tables. A *table* is a
range of cells with related data. For example, a grocery list with quantities is
a table. Your spreadsheet may have only one table in it, or it may have a hun-
dred tables or more. Tables can be as small as two cells or as big as, well, a
40-story skyscraper.

If you have more than one table that is related, such as a monthly budget, you can stack the tables into *sheets*. By using sheets, you have the ability to add or otherwise manipulate your data in three directions: vertically, horizontally, and by depth.

Inputting Your Data

To open your spreadsheet, choose File⇨New⇨Spreadsheet. A grid of cells appears, with toolbars and a main menu (refer to Figure 8-1). This is your spreadsheet.

Notice that one cell has a dark frame around it. This is your *active cell*. When you type and enter data into your spreadsheet, Calc places the data in the active cell. The dark frame around the cell is called the *active cell pointer*.

Calc assigns each cell an *address,* which is the column name of the cell, followed by the row name — for example, A1 or Z4026. You refer to a range of cells by using the cell names of the upper-left cell and the lower-right cell, separated by a colon — for example, A1:Z4026.

pg 96

Entering your data

To enter data into a cell, just start typing. Your data appears within the active cell. When you press Enter, Calc moves the active cell pointer to the cell below. To enter your data in a different direction, press an arrow key instead of pressing Enter after entering your data. The active cell pointer relocates accordingly.

Want to type a whole lot of text in a single cell? Calc handles text in clever ways. Don't worry if your text is longer than the width of the cell. The text shows in the next cell, as long as that cell is empty. And, if that cell is not empty, you can always double-click the cell with your text, and your full line of text appears.

Editing your data

Entering data is easy with Calc, but what if you want to change what you entered? Fortunately, editing data is just as easy.

To edit the contents of the active cell, follow these steps:

1. **Double-click the cell that you want to edit.**

   This transforms the cell into the active cell and causes a cursor to appear within the cell.

2. **Move the cursor with the arrow keys to where you want to edit.**

   You can also click anywhere in your data, and the cursor repositions itself.

3. **Type in your change.**

4. **Press Enter.**

Using Insert mode and Overwrite mode

Do you like to click buttons, even when you don't know what they do? If the answer is yes, you need to know about Insert and Overwrite modes. Getting stuck in Overwrite mode is no fun. But read on to understand more about the two modes.

Calc has two modes of editing: Insert mode and Overwrite mode. In Insert mode, the text is inserted at the location of the cursor, pushing existing text to the right. In Overwrite mode, text overwrites other text that exists at the location of the cursor. Insert mode is the default mode. You can toggle between Insert mode and Overwrite mode by clicking the mode box in the status bar (the bar at the bottom of your window). The box shows INSRT or OVER.

If INSRT or OVER is not displayed in the status bar, double-click a cell so that a cursor appears. This causes either INSRT or OVER to appear in the status bar.

Deleting the contents of the active cell

To delete the contents of a cell, click the cell that you want to delete and press Backspace. The entire contents of the cell are deleted.

Filling cells automatically

Calc has a nifty feature for automatically inputting values. If you want to enter numbers sequentially or in regular multiples (such as 2, 4, 6, 8, and so on) but you don't want to type each one individually, that's no problem. Put Calc to work for you.

To automatically input numbers sequentially into your spreadsheet, perform the following steps:

1. **Type the number that you want to begin with in the active cell.**

   For example, if you want your numbers to read 5, 6, 7, 8, and so on, type **5**.

2. **Return the active cell to the cell that contains your number.**

   Your active cell moved when you typed your number. Just press the appropriate arrow key, or click the cell with the number that you just typed.

3. **Click and drag the small square in the lower-right corner of the active cell pointer, as shown in Figure 8-2, and drag either up, down, or across the cells.**

Figure 8-2:
The Autofill tab is a small square in the lower-left corner of the active cell. Clicking and dragging the square autofills your cells with sequential numbers or multiples.

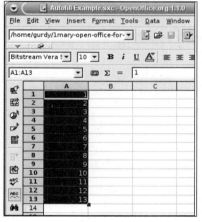

Dragging up or to the left counts backward. Dragging down or to the right counts forward. Your range is outlined in red, and a box appears showing the value for the farthest cell. When you release the mouse, your numbers appear.

When you have a row or column of numbers, you can select the numbers by clicking in the top cell and dragging the mouse to the bottom cell. Selected cells appear shaded. When your numbers are selected, you can automatically fill a whole table, if you want. Just pull on the Autofill tab of the active cell and drag. Of course, few people really need a whole table of auto-filled numbers, but you may be the exception.

To automatically input numbers in multiples, perform the following steps:

1. **In two adjacent cells, type the multiple that you want to use.**

    For example, type **5** in cell A1 and **10** in cell A2.

2. **Select cells A1 and A2 by clicking cell A1 and dragging the mouse to cell A2.**

3. **Click and drag the small square in the lower-right corner of the active cell pointer.**

4. **Drag the mouse down over the rows.**

    When you release the mouse button, the multiples are entered into your cells.

Moving and Grooving in the Grid

Spreadsheets can range in size from the smallest four-cell miniatures to gargantuan, but friendly beasts. Fortunately, getting around even the biggest spreadsheets is no problem. You can navigate with either the mouse or the keyboard.

Scurrying around your grid with your mouse

You can manipulate the grid with your mouse in the following ways:

- Dragging the scroll bars shows rows and columns that are out of view.
- Clicking and holding the arrow symbol on a scroll bar allows you to proceed line by line through rows or columns.
- Clicking and holding the space that's adjacent to the arrow symbol on a scroll bar allows you to proceed page by page through rows or columns.

Let your fingers do the walking

Using your arrow keys to navigate through your document cell by cell gets you around your document easily. But if your document is large, you need more than just the arrow keys to reach your destination efficiently. Press the following keys or key combinations to quickly navigate through your document:

- **Page Up or Page Down:** Pages through your document.
- **Home:** Moves the active cell pointer to the first column of a row.
- **End:** Moves the active cell pointer to the last column of a row.
- **Ctrl+Backspace:** Finds the active cell.
- **Ctrl+arrow (Ctrl plus any arrow key):** Zips around your spreadsheet.

  If the active cell is in a table (and not the last entry in the direction that you want to head), Calc moves to the last filled cell of the table in the direction of the arrow. If the active cell is empty, Calc moves to the first filled cell that it encounters in the direction of the arrow. If no more filled cells exist in the direction of the arrow, Calc moves the active cell to the last (or first) cell of the spreadsheet. This is either row 32000 or row 1, or column IV or column A.

If pressing Ctrl+arrow mysteriously stops you at an empty cell when you expect it to take you to the beginning or end of a column or row, or to stop at a cell with data, the cell where it stopped may look empty but actually contain unseen blank spaces or other invisible items. You can clear the cell by pressing Backspace.

Managing Columns and Rows

When creating a new spreadsheet, Calc assigns each column a standard width of about ⁹⁄₁₀ of an inch (on our monitor, anyway). But, needless to say, your data does not always conform to those dimensions. Some columns may contain lots of text. Other columns may have only a single digit in them. Calc allows you to easily change the widths of your columns and even change the heights of your rows.

Also, creating a spreadsheet can be a very organic process: One column or row may need to grow into three or five — like the trunk of a tree becoming branches and twigs. You'll no doubt want to add or even prune some rows or columns.

Changing column widths and row heights

To change column widths and row heights using the mouse, perform the following steps:

1. **Click the line that separates two column names or row names, as shown in Figure 8-1. Choose the line that is to the right of the column that you want to resize (or below the row that you want to resize).**

   For example, the line between columns D and E resizes column D, and the line between rows 3 and 4 resizes row 3. The mouse pointer changes to a double-headed arrow.

2. **While holding down the mouse button, drag the line to the desired column width or row height.**

We know a quick mouse method for changing column widths and row heights. We give it two thumbs up! Double-click the line separating the two column names or row names that is to the right of the column that you want to resize (or below the row that you want to resize), as shown in Figure 8-1. Calc optimizes the column width or row height according to the data that's currently in that column or row.

To change column widths and row heights by using the main menu, follow these steps:

1. **Click a cell in the column or row that you want to resize.**

2. **Choose Format⇨Column⇨Width to open the Column Width dialog box. Or, choose Format⇨Row⇨Height to open the Row Height dialog box.**

3. **Enter the desired size of your column or row.**

4. **Click OK.**

   Make sure that you like the new column or row size.

To change column widths and row heights by using a sometimes faster main menu method, perform the following steps:

1. **Click a cell in the column or row that you want to resize.**

2. **Choose Format⇨Column⇨Optimal Width, or choose Format⇨Row⇨Optimal Height.**

3. **Use the up or down arrows in the Add list box to select how much width or height to add to the column or row, or enter a value in the Add list box instead.**

Want to quickly change the formatting of your columns or rows back to their default dimensions? Just double-click the line that separates the two column names or row names (refer to Figure 8-2). Be sure that the line is to the right of the column or below the row that you want to resize. Your column or row resizes to the default size.

You can also perform the following steps to return your columns and rows to their default sizes:

1. **Place the active cell pointer in a cell in the column or row that you want to restore to the default size.**

2. **Choose Format⇨Column⇨Width, or choose Format⇨Row⇨Height.**

   The Column Width dialog box or Row Height dialog box appears.

3. **Select the Default Value check box.**

4. **Click OK.**

Adding columns and rows

To add columns or rows in between other columns or rows, follow these steps:

1. **Select a cell or a range of cells to the right of the column that you want to add, or below the row that you want to add.**

   Calc inserts one row or column for each row or column that you selected.

2. **Choose Insert⇨Columns, or choose Insert⇨Rows. You can also long-click (click and hold a few seconds) the Insert Cells button on the Main toolbar. If the Main toolbar is not visible, choose View⇨Toolbars⇨ Main Toolbar to make it appear.**

   The floating Insert Cells toolbar appears.

3. **On the Insert Cells toolbar, click the Insert Columns button or the Insert Rows button.**

   Calc renames all the columns or rows so that they are still in alphabetical or numerical order.

Deleting columns and rows

Perhaps you want to prune a few twigs here and there. To delete columns or rows, follow these steps:

1. **Select at least one cell in each column or row that you want to delete.**

2. **Choose Edit⇨Delete Cells to open the Delete Cells dialog box.**

3. **Select the Delete Entire Column(s) check box or the Delete Entire Row(s) option button.**

4. **Click OK.**

   Calc then renames all the columns or rows as though the deleted rows never existed.

Hiding columns and rows

Just for fun, try making a column or row disappear. Yes, this is possible. It is formally known as *hiding.* This can be useful when you want to print different versions of your spreadsheet for different clients, but you don't want go to the trouble of creating new tables.

To hide a column or row, follow these steps:

1. **Click and drag the line that separates the two column or row names.**

2. **Drag the column or row line beyond the line of the preceding column or row.**

   For example, click the line between rows H and I, and drag that line to column C.

   Your columns now read A, B, C, I, J, and so on. Don't worry, Calc has not devoured your columns. You can get them back whenever you want — we hope. (Just kidding.)

You can also hide a column or row by following these steps:

1. **Select the cells in the columns or rows that you want to hide.**

2. **Choose Format⇨Column⇨Hide, or choose Format⇨Row⇨Hide.**

Hidden columns or rows are restored to the default size. If your rows or columns are resized and you don't want to resize them a second time, do not hide them.

Restoring hidden columns and rows

Hidden columns or rows are easy to find.

- If spreadsheet column rows or numbers are missing, such as in the sequence A, B, C, D, J, K, the missing rows or numbers are hidden.

- Calc highlights the line between two columns where hidden columns exist.

✔ To restore hidden columns, use one of the following methods:

- Double click slightly to the *right* of the highlighted line between the two visible column names that surround the hidden columns.

- Select a group of cells on both sides of the hidden columns, and choose Format⇨Column⇨Show.

  For example, if columns D and E are hidden, select cells in column C and column F and then choose Format⇨Column⇨Show.

✔ To restore hidden rows, use one of the following methods:

- Double click slightly *below* the highlighted line between the two visible row names that surround the hidden rows.

- Select a group of cells on both sides of the hidden rows, and then choose Format⇨Row⇨Show.

  For example, if rows 12 and 13 are hidden, select cells in row 11 and row 14 and then choose Format⇨Column⇨Show.

If the double-headed arrow is centered directly on the line and not slightly off center to the right for columns or below for rows, you could double-click forever and not see those hidden columns or rows. (Gulp!)

Crash! Boom! Quick, Save!

After you create, format, and edit your spreadsheet, you probably want to save it as well. Saving is easy in Calc.

Choosing File⇨Save opens the Save As dialog box the first time that you choose this command. Click the Up One Level button or double-click folder names to navigate to the folder that you want to save your file. Or create a new folder by clicking the Create New Directory button and typing a folder name. Then type in a name for your file in the file name box. Be sure that the Automatic File Name Extension check box is selected. And unless you are exporting your final data to Microsoft Excel, you probably want the File type to be OpenOffice.Org 1.0 Spreadsheet.

Does more than one person use your computer? Want to keep your spreadsheet safe, secure, and secret? If so, select the Save with Password check box. When you enter Save, a dialog box appears requesting you to enter a password twice. Be sure to remember this password, because the next time that you open your spreadsheet, you will be asked for it.

Be sure to save frequently while using OpenOffice.org. You never know when a bolt of lightning may strike or when a tennis ball may land on the on/off switch of your surge protector. For faster saving, press Ctrl+S.

For those who just can't remember to save (and have paid the price by losing hours of work), Calc offers an AutoSave option. And why not always create a backup copy of your spreadsheet, as well? Calc offers this option, too.

To activate the AutoSave and the backup options, perform the following steps:

1. **Choose Tools⇨Options⇨Load/Save⇨General.**

   This opens the Options-Load/Save-General dialog box, as shown in Figure 8-3.

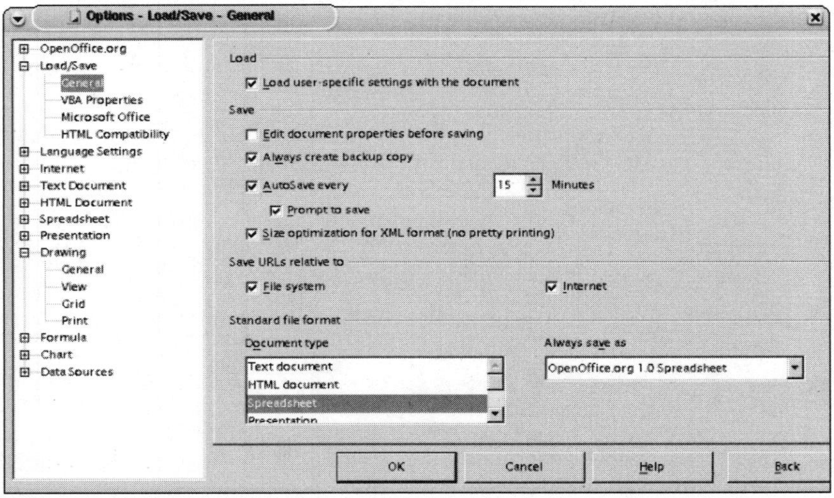

Figure 8-3:
The Options-Load/Save-General dialog box has lots of useful items.

2. **To activate AutoSave, select the AutoSave Every check box and type in or scroll to enter the appropriate AutoSave interval, in minutes. Select the Prompt to Save check box if you want your computer to ask you for permission to save each time.**

   Prompting can be annoying, but if you like to revert to a previous version of your spreadsheet, prompting may be the ideal option for you.

3. **To automatically save a backup copy every time you save your spreadsheet, select the Always Create Backup Copy check box.**

   If some calamity occurs and you need to access this backup copy, you can find it in a folder called backups. If you do not readily see this folder on your computer, choose Tools⇨Options⇨OpenOffice.Org⇨Paths. Then search for Backups in the list of paths to see where your Backups folder is located.

4. **Click OK.**

Chapter 9

At Home on the Range

Spreadsheets are famous for having beautiful columns of numbers — all with two decimal places and maybe some with dollar signs or other currency signs. Spreadsheets often have nice-looking titles and column headings where the text may be enlarged or in boldface. How do you get the look you want? You format.

To format *ranges* (collections) of cells, you need to know how to readily select the ranges. A range can be as small as one cell or as large as your entire spreadsheet. After you select your range, you can manipulate all those cells in one fell swoop. Whether you want to drag and drop, format, or make other changes, knowing the ways to select your cells is important. And, because your ranges may not just be on a single sheet but may span many sheets, we discuss how to select sheets and provide a basic understanding of sheets as well in this chapter.

Selecting Your Cells

Suppose that you want to edit large groups of data at the same time. You may also want to delete the contents of many cells all at once. Calc allows you to select large blocks of cells and move them around your spreadsheet — or format them in different ways. You can apply formulas to selected cells. You can even select several blocks of cells at the same time. For faster selection, try using the keyboard method of selecting cells. Two keystrokes can select even the largest table of data.

Selecting a range of cells

Calc allows you to select cells in a variety of ways. To select a range of cells using the mouse, follow these steps:

1. **Click one of the four corner cells of the range that you want to select.**

2. **Hold the mouse button down, and drag the mouse to the diagonal corner cell of the range.**

   The cells that are selected appear shaded, as shown in Figure 9-1.

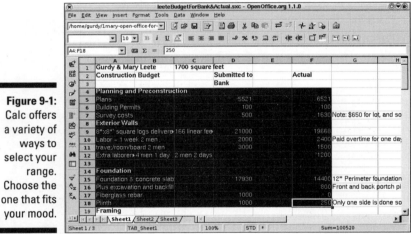

Figure 9-1: Calc offers a variety of ways to select your range. Choose the one that fits your mood.

Do not drag the active cell from its lower-right corner. This is the Autofill handle, and cells that are selected when you release the mouse are autofilled with new data.

To select a range of cells using the keyboard, follow these steps:

1. **Click one of the four corner cells of the range that you want to select.**

2. **Press and hold Shift while moving the arrow keys in the direction of the cells that you want to select.**

   The selected cells appear shaded, as shown in Figure 9-1.

Selecting a large range of cells

When your spreadsheet is quite large, clicking and dragging the mouse or using arrow keys while pressing Shift to select cells is not practical. (Remember, you could have a 40-story-high spreadsheet.)

To select a large range of cells while using the mouse, follow these steps:

1. **Click one of the four corner cells of the range that you want to select.**

2. **Click the Selection Options box in the Status Bar (at the bottom of your window) until the box displays** EXT.

   The box may display ADD, or it may show STD (refer to Figure 9-1).

3. **Use the scroll bars to locate the opposite diagonal corner of the range of cells that you want to select, and click that cell.**

   Calc selects the range.

To select a large range of cells using the keyboard, follow these steps:

1. **Position your active cell pointer at the upper-left corner of a range of cells that you want to select.**

2. **Press Shift+Ctrl+→.**

   This automatically selects all cells in the first row up to the first empty cell.

3. **Press Shift+Ctrl+↓.**

   This automatically selects all the rows of your table down to the first empty cell in the last column.

To select a large range of cells with the keyboard by typing the cell addresses, follow these steps:

1. **Locate the sheet area to the left of the input line.**

2. **Type in the cell addresses of two diagonal corners of the range separated by a colon. (For example: C1:F35.)**

3. **Press Enter.**

   Calc selects the range.

Selecting noncontiguous ranges of cells

You can select several ranges that are not next to each other (*noncontiguous*). To select a noncontiguous range of cells using the mouse, follow these steps:

1. **Click the Selection Options box in the Status Bar until it displays** ADD.

2. **Click and drag to select a block of cells.**

3. **Repeat Step 2 to select as many noncontiguous ranges as you want.**

   If you select a cell that is already selected, this method deselects that cell.

Using the ADD feature, you can easily select any cells you want in any arrangement you desire — even the pattern that's shown in Figure 9-2.

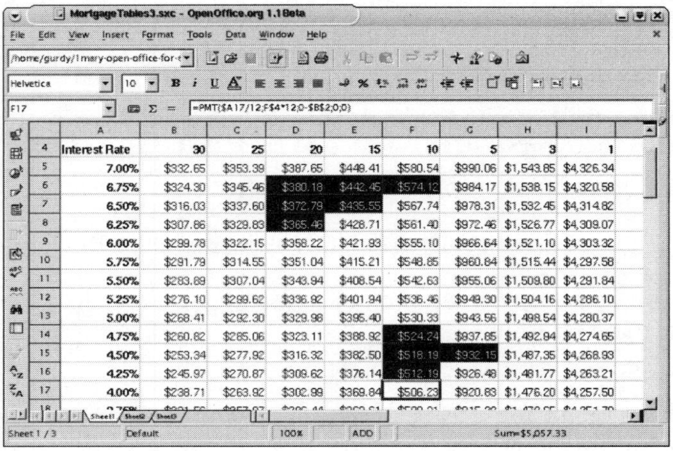

Figure 9-2:
You can select any configuration of cells using the ADD option.

To select a noncontiguous range of cells using both the keyboard and the mouse (a hybrid method), follow these steps:

1. **Click and drag to select a range of cells, and then release the mouse button.**

2. **Press Ctrl while repeating Step 1.**

Selecting one, many, or all columns or rows

To select a single row or column, click the row number or column name.

To select several rows or columns, follow these steps:

1. **Click the first row or column that you want to select.**

2. **Press and hold Shift, and click the last row or column that you want to select.**

To select the entire active sheet, choose Edit⇔Select All or press Ctrl+A. You can also click the square at the upper-left corner of your sheet, which is the junction of both the column names and row names.

Copying, Pasting, Cutting, Dragging, and Dropping Your Cells

When you have your cells selected, it's child's play to cut and paste them, drag and drop them, and move them all around.

Copying and pasting cells

To copy and paste a range of cells, follow these steps:

1. **Select the range of cells that you want to copy.**

2. **If the Function Bar is not visible, choose View⇨Toolbars⇨Function Bar to make it appear.**

3. **Choose Edit⇨Copy, press Ctrl+C, or click the Copy button on the Function Bar.**

4. **Select the cell that you want to paste the upper-left corner of your range into.**

5. **Choose Edit⇨Paste, press Ctrl+V, or click the Paste button on the Function Bar.**

Cutting and pasting cells

To cut and paste a range of cells, follow these steps:

1. **Select the range of cells that you want to copy.**

2. **Choose Edit⇨Cut, press Ctrl+X, or click the Cut button on the Function Bar. (If the Function Bar is not visible, choose View⇨Toolbars⇨ Function Bar to make it appear.)**

3. **Select the cell that you want to paste the upper-left corner of your range into.**

4. **Choose Edit⇨Paste, press Ctrl+V, or click the Paste button on the Function Bar.**

Dragging and dropping cells

You may find this is the most enjoyable way to cut and paste. Once you know how to drag and drop, you may want to do nothing else.

1. **Click the Selection Options box in the Status Bar until the box displays** STD.

   You can only drag and drop single cells or standard rectangular ranges.

2. **Click and drag to select a range.**

3. **Click anywhere in the selected area, and drag the entire range to a new location.**

Formatting Numbers and Text

One of the first things that you probably want to do when you create your spreadsheet is to format your numbers. Your numbers may be quantities, dollars, or percentages. If they are dollars, you may want to see the dollar signs — or maybe you don't — but you probably don't want to see more than two numbers after the decimal points. A tenth of a penny just clutters your beautiful spreadsheet. Calc's formatting abilities are as impressive as they are easy to use.

You can format your numbers in two ways: using the Object Bar or using the Format Cells dialog box.

Formatting numbers with the Object Bar

Locate the Object Bar shown in Figure 9-3. This toolbar appears just above the Formula Bar in your window. If the Object Bar is not visible, choose View⇨Toolbars⇨Object Bar to make it appear.

To format numbers with the Object Bar, follow these steps:

1. **Select the cell or range of cells that you want to format.**

   You can select a range using any of the numerous techniques described in the "Selecting Your Cells" section earlier in this chapter.

   The selected cells appear shaded.

2. **From the Object Bar, click one of the following buttons for the formatting style that you want to use:**

   • **Currency:** Shows your numbers with dollar signs and two decimal places. This format is commonly used on the top row of a table and in the Total rows. Dollar signs throughout an entire table may look messy.

- **Percentage:** Places a percentage sign after your number, along with two decimal places. If you do not want the decimal places, you can omit them by clicking twice on the Number Format:Delete Decimal Place button (three buttons to the right).

- **Number Format:Standard:** If you goof using the other formats and want things to look the way that they did from the start, this button returns the cell to the standard format. This is important because simply deleting data does not delete the underlying format of the cell. You must use this button to eliminate a format from a cell.

- **Add Decimal Place:** Adds an additional decimal place each time you click the Add Decimal Place button. To format currency without currency signs, click this button twice to add two decimal places to your number.

- **Delete Decimal Place:** Deletes a decimal place each time you click the Delete Decimal Place button.

- **Decrease Indent:** Moves your numbers slightly to the left each time that you click this button so that you can line up your numbers with your text. Remember, Calc left-justifies text in the cell and right-justifies numbers. If you don't want that crooked look in your columns, you need to either left-justify your numbers or right-justify your text. Changing the indent does not change your numbers' ability to act as numbers.

- **Increase Indent:** Moves your numbers slightly to the right each time that you click this button so that you can properly line up data in a column.

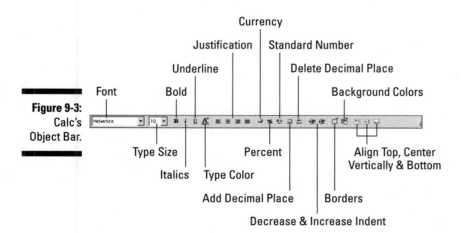

Figure 9-3:
Calc's
Object Bar.

When you format your numbers, any subsequent change of the data in that cell also reflects that same format. Even if you delete the contents of the cell, the next time that you enter data into the cell, the same format appears. To return a cell to its original format, you must select the cell and click the Number Format:Standard button.

Adding style with the Object Bar

Want to change your font type, size, and style right from the Object Bar? Calc makes formatting text easy. To choose your font type, size, and style, follow these steps:

1. **Click the cell that you want to format. Or select a range of cells.**

   The selected cells appear shaded.

2. **Select your font from the Font Name list box on the Object Bar.**

   If the Object Bar is not visible, choose View⇨Toolbars⇨Object Bar to make it appear.

3. **Choose the font size from the Font Size list box on the Object Bar.**

   Calc resizes the rows to accommodate the larger or smaller sizes of type.

4. **Choose your style.**

   Choose either boldface, italic, or underline, or choose the color for your type by clicking the appropriate button on the Object Bar.

Formatting using the Format Cells dialog box

The Format Cells dialog box can do everything that the Object Bar can do — and more. For example, if you are from Finland and your spreadsheet is showing the American dollar sign, this is probably not what you want. Or, suppose that you are a scientist, and you need to view your numbers in scientific notation. What if you just want to know what day of the week that you were born on? Try the Format Cells dialog box, shown in Figure 9-4.

Choosing a number format

To format numbers, dates, or more, follow these steps:

1. **Select the cell or range of cells that you want to format.**

2. **Choose Format⇨Cells or right-click anywhere in the selected area, and choose Format Cells from the shortcut menu that appears.**

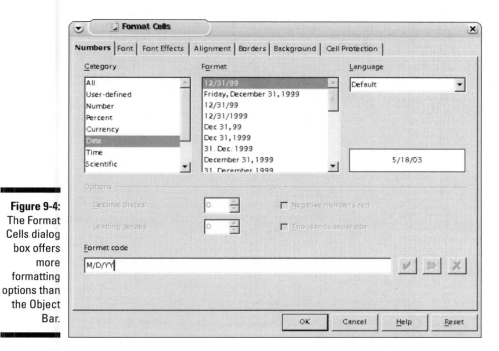

Figure 9-4:
The Format
Cells dialog
box offers
more
formatting
options than
the Object
Bar.

3. **Click the Numbers tab.**

4. **Choose All from the Category list.**

5. **To view the formats, scroll through the Format list.**

6. **Click the format that suits your needs. For scientific notation, click one of the numbers with the E in the middle of it. (If you're a scientist, you'll recognize it.)**

   And, more importantly, to find out what day you were born on, choose the `Friday, December 31, 1999` format.

7. **Click OK.**

For example, to find the day you were born, type **6/12/71**, and Calc automatically displays `Saturday, June 12, 1971.` Maybe you will find, like we did, that your whole family was born on the same day of the week!

If you choose a long format such as the day and date format in our birthday example, you may be disappointed to see that instead of your birthday, the symbol ### appears. Don't fret. Calc is just informing you that it cannot fit everything it needs to display in your narrow column. Just make your column wider to see everything. To make your column wider, click and drag the line between two column headings. For example, if your formatted cell is in column B, drag the line between heading B and heading C. Or double-click the line and the column resizes automatically.

Getting the right look for your money

Another great function of the Format Cells dialog box is its ability to change currency signs.

Want to use the Dutch guilder? Or Euros instead of boring dollars? If you live in beautiful Holland or elsewhere in Europe, you probably want to do that. And while you're at it, you probably don't want to read English dates if you are Russian or Norwegian, or if you speak Spanish. Fortunately Calc allows you to choose from a wide array of currencies and languages. Follow these steps to translate your currency, dates, and more:

1. **Select the cell or range of cells that you want to format.**

2. **Choose Format⇨Cells.**

3. **In the Format Cells dialog box, click the Numbers tab.**

4. **Choose your language from the Language list box.**

5. **Choose All from the Category list.**

6. **Scroll through the Format list, and choose your currency format.**

   The correct currency symbols automatically appear in the list.

   If you want, choose a date format.

To AutoCorrect or not to AutoCorrect

As you type your text into the cells of your active sheet, you may notice that when you move to the next cell, the text that you typed may change. Perhaps the first letter suddenly becomes capitalized. Or perhaps you typed **abotu** and Calc changed it to about.

Hopefully, Calc is changing things to your liking. But if abotu is the name of a Brazilian butterfly and you do not want it changed, or if you are in a particularly touchy mood and you feel like your computer is criticizing you, you may want to modify the options of AutoCorrect.

Turning off automatic capitalization

Some options you probably want to keep, for example, COrrect TWo INitial CApitals. But other options, such as Capitalize the First Letter of Every

Sentence, may drive you batty. The problem is that many words that you type into your spreadsheet are not sentences, but data items. And you may not want all your data items capitalized.

To turn off automatic capitalization, follow these steps:

1. **Choose Tools⇨AutoCorrect to open the AutoCorrect dialog box.**

2. **Click the Options tab to view the list of Options, as shown in Figure 9-5.**

3. **To change any option, select or deselect the appropriate check box.**

   Most options are self-explanatory. However, the Automatic *bold* and underline option automatically changes the style to bold if your text is surrounded by *s or underlines your text if it is surrounded by _s. Be sure to deselect the Capitalize First Letter of Every Sentence check box.

4. **Click OK.**

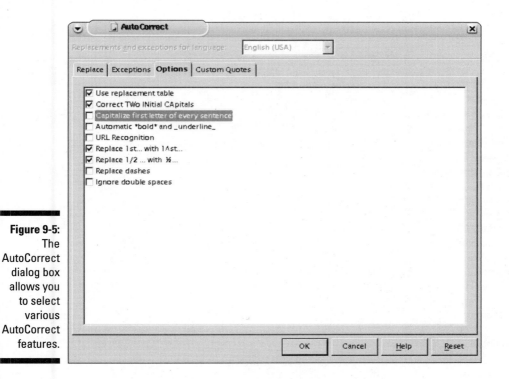

Figure 9-5:
The
AutoCorrect
dialog box
allows you
to select
various
AutoCorrect
features.

Adding a shortcut or common misspelling to the replacement table

The replacement table is not just for misspellings. In fact, the first entry in the list is an easy way of getting the copyright symbol. In your spreadsheet, you can simply type **(C)** and the copyright symbol (©) appears automatically. Another use for this table is to create shortcuts. Suppose that you need to type the word *supermarket* many times in a spreadsheet. You can create a shortcut for it by typing **su**.

To add to the replacement table, follow these steps:

1. **Choose Tools⇨AutoCorrect.**

   The AutoCorrect dialog box appears.

2. **Click the Replace tab.**

   Glance at the replacement table, as shown in Figure 9-6. Commonly misspelled words are listed in the list box on the left and their correct spellings in the list box on the right.

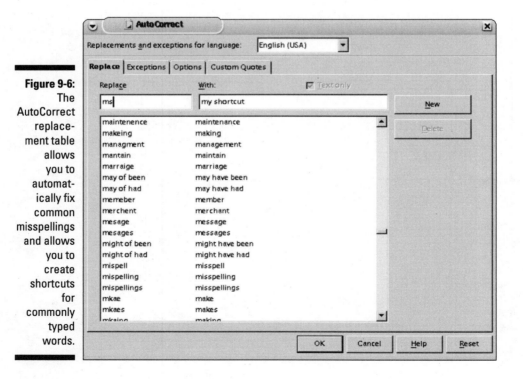

Figure 9-6: The AutoCorrect replacement table allows you to automatically fix common misspellings and allows you to create shortcuts for commonly typed words.

3. **If the replacement list is empty, choose English(USA) from the list box.**

   A replacement table appears that contains many common misspellings. Other languages may need to be entered manually.

4. **Type your new commonly misspelled word or shortcut into the Replace line.**

   If a term is already in that line, just select the term and delete it. (This does not delete it from the replacement table.)

5. **Type the text that you want to use as the replacement into the With box.**

   If text exists in the With box, then your term already exists in the replacement list. You can modify the text in the With box, if you want.

6. **Click the New button or Replace button to enter your words into the replacement list.**

   If the New button is not active, your new shortcut or common misspelling is probably already in the replacement table. You need to either choose a new term to replace, or modify the text in the With box.

Want to play a practical joke? Type **the** in the Replace box, and type **turtle** in the With box. Click the New button, and then click OK. Then let someone use your program. Every time he or she types **the**, the computer automatically changes it to `turtle`. Pretty funny? Maybe not, but you didn't learn it from us.

Deleting items from the replacement table

If your name happens to be a commonly misspelled word, or if you just played a practical joke on someone and now need to fix it, you may want to delete items from the replacement table, which you can do by performing these steps:

1. **Choose Tools⇨AutoCorrect, and click the Replace tab in the AutoCorrect dialog box.**

2. **Select the item that you want to delete from the table. Or, just type the item into the Replace box, and AutoCorrect selects it for you.**

3. **Click the Delete button.**

   Clicking the Reset button (instead of the Delete button) does not delete your additions to the replacement table; it only erases your current entry.

Spell-checking

If you're like us, you may make lots of spelling mistakes, and you appreciate a subtle hint from the computer that something may be awry. A simple red underline of a misspelled word is a nice feature. Of course, if your data consists of text-like product codes instead of complete words, you may be seeing lots of red.

To toggle the Automatic Spellchecking feature on or off, simply click the Automatic Spellchecking button on the Main toolbar, as shown in Figure 9-7. You can also choose Tools⇨Spellcheck⇨AutoSpellcheck.

Figure 9-7:
Click the Automatic Spell-checking button on the Main toolbar to toggle automatic spell-checking on or off. A wavy red line appears below suspected misspellings.

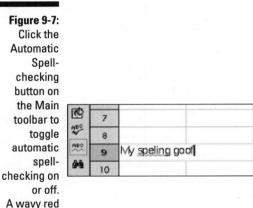

You also have the option to spell-check the entire document with the help of a dialog box and an automatic dictionary that suggests revisions. Just click the Spellchecking button on the Main toolbar or choose Tools⇨Spellcheck⇨ Check to open the Spellcheck dialog box.

Seeing Sheer Simplicity in Sheets

When you create your spreadsheet (also called a *worksheet*), Calc creates a three-dimensional workbook that is a collection of stacked sheets. The sheets are given default names of sheet1, sheet2, and sheet3, and tabs with the names of each sheet are located near the lower-left corner of the spreadsheet window. Click the appropriate tab, and a new spreadsheet appears.

The maximum number of sheets that Calc allows in a single workbook is 256. You can add sheets, delete sheets, name sheets anything you like, and manipulate sheets in a variety of ways. You can enter data into one sheet and have the data simultaneously be entered into all the selected sheets. Knowing how to use sheets can make life a breeze — instead of a tornado.

Adding sheets

When you use up the three sheets that Calc supplies in every new spreadsheet document, you need to add some more.

To add a sheet, follow these steps:

1. **Click a sheet name that is located either before or after where you want to add new sheets.**

   Sheet names are located on tabs near the lower-right corner of the spreadsheet window, as shown in Figure 9-8.

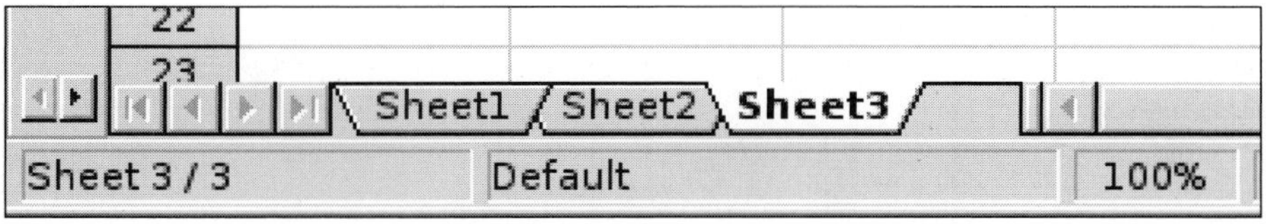

Figure 9-8:
Selected sheet name tabs appear white, and deselected sheet name tabs appear shaded. Click the tabs to select or deselect them.

2. **Choose Insert⇨Sheet to open the Insert Sheet dialog box. You can also right-click the sheet name and choose Insert Sheet from the shortcut menu that appears.**

3. **Choose the appropriate option button to position the new sheet(s) either before or after the active sheet.**

4. **Indicate how many sheets you want to add and click OK.**

   You can also specify the name of a single sheet. (If you already have a spreadsheet in another file that you want to insert into your workbook, select the From File option button and type in the file address, or click Browse and select your file.)

Scrolling through sheets

When you have more than just three sheets in your workbook, some of the sheet name tabs may be out of view. To scroll through your tabs, click the arrow buttons that are to the left of the tabs. You can also display more tabs at once by moving the vertical bar between the sheet names and the active sheet scroll bar. Move the vertical bar to the right, making the scroll bar shorter.

Entering data into more than one sheet simultaneously

You can enter data into more than one sheet simultaneously when more than one sheet is selected (which we describe in the next section). Then type your data into any cell of the active sheet. The data is recorded in the same place on all selected sheets.

Selecting sheets

Sheet names appear on tabs that are located near the lower-right corner of the spreadsheet.

Selected sheet tabs appear white, and deselected sheet tabs, are shaded as shown (refer to Figure 9-8).

To select a single sheet, simply click its name, and that sheet becomes the active sheet. To select several sheets simultaneously, press and hold Ctrl while clicking the name tab for each sheet that you want to select. Each tab that you click appears white, indicating that it is selected.

If you have lots of sheets and want to select many of them, follow these steps:

1. **Click the first sheet name of a group of sheets that you want to select.**

   This becomes the active sheet.

2. **Press and hold Shift, and click the last sheet name that you want to select.**

   Calc selects all the sheets between the active sheet and the last sheet name that you chose.

To select all of your sheets, follow these steps:

1. **Right-click any sheet name.**

2. **Choose Select All Sheets from the shortcut menu that appears.**

Deselecting sheets

To deselect one sheet at a time, press Ctrl while clicking the sheet name that you want to deselect.

To deselect a large group of sheets, press and hold Shift while clicking the last sheet that you want to remain selected. Calc keeps all sheets between the active sheet and the sheet that you Shift+click selected, while deselecting all other sheets.

To deselect all sheets except the active sheet, Shift+click the active sheet name.

Renaming sheets

To rename sheets, follow these steps:

1. **Select the sheet that you want to rename.**

2. **Choose Format⇨Sheet⇨Rename.**

   The Rename Sheet dialog box appears. You can also right-click any sheet name tab and choose Rename from the shortcut menu that appears.

   (If the Rename option does not appear on the Sheet menu or the short-cut menu, you have more than one sheet selected. Calc can only rename one sheet at a time. In this case, you need to first deselect all but the one sheet that you want to rename.)

3. **In the Rename Sheet dialog box, type in the new name and click OK.**

Moving and copying sheets

You can move a sheet to change the sheet's order among all the sheets. To move sheets using the mouse, follow these steps:

1. **Select the sheet or sheets.**

2. **Drag the sheet or sheets to a new location within the sheet name tabs.**

You can copy an entire sheet, instead of copying the data within the sheet. To copy sheets using the mouse, follow these steps:

1. **Select the sheet name or names.**

2. **Ctrl+click and drag the copied sheet or sheets to a new location within the sheet name tabs.**

To move or copy sheets using the main menu, follow these steps:

1. **Select the sheet name or names that you want to move or copy.**

2. **Choose Edit➪Sheet➪Move/Copy. (Or position the mouse on a selected sheet name and right-click. Then choose Move/Copy Sheet from the pop-up menu.)**

   The Move/Copy Sheet dialog box appears.

3. **Select the Copy check box to copy your sheet(s). Deselect this check box to move your sheet rather than copy it.**

4. **Click the name of the sheet that you want to insert — either the origi-nal sheet or its copy — and click OK.**

Deleting sheets

To delete one or more sheets, follow these steps:

1. **Select one or more sheets that you want to delete.**

2. **Choose Edit➪Sheet➪Delete.**

   A dialog box appears asking if you are sure that you want to perma-nently delete the current sheet(s).

3. **If you are sure that you want to delete those sheets that are selected, click the Yes button.**

When deleting sheets, Calc deletes all the selected sheets. Double-check to make sure that only the sheets that you want to delete are selected. Selected sheet tabs appear white, and deselected sheet tabs appear shaded.

Chapter 10

Knock on Wood and Print!

. . . .

In This Chapter

▶ Using Page Preview mode

▶ Adding headers and footers

▶ Inserting page breaks

▶ Printing or suppressing sheets and grids

▶ Scaling and orienting your printout

. . . .

*W*ouldn't it be convenient if all you needed to do was press a button and your spreadsheet would print exactly how you wanted it? Calc spreadsheets are easy to print, but you still need to find out about some basics. After you do that, printing can be fast and fun.

Previewing Your Printout

Ready to print? The first thing that you want to do is preview your printout. Whether your spreadsheet is a giant or a Lilliputian, you still want to see what it looks like before you print it. To preview your spreadsheet before printing, follow these steps:

1. **Choose File⇨Page Preview.**

   Your window changes to show the first page of your printout.

2. **To see each subsequent page, click the Next Page button.**

Look at your page carefully. You'll probably want to adjust the page breaks to make your tables look right. We explain how to do that later in this chapter. Also, your header probably says sheet1, unless you specified otherwise. You probably want to change that, as well.

Customizing Your Headers and Footers

You can customize your headers and footers, either from the Page Preview window or from the main menu.

To customize your headers or footers, perform the following steps:

1. **Choose Format⇨Page. Or, if you are viewing a Page Preview window, click the Page Format button.**

   The Page Style dialog box appears.

2. **Click the Header tab or Footer tab, depending on which one you want to customize.**

   Several check boxes and margin settings appear.

3. **If you don't want Calc to automatically generate any header or footer, deselect the Header On check box or Footer On check box. Or, if you want a header or footer, but you want a *different* header or footer for left pages and right pages, deselect the Same Content Left/Right check box.**

4. **To create a customized header or footer, click the Edit button.**

   The Header dialog box or Footer dialog box appears, as shown in Figure 10-1, depending on your choice in Step 2. The Header dialog box or Footer dialog box contains three text boxes: Left Area, Center Area, and Right Area. It also contains seven buttons.

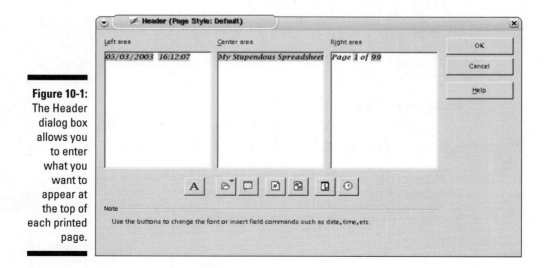

Figure 10-1:
The Header dialog box allows you to enter what you want to appear at the top of each printed page.

5. **Enter your text into any of the three text boxes, and/or select one or more of the three text boxes by clicking in it so that a cursor appears. Then click one of the following buttons:**

   - The File Name button inserts your filename on each page in the text area that you select.

   - The Sheet Name button inserts the name of your sheet as a heading.

   - The Page button inserts the page number on each page in the text area that you select.

   - The Pages button inserts the total number of pages in the document on each page.

   - The Date button inserts the current date on each page.

   - The Time button inserts the current time on each page.

6. **If you want to format any of the text in the three text boxes, apply these steps:**

   1. Select the text that you want to format, and click the Text Attributes button to open the Text Attributes dialog box.

   2. Specify the font type, size, and style.

   3. Click the Font Effects or Font Position tab and choose attributes from the panels, such as color, shadow, scaling, and spacing.

   4. Click OK in the Text Attributes dialog box.

7. **Click OK in the Header dialog box or Footer dialog box.**

8. **To complete the process, or put some finishing touches, choose from the following:**

   - To specify fancy backgrounds and borders for your headers or footers, click the More button.

   - If you're finished formatting, click OK in the Page Style dialog box.

You can inspect your handiwork in the Page Preview window.

Dealing with Page Breaks

When printing your spreadsheet, you need to consider page breaks. With a little manipulation, you can sometimes squeeze all your columns or rows onto a single page. Or, you can break your pages at logical points. A little preparation before printing can make all the difference.

The first thing to do is find out where Calc is planning to automatically place the page breaks. You can view automatic page breaks by viewing your document using File⇨Page Preview, but if you want to view the page breaks and adjust them as well, use Page Break Preview.

Adjusting page breaks with Page Break Preview

To view and adjust page breaks for the entire document — or at least several pages at a time — perform the following steps:

1. **Choose View⇨Page Break Preview.**

   This reduces your view to 60 percent so that more of your spreadsheet is visible, and the page breaks are clearly marked, as shown in Figure 10-2.

2. **Adjust your page breaks in the following ways:**

   - Click and drag the page breaks to your liking.

   - Resize your rows or columns to fit either inside or outside the page break lines.

   - Inserting a manual page break as described below.

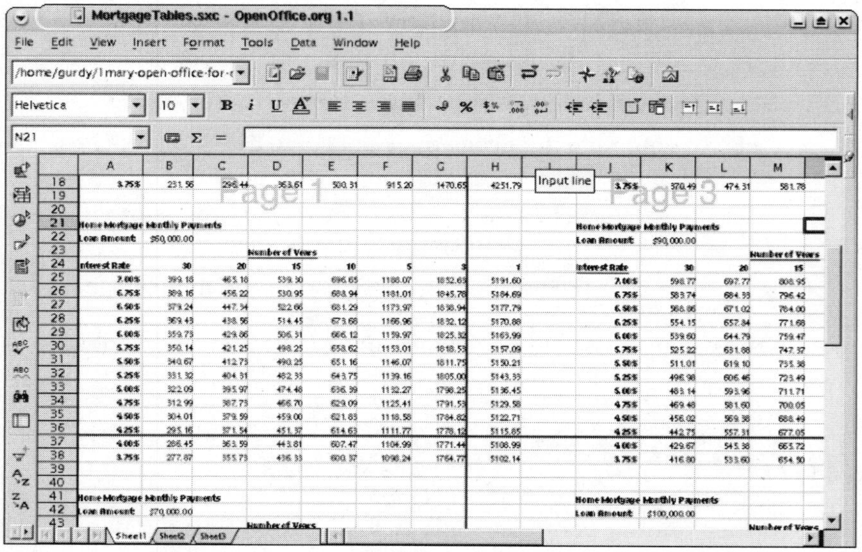

Figure 10-2:
Using Page Break Preview allows you to see and adjust your page breaks easily.

3. **Choose View⇨Page Break Preview again to deselect Page Break Preview and return to normal mode.**

You can adjust your page breaks in the normal viewing mode just as in Page Break Preview. Page breaks in the normal viewing mode are slightly thickened grid lines, but they only appear after the first time you exit Page Preview or Page Break Preview, or define print ranges.

Inserting manual page breaks

To insert manual page breaks, do the following:

1. **Place the active cell pointer either above your desired horizontal page break or to the left of your desired vertical page break.**

2. **Choose Insert⇨Manual Break⇨Row Break, or choose Insert⇨Manual Break⇨Column Break.**

Orienting your printout sideways

If your spreadsheet is wider than it is tall, it may fit into a single sheet of paper if it is oriented *sideways.*

To orient your printout sideways, follow these steps:

1. **Choose Format⇨Page.**

   The Page Style dialog box appears.

2. **Click the Page tab.**

3. **Select Landscape in the Orientation section.**

   Note that the Paper format width and height values adjust to their proper sizes.

4. **Click OK.**

   You also need to tell your printer to print in landscape format. See the section "Printing Your Spreadsheet," later in this chapter.

Scaling your printout

What if you want your spreadsheet to print onto a single piece of paper, but it's just too big and nothing that you do can squeeze it on? Calc offers a solution for everything. Just scale your printout down. (With a high-resolution printer and a magnifying glass, you're all set!) You can scale your printout down to whatever percentage you desire.

To scale your printout, perform the following steps:

1. **Choose File⇨Page Preview to enter the Page Preview mode (if you are not already in Page Preview).**

2. **Click the Page Format button.**

   The Page Style dialog box appears.

3. **Click the Sheet tab in the Page Style dialog box.**

4. **In the Scale section, do one of the following:**

   • Select Reduce/Enlarge Printout and select the percentage from the list box.

   • Select Fit Printout on Number of Pages and select the number of pages from the list box. (Try starting with 1. If you have a large spreadsheet, it's good for a laugh.)

5. **Click OK.**

   Your new preview appears. What do you think?

6. **Repeat Steps 1 through 5 as needed until you like the look of your printout.**

Printing a Selection

Suppose that your spreadsheet is humongous and you only want to print a small section of it. Calc makes this easy. To print a section, follow these steps:

1. **Select the range of cells that you want to print.**

2. **Choose File⇨Print.**

   The Print dialog box appears.

3. **In the Print Range section, select the Selection option button.**

4. **Click OK to start printing.**

If you want to print lots of specific selections, do the following:

1. **Select the range for your first page, and choose Format⇨Print Ranges⇨Define.**

   Notice that page breaks appear as thickened grid lines.

2. **If you want to print another print range, select your next range, and choose Format⇨Print Ranges⇨Add.**

3. **Repeat Step 2 until all of your print ranges have been selected.**

4. **Choose File⇨Print.**

5. **Click OK.**

   Calc prints whatever is in the print ranges and starts each print range on a separate page.

To cancel your print ranges, choose Format⇨Print Ranges⇨Remove.

Printing or Suppressing Sheets and Empty Pages

Calc prints all your nonempty sheets and also all your empty pages, unless you tell it otherwise. To specify the sheets that you want to print, or to tell Calc to skip empty pages, follow these steps:

1. **Select the sheets that you want to print.**

   To select more than one sheet, you press Shift and click the sheet name tabs.

2. **Choose File⇨Print.**

   The Print dialog box appears.

3. **Click the Options button.**

   The Print Options dialog box appears.

4. **To print only selected sheets, select the Print Only Selected Sheets check box. To skip printing empty pages, select the Suppress Output of Empty Pages check box.**

5. **Click OK to return to the Print dialog box.**

6. **Click OK to start printing.**

If you don't want to perform these steps every time you print, you can set these options more permanently by choosing Tools⇨Options to display the Options dialog box. Expand the Spreadsheet menu by clicking the plus sign next to Spreadsheet and click Print. On the Options-Spreadsheet-Print panel that appears, perform Steps 4 and 5.

To Print or Not to Print

The majority of people who print spreadsheets consider the grid to be extraneous clutter. But you may be different. Or you may want to show or suppress notes, graphics, charts, drawing objects, formulas, or even zero values, as well. That all adds up to lots of flexibility! To set these printing options, follow these steps:

1. **Choose File⇨Page Preview to enter the Page Preview mode.**

2. **Click the Page Format button.**

3. **Click the Sheet tab.**

4. **In the Print section, select the check boxes of the items that you wish to print, and deselect the check boxes of the items that you want to suppress printing.**

   The choices are Column and row headers, Grid, Notes, Objects/graphics, Charts, Drawing objects, Formulas, and Zero values.

5. **Click OK, and look at your preview.**

   Are you sure you want that grid?

Printing Your Spreadsheet

Finally, you are ready to print. You have previewed your pages, and everything looks great. And you've loaded your printer cartridge with a hypodermic needle full of ink (and cleaned up the extra squirts that dripped on your keyboard, mouse, table, and floor). Follow these steps to print your spreadsheet:

1. **Choose File⇨Print.**

   The Print dialog box appears.

2. **Select the printer that you are using.**

   If your printer does not appear on the drop-down list, you need to install the printer driver according to the manufacturer's instructions.

3. **Click the Properties button to open the Properties of Your Printer dialog box.**

   This dialog box varies among printers, but you can generally continue with the next steps.

4. **Choose your paper size (8½×11 inches is standard U.S. letter size), orientation (landscape is sideways, of course), and scale (normally 1).**

   If you chose the landscape orientation for your page setup, be sure to choose landscape orientation for your printer here, as well.

5. **Choose the pages that you want to print, or print all the pages.**

   Refer to the instructions in the section "Printing a Selection," earlier in this chapter, to print just a selection.

6. **Click OK.**

   Hold your breath, cross your fingers, knock on wood, and listen for that soothing sound of whirling gizmos that magically make numbers and letters appear on paper right in front of your eyes.

Chapter 11

Snazzing Up Your Spreadsheet

· ·

In This Chapter

▶ Using AutoFormat for a professional look

▶ Adding borders and backgrounds

▶ Freezing headings

▶ Splitting windows and floating frames

▶ Inserting OLE objects

▶ Adding graphics

▶ Using Notes

· ·

Calc's formulas and database abilities are fabulous, but its graphics are also amazing. Why settle for ordinary spreadsheets when you can insert all kinds of graphic aids into them? Add borders, backgrounds, and shadows for 3-D styles that make your tables pop-out from the screen or page. Or let Calc automatically format your tables for an appealing look that suits you. Also, try out floating frames, splitting windows, and freezing column and row headings to organize your information more optimally.

Just a few touches can make all the difference. It can set you apart from the crowd by giving your spreadsheet that professional look and functional edge it needs in today's highly competitive business world — and perhaps even get you that richly deserved promotion.

Getting that Professional Look with AutoFormat

AutoFormat is the most quick and easy method for beautifying your spreadsheet and getting it the attention it deserves. See Figure 11-1 for an example of a table that was created with the AutoFormat feature. To AutoFormat your spreadsheet, follow these steps:

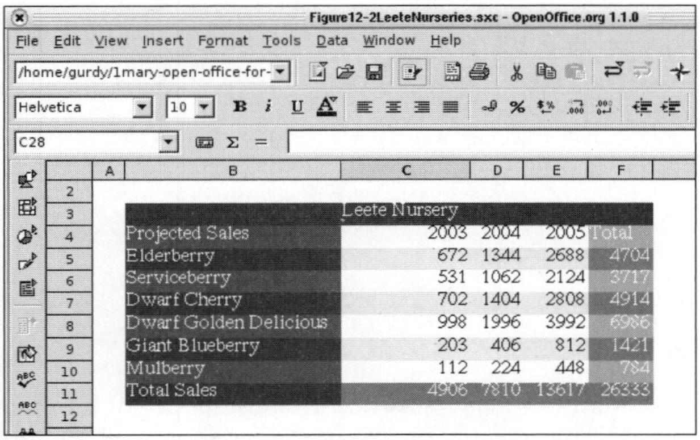

Figure 11-1: The AutoFormat feature makes every table look good.

		Leete Nursery			
Projected Sales		2003	2004	2005	Total
Elderberry		672	1344	2688	4704
Serviceberry		531	1062	2124	3717
Dwarf Cherry		702	1404	2808	4914
Dwarf Golden Delicious		998	1996	3992	6986
Giant Blueberry		203	406	812	1421
Mulberry		112	224	448	784
Total Sales		4906	7810	13617	26333

1. **Select the cells that you want to AutoFormat.**

   Be sure that you select enough cells. AutoFormat does not appear on the Format menu unless you select a range that's at least three cells wide and three cells high.

2. **Choose Format⇨AutoFormat.**

   The AutoFormat dialog box appears.

3. **Choose your format type from the Format list.**

   Calc shows an example of the format in the center of the dialog box. Take a look at all the formats. Which do you like best? Our favorite is the Yellow.

   If your cells are specifically formatted in any way, you could be in danger of losing those formats unless you tell AutoFormat not to change the formats.

4. **To retain your formats, click the More button and deselect the Number Format check box and Font check box. You could also deselect the Autofit Width and Height check box if you don't want your columns and rows to change sizes.**

5. **Click OK, and view your new table.**

Like it? If not, it's easy to change. And remember, you can refine the look of your autoformatted table by changing your font type and font size and styles. For more information about formatting your text, see Chapter 4.

Going Bananas with Backgrounds and Borders

If the AutoFormat feature does not provide precisely what you envisioned for your tables, you can design your own look — and even add those shadows for the 3-D look.

Adding font and background colors

The world is a rainbow of colors. Why stick to black and white? To change font and background colors of a table or your entire spreadsheet, first select the cells of your table that you want to color, and then click the Background Color button or the Font Color button from the Object Bar, and select your background color or font color from the pop-up swatches.

You may want to select different colors for your titles and headings than for the body of your table.

For maximum readability, choose either a light background color with dark font, or a dark background with a light font.

Creating a background with a graphic

Want to use that great picture of yours as a background for your table? Or use a nice texture to add interest? To create a background with a graphic, first you need to insert the graphic. You insert graphics into Calc in the same way you insert graphics into Writer, which we cover in Chapter 5.

After you insert, resize, and place your graphic just where you want it, choose Format⇨Arrange⇨To Background. Your grid lines appear, if they are visible in your spreadsheet, along with any data that was beneath your graphic.

To modify or delete your background, first you need to select it with the Navigator and then you can delete, resize, or modify it. The Navigator works the same in Calc as it does in Writer. Check out Chapter 3 for complete details.

Adding borders and a 3-D look

Suppose you want your table to have colored borders and look like it's jumping out of the page toward you. Calc allows you to vary the line width and color of your grid and create borders of varying thicknesses and types wherever you desire. It also allows you to format shadows for a 3-D effect as shown in Figure 11-2. In fact, the possibilities are endless.

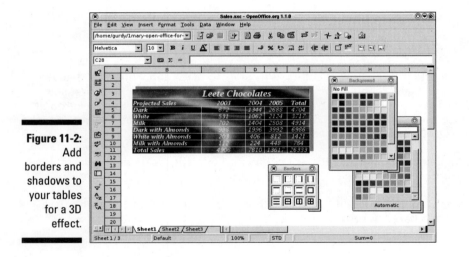

Figure 11-2:
Add borders and shadows to your tables for a 3D effect.

For a simple black grid or border, just select the range of cells to be bordered or gridded, and then click the Border button and select from the range of line arrangement options.

For borders with colors and/or shadows, perform the following steps:

1. **Select the range of cells to be bordered or gridded.**

2. **Choose Format➪Cells.**

   The Format Cells dialog box appears.

3. **Click the Borders tab.**

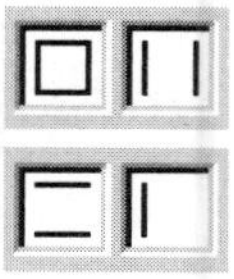

4. **Select your line arrangement from the Default boxes, or click in the User-Defined area to create your own line arrangement.**

5. **Select the line style and line color from the list boxes. (Watch out! Don't confuse the Shadow Color list box with the Line Color list box!)**

6. **If you want a shadow to appear, select a shadow style, position, and color. Go ahead, it looks great!**

7. **Click OK.**

Look good? Now you'll probably want to do the same thing with all your tables!

Now that you have grid lines formatted on your table, you may want to do away with them elsewhere on your screen, as shown in Figure 11-2. To do that you need to change some options.

Setting Up Your Viewing Options

Want to change the color of the grid on your screen? Or do away with it alto-gether? Or make all your zeros disappear? Or get them back again if they are already done away with? Follow these steps to modify your View options:

1. **Choose Tools⇨Options.**

The Options dialog box appears.

2. **Expand the Spreadsheet menu by clicking the plus sign beside the word Spreadsheet in the list on the left side of the dialog box.**

The Spreadsheet menu expands.

3. **Click View.**

The Options-Spreadsheet-View panel appears, as shown in Figure 11-3.

Options changed in one document apply to every document.

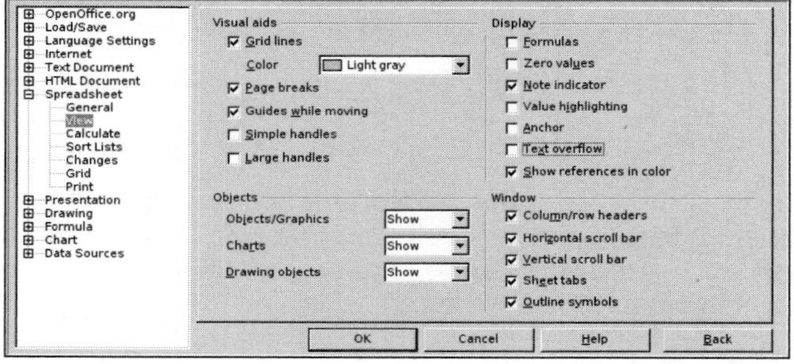

Figure 11-3: Calc allows you to set many viewing options.

4. **Do any of the following in the Visual Aid section:**

   - Select or deselect Grid Lines to show or hide the grid lines. (Hiding the grid lines can make your tables look more appealing when using borders. See Figure 11-2 earlier in this chapter.)

   - Choose a new color for the grid lines from the Color list box.

   - Deselect Page Breaks to suppress the thickened page break line.

   - Select Guides while moving if you want to see guides when you move inserted objects.

   - Select Simple Handles or Large Handles to change the handle style for your inserted objects.

5. **Do any of the following in the Display section:**

   - Select Formulas to display formulas instead of values in a cell. (For more about formulas, refer to Chapter 12.)

   - Deselect Zero Values to make all zero values on your spreadsheets disappear.

   - Select or deselect Note Indicator to show or hide the small triangle in the top right hand corner of a cell containing a note. (See more about Notes in the section "Adding notes" later in this chapter.)

   - Select Value Highlighting to have cells with formulas highlighted in green, and cells with numbers in blue, and cells with text in black.

   - Select or deselect Anchor to show or hide the anchor of an inserted object.

   - Select or deselect Text Overflow to show or hide the text overflow symbol (a small triangle in the right side of the cell which appears when text overflows the cell while the cell to the left of it is non-empty).

   - Select or deselect Show References in Color to allow all cell ranges to be highlighted in color when editing formulas. (For more on Formulas, see Chapter 12.)

6. **Choose Hide, Placeholder in the Charts, Drawing Objects, or Objects/Graphics list boxes if you want to hide or replace your objects temporarily with an empty frame. Or choose Show to show your Charts or Drawing Objects or Objects/Graphics.**

   Placeholders are traditionally used when you have lots of objects in your spreadsheet and they are slowing down your computer. With today's fast processors, it is normally is not necessary to use placeholders.

7. **Deselect Column/row headers, Horizontal scroll bar, Vertical scroll bar, Sheet tabs or Outline Symbols if you want to eliminate any or all of them from view. (You can always come back to this section and select them again to show them.)**

8. **Click OK.**

Functional Fun

Another way to impress your boss — or just improve your productivity — is to split your windows, freeze your headings, use floating frames or add notes to a cell that pop-up when you want them to.

Freezing column and row headings

Ever scroll down a very large spreadsheet and suddenly not know which column pertains to what data, because your column headings scrolled off the top of the screen? Or maybe it was your row headings that scrolled off to the left. Calc can freeze those headings so that you never have that problem.

To freeze column or row headings, follow these steps:

1. **Place your active cell in the row below the column headings that you want to freeze and in the column to the right of the row headings that you want to freeze.**

   If you don't want to freeze any row headings, place your active cell in column A. Or if you don't want to freeze any column headings, place your active cell in Row 1.

2. **Choose Window⇨Freeze.**

3. **To unfreeze your headings, choose Window⇨Freeze again to halt the effect.**

Splitting your window

Splitting your window is similar to freezing your headings, except Calc also splits the scroll bars and allows you to see all columns and rows in each window. You can use this feature to line up and compare data from different tables, or view data from far off sections of your spreadsheet at the same time. In general, you have more control over what's on your screen. To split your windows, follow these steps:

1. **Place your active cell in the row where you want to split your window and in the column where you want the split to occur.**

   If you want to split your rows and not your columns, place your active cell in column A. Or, if you want to split your columns only and not your rows, place your active cell in row 1.

2. **Choose Window⇨Split.**

   Note that you now have more than one scroll bar on at least one side of your window. And you can scroll through the entire sheet by using any of the scroll bars.

Typing data into a field on one side of the split automatically records in the other quadrants of the split. In other words, it is still just one sheet; you just see it as if it were four (or two).

3. To deactivate your split window, choose Window⊳Split again.

Using floating frames

Want to work in more than one spreadsheet at a time? Use floating frames to read in another spreadsheet and float that spreadsheet in a draggable window inside your spreadsheet window, as shown in Figure 11-4. You can work inside your floating frame just as you can work in your main window. Changes are saved to the original file of the floating frame (if you want them to be) as well as to the file of the main window.

To open a floating frame, follow these steps:

1. Place your active cell where you want your floating frame to appear.

2. Choose Insert⊳Floating Frame. Or long-click (click and hold) the Insert Object button on the Main toolbar so that the floating Insert Object ToolBar appears and click on the Insert Floating Frame button.

The Floating Frame Properties dialog box appears.

3. Type in a name for your floating frame.

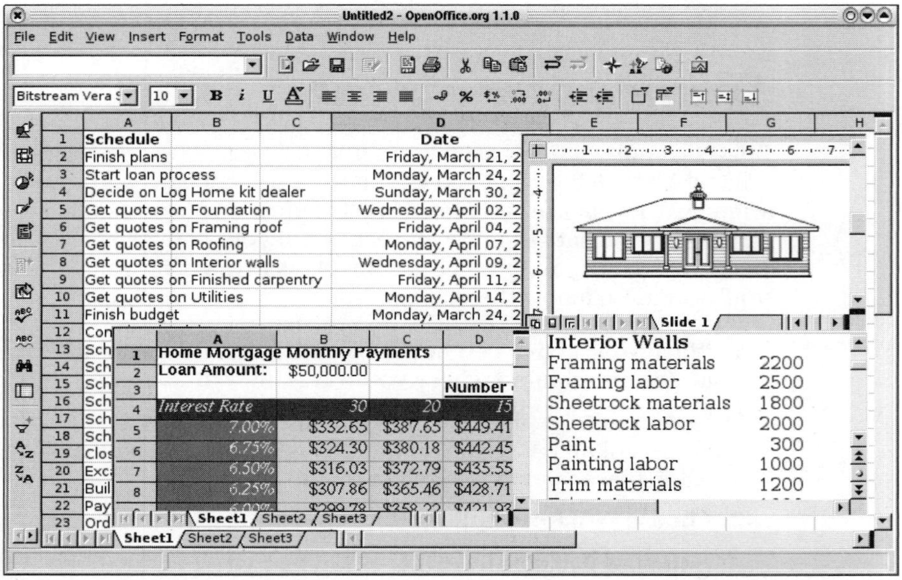

Figure 11-4:
A floating frame is a spreadsheet within a spreadsheet.

4. **Click the Browse button next to the contents line.**

    The Select File for Floating Frame browser window appears.

5. **Browse through your files, and double-click the spreadsheet file, text file, presentation file, or graphic that you want in your floating frame.**

6. **Click the Open button.**

7. **Click OK in the Floating Frame Properties dialog box.**

Move or resize your floating frame just as you would any graphic. If your floating frame is not selected, use the Navigator to select it.

To save your floating frame, choose File⇨Save All. This saves all your changes in every floating frame and your document. If the Save All option does not appear in the File menu, choose Save instead. (Save All only appears when more than one window needs to be saved.)

Adding notes

Notes are a great tool to use in any spreadsheet. They allow you to describe what is going on in a particular cell, but they don't take up precious space around the cell. They are embedded into the cell and pop-up only when you want to read them, as shown in Figure 11-5.

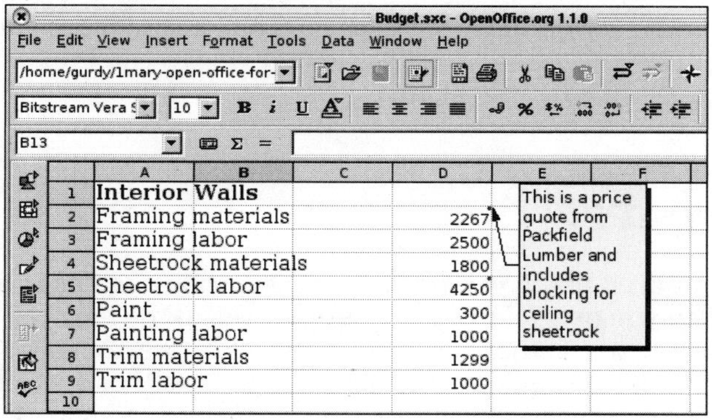

Figure 11-5:
Add notes that pop-up whenever you want to read them.

To add a note to a cell, perform the following steps:

1. **Click the cell where you want to add a note.**

2. **Choose Insert⇨Note.**

    A Note text box appears with a blinking cursor and an arrow pointing to the active cell.

3. **Type in your note.**

4. **Click anywhere outside the note.**

> The note vanishes, but a *Note Indicator* — a red and blue triangle — appears in the upper right hand corner of the cell containing the note.

To read a note, pass the pointer over the Note Indicator and the note pops up, or right-click the cell to bring up the context menu, and choose Show Note.

Making Terrific Text

You can make lots of nice effects with text. You can use the Object Bar to select your font type and size, and you can choose boldface, italic, underlined, or colored text. You can center your text horizontally or vertically within its cell, indent it, or justify it to the left, right, top, or bottom. You can give your cells borders or background color — all this can be done from the Object Bar. If the Object Bar is not visible, choose View⇨Toolbars⇨Object Bar.

You can also use styles in Calc. Just set up your styles. Then with one click, your font type, font size, indentations, and so on are all formatted for you. You can create different styles for different headings, titles, and data. For complete information about styles and formatting check out Chapter 4.

You can do even more things with your text. How about typing several lines of text in one cell? Or you can get fancy with slanted or upside-down text. Or you can use the full power of Writer as an OLE object and place your text anywhere you want in your spreadsheet without having to conform to the grid. With Calc, the sky's the limit — almost.

Multiline text

You probably noticed that if you try to type more than one line of text into a single cell, when you press Enter the cursor moves to the next cell and not to the next line of text within the same cell, as you may have hoped. Fortunately, Calc has ways to enter line breaks within single cells, either automatically or manually. As far as we can tell, you can have as many line breaks as you want in a cell. So, if you want to put a whole book into a single cell, go right ahead.

To manually enter line breaks within a cell, type your text into a cell, and press Ctrl+Enter where you want the line break to occur. The whole row enlarges to accommodate the extra line of text.

To automatically enter line breaks within a cell, follow these steps:

1. **Choose Format⇨Cell.**

   The Format Cells dialog box appears.

2. **Click the Alignment tab.**

3. **Select the Line Break check box.**

4. **If you want automatic hyphenation, select the Hyphenation Active check box.**

5. **Click OK.**

Using OpenOffice.org Writer as an OLE object

OLE stands for *object linking and embedding*. One of the best features of OpenOffice.org is how it can integrate all its various modules. With a click or two of the mouse, you can have the writing program, the drawing program, or the presentation program function embedded within your spreadsheet, as shown in Figure 11-6.

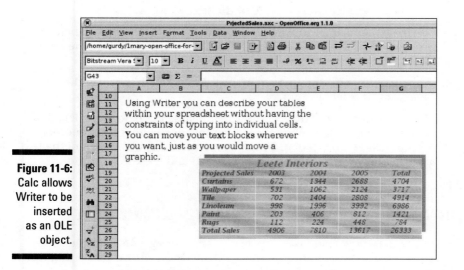

Figure 11-6: Calc allows Writer to be inserted as an OLE object.

Opening the Writer program within OpenOffice.org's Calc program is especially useful. You then have the power to fine-tune your text without the restrictions of dealing with cells. Suppose that you have a chart or table and you want text to appear above, below, and around your chart or table. By typing your text into the Writer program and dragging the text to its precise location, you have more power to fine-tune the look of your spreadsheet and your printout.

When using Writer as an OLE object, hiding the grid lines of your spreadsheet to make your text more readable is a good idea. For the know-how on hiding the grid, see the section "Setting Up Your Viewing Options."

Follow these steps to insert text as an OLE object:

1. **Choose Insert⇨Object⇨OLE Object, or long-click (click and hold) the Insert Object button on the main toolbar until the Insert Object floating toolbar appears, and then click the Insert OLE Object button.**

   The Insert OLE Object dialog box appears.

2. **From the list of OLE objects, choose OpenOffice.org 1.1.0 Text.**

   A miniature Writer window appears and the toolbars and main menu changes to Writer toolbars and main menu. A cursor appears in the window.

3. **Type your text and format it however you want.**

4. **Drag and resize the new text window to the size you want.**

5. **To return to Calc, click outside of the text window.**

   The main menu and toolbars return to the Calc menu and toolbars. The text that you inserted is now free of the text window and can be resized or dragged anywhere in Calc.

6. **If you need to edit the text again, just double-click it or use the Navigator to select it.**

   The OpenOffice.org Writer window reappears. If you double-clicked the text and the OpenOffice.org Writer window does not appear, another object must be on top of it. Simply move the other objects off of the text and double-click the text again, or forget it and use the Navigator.

Slanted, vertical, or upside-down text

Feeling like the whole world is topsy-turvy? Display how you feel with slanted or upside-down text or numbers. Actually, slanted text can be very useful when labeling charts or adding row titles to tables. You can slant your text (or align it vertically) in two ways: using Calc, or using Draw as an OLE object. If you don't want your text to slant, but just want to align it vertically, you can also use Writer as an OLE object.

To create vertically aligned text by using Writer as an OLE object, perform the steps in the previous section to create your OLE object and type and select your text. Then choose Format➪Character and click the Position tab and choose either 90 degrees or 270 degrees and click OK.

To create slanted, vertical, or upside-down text, you can use Draw as an OLE object and create a text box to enter your text, and then use the rotation tool. See Chapter 18 for complete details.

To create slanted, vertical, or upside-down text (or numbers, of course) by using Calc, follow these steps:

1. **Select the cell or range of cells that you want to format as slanted, vertical, or upside-down.**

2. **Choose Format➪Cells.**

   The Format Cells dialog box appears.

3. **Click the Alignment tab.**

4. **Turn the wheel in the Text Direction section to the alignment that you want, or type the number of degrees in the Degrees box, or use the arrow keys in the Degrees box to scroll though the numbers.**

5. **To align your text to the bottom, middle, or top of the cell, open the Vertical list box in the Text Alignment panel and choose Bottom, Middle, or Top.**

   Your upside-down text looks a bit better if you align it to the top or middle of the box, instead of the bottom. In Figure 11-7, we aligned all the text to the middle.

Figure 11-7:
Go wild with slanted or upside-down text.

6. **Click the Text Extension Inside Cells button under Reference Edge.**

   If you do not select this button, your rotated text can end up anywhere from here to China. (Or there to North America, if you are already in China.)

   7. **Click OK.**

   8. **Type in a cell, and press Enter.**

   Your text slants, flips, or stands vertically — whatever you designated.

Ready for a practical joke? Select all the cells in the sheet and format them for upside-down data. Then let a coworker use your spreadsheet. Funny? Hopefully that coworker is not your boss.

Adding the Art

Art can really spruce up a spreadsheet and make a statement. Art can be added in several ways:

- ✔ Art can be imported by choosing Insert⇨Graphics⇨From File, or clicking the Insert Graphics button on the Main toolbar. This brings up the Insert Graphics dialog box. Chapter 5 covers importing graphics in detail.

- ✔ Art can be copied and pasted into your spreadsheet. For instance, you can create it in the Draw program and copy and paste it into your spreadsheet.

- ✔ Art can be created in Calc, using Draw as an OLE object. Just long-click the Insert Object button on the Main toolbar and click the Insert OLE object button, and then choose OpenOffice.org 1.1.0 Drawing from the list box in the Insert OLE Object dialog box. Then draw as you please in the window that appears, and when you click outside the window, the window vanishes and your drawing remains.

- ✔ Art can also be created in Calc using the Draw Functions floating toolbar. This toolbar offers a small smattering of what the Draw program offers, but if you don't need much, it's handy. Click the Show Draw Functions button on the Main toolbar to use this Draw toolbar.

- ✔ Art can be used from the Gallery. Choose Tools⇨Gallery to see those levitating donuts and more, or click the Gallery button on the Main toolbar. For complete information see Chapter 5.

When selecting your art to move or resize it, either double-click it, or use the Navigator. (For details on the Navigator, check out Chapter 3.)

Sometimes you want your art to stay put near a specific cell. Other times, you may want it positioned on a page regardless of how many rows or columns get inserted above it, or to the right. This is called *anchoring*. To anchor your art (or OLE object) either to a cell or to a page, follow these steps:

1. **Click your object to select it, or use the Navigator to select it.**

2. **Right-click your object to bring up the shortcut menu and choose Anchor ⇨To Cell to anchor your object to a cell. Or choose Anchor ⇨ To Page to anchor your object to the page.**

    The anchor appears, indicating what cell or what page your object is anchored to.

3. **If you don't want to continuously see the anchor, click the Anchor button on the Object Bar.**

    The anchor disappears from view.

Chapter 12

Making Calculations

- -

In This Chapter

▶ Creating formulas

▶ Generating formula arrays

▶ Nesting functions

▶ Creating conditional formulas

- -

*N*ow it's time to explore the deeper powers of Calc. Calc takes you far beyond addition and subtraction. Its ready-made functions span a whole range of statistics, business, mathematics, and computing. And the AutoPilot:Functions allows you to use and combine these formulas with ease. And if that's not enough for you, you have complete control to create your own formulas as well.

Formula Basics

Almost every spreadsheet contains formulas. Some spreadsheets use formulas just to generate totals. Other spreadsheets use more complex formulas, such as for subtracting cost of goods sold from sales to generate net income, and then for multiplying net income by the tax rate to roughly calculate taxes. Other spreadsheets, like the mortgage tables that are shown in Figure 12-5 (coming up later in this chapter), are almost entirely generated by formulas.

Creating a formula can be as simple as clicking the Sum button on the Formula Bar. Or you can allow Calc to automatically enter formulas, using AutoPilot: Functions, or you can type formulas into cells yourself.

If you want to type your own formula, Calc requires each formula to begin with an equal sign. An example of simple addition is the formula =1+1 . Formulas can contain numbers, or they can refer to cell addresses. For instance, the formula =1+1 returns the same value, 2, as the formula =A1+A2 if cells A1 and A2 both contain the number 1.

When you type in a formula and press Enter, the formula seems to disappear. What you see is the value that the formula generates. Even though the formula seems to disappear, Calc remembers it. You can see the formula in the Input line of the Formula Bar. (If the Formula Bar is not visible, choose View⇨ Toolbars⇨Formula to make it appear.)

Figure 12-1:
Keep your
Formula Bar
visible while
working
with
formulas.

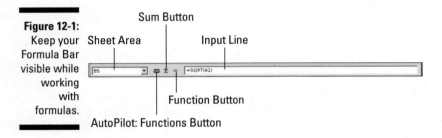

Sum Button

Sheet Area   Input Line

Function Button

AutoPilot: Functions Button

The Formula Bar as shown in Figure 12-1, contains the following items:

- **The Sheet Area list box:** This box displays the addresses of selected cells and stores any ranges that you name. (See the section "Naming ranges" in this chapter.)

- **AutoPilot: Functions button:** This brings up the AutoPilot: Functions dialog box which lists 365 different functions (if we counted correctly) in ten different categories, such as Financial, Statistical, Mathematical, and Date&Time. These functions offer a wide range of applications. You can create your own mortgage tables, calculate standard deviations, and manipulate text and data in a variety of ways. You can even find out the date of Easter Sunday in the year 5032! (It's always good to plan ahead.)

- **Sum button:** This totals the ranges that you specify, either by entering the ranges, or clicking and dragging a colored border around the cells you want to total. Or you can click the Sum button in a cell below a column of numbers to automatically total the column. Or click the Sum button in a cell to the left of a row of numbers to automatically total the row.

- **Function button:** Inserts the first character of a formula, an equal sign, into the active cell. The rest of the formula can then be added in the Input line.

✔ **The Input Line:** This line shows the formula that resides in the active cell, if there is one; otherwise it displays the value. To type or edit your formula, you do so from the Input line when the cell is selected. (Or, you can double-click the cell, and type or edit the formula right in the cell.)

✔ **Cancel:** This button appears when you are entering or editing a formula. Click it to delete the formula from the cell.

✔ **Accept:** This button also appears when you are entering or editing a formula. Click it to insert your completed formula into the cell. (This is the equivalent of pressing Enter.)

Adding, Subtracting, and More

Learning to add and subtract is the core of your mastery of the formulas and functions of Calc. You can gain the basic skills that are necessary to unleash the awesome power of Calc from the ins and outs of simple addition.

Adding and other arithmetic

You can perform basic addition and subtraction in a cell simply by typing **=4+6+9+7+3–2–5+1** and so on.

Multiplication and division are not much different, although you can incorporate parentheses into your equation. An example is **=(2+(5*3)–4)/2**. Nesting parentheses is fine. You can make your formula as short or as long as you want — almost. Calc does have an upper limit, but it's astronomically large.

You can mix and match cell addresses with numbers. For example, you can enter the formula **=C3/(2*D6)**. Calc easily distinguishes between numbers and cell addresses.

If ### appears in your cell instead of your expected value, you need to make the column wider. Calc needs more space to enter the value.

Adding with the Sum function

When adding a long column of numbers, typing each cell address followed by a plus sign can be tedious, so Calc provides the Sum function. You can use this function in two ways: by using the Sum button on the Formula Bar or by typing the function into a cell.

Using the Sum button

To add or subtract using the Sum button, perform these steps:

1. **Place your active cell where you want your total to appear.**

2. **Click the Sum button.**

A colored border appears around the cells that Calc guesses that you want to add. For instance, if your active cell is below a column of numbers, the border appears around the column of numbers.

Also, the formula is visible in your active cell. All formulas begin with an equal sign followed by the formula type — in this case, SUM. Then the range of cells is listed in parentheses.

3. **If Calc has not guessed correctly and the border does not surround any or all of the cells that you want to add, place your cursor over the border so that the cursor changes to a pointing hand (not a plus sign), and click and drag the border to the first value that you want to include in your sum.**

Don't worry if your border extends downward and you want to sum rows (across) instead. Changing the shape of the border is discussed in the next step.

4. **If the border still does not surround all the cells that you want to add, click and drag the tiny square at the lower-right corner of the border over the cells that you want to add.**

Your cursor changes to a plug sign (+) as you position it over the tiny square. As you drag, the border expands or contracts to surround the range of cells that you want to add.

Be sure that the border does not include the active cell. If it does, it means that you are trying to use your sum as a value in your sum. This is known as a *circular reference*. Just like everyone else, computers don't like to go around in circles. In this case, Calc gives you an error message.

5. **Press Enter or click the Accept button on the Formula Bar.**

Your sum appears in the active cell.

If #VALUE! appears in your active cell instead of your total, Calc found some invalid data that it could not add. Calc ignores text and empty cells, but it does not always ignore formulas. If #VALUE! appears, look for an invalid formula in the sum range. Then delete or move the invalid formula. Let's keep Calc happy.

Canceling a Sum or Formula

If you are in the middle of creating a sum or other formula and decide to cancel it, just click the Cancel button on the Formula Bar. This button only shows when you are in the middle of creating or editing a formula. Clicking the button causes the colored border to vanish, and the formula disappears from the active cell.

If you have already finished creating a sum and want to delete it, click the cell that the total is in and press Backspace. Poof! The sum vanishes.

Entering the Sum function manually

Some people like things automated, and some don't. Calc caters to both predilections. If you would rather just type in the formula and not have to click and drag on tiny colored borders, you can do that. To enter the Sum function manually, follow these steps:

1. **Click in the cell where you want your total to appear.**

2. **Type** =Sum(**. (Don't type the period!)**

3. **Type the range of cells that you want to add.**

   For example, if you want to add cells A1 through A5, then type A1:A5.

4. **Type**) **and press Enter.**

   Your formula disappears from the cell (but not the Input line), and in its place is the total.

Rocketing into Orbit with Functions

Now it's time to blast off and really have fun. Don't worry about the ins and outs of the laws of aerodynamics; your AutoPilot takes care of everything. Walking on the moon is no less stunning than the heights to which Calc can take you.

Using the AutoPilot:Functions dialog box

The AutoPilot:Functions dialog box, shown in Figure 12-2, has scads of formulas to choose from. And all of them are infinitely useful. The formulas cover the following topics:

- ✔ Database
- ✔ Date&Time
- ✔ Financial
- ✔ Information
- ✔ Logical
- ✔ Mathematical
- ✔ Array
- ✔ Statistical
- ✔ Spreadsheet
- ✔ Text

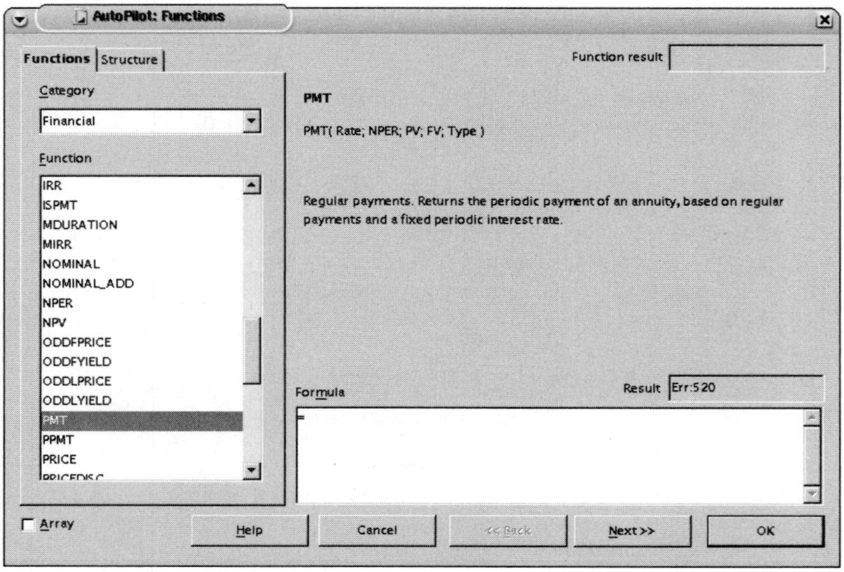

Figure 12-2:
The
AutoPilot:
Functions
dialog box
offers 365
functions.

We count 365 functions in all. One for each day of the year? Plus, you can add functions as well. Combinations and permutations of these functions provide Calc with a scope of computational abilities that is almost unlimited.

To use a function from the AutoPilot: Functions dialog box, perform the following steps:

1. **Select a cell that does not have a formula in it.**

   To modify a function instead of inserting a new one, follow the steps for modifying a formula, which are presented in the section "Editing functions," later in this chapter.

2. **Choose Insert⇨Functions, or click the AutoPilot button on the Formula Bar. If the Formula Bar is not visible, choose View⇨Toolbars⇨ Formula Bar to make it appear.**

   The dialog box should look similar to Figure 12-2, which shows the Functions tab displayed. If the Structure tab is active instead of the Functions tab, your active cell probably contains a formula. Click the Cancel button to return to your active sheet and either choose another active cell or press Backspace to delete the contents of the active cell. Then return and perform Step 2.

3. **Choose a category from the Category list box, and select a function from the Function list.**

   The name and description of that function appear, as shown in Figure 12-2. Also, the list of arguments that the function needs to return a value appears. For instance, the PMT function returns the periodic payment of an annuity. That's bank jargon for "calculates mortgage payments and other similar investments." As shown in Figure 12-2, this function requires Rate, NPER, PV, FV, and Type to return a value. The following step provides more information about these arguments.

4. **Double-click a function from the Function list.**

   Input boxes appear so that you can insert values into the function. Some functions, such as NOW in the Date&Time category, do not require information to return a value. No input box appears. Just click OK, and you see the date and time in the active cell. Other functions require many values, such as the PMT function that is shown in Figure 12-3.

5. **Insert your values or cell references into the input boxes for your function.**

   Sometimes figuring out exactly what the function expects can be tricky. For instance, Rate, as shown in Figure 12-3, applies to the rate for the monthly period, not the yearly period. In this case, an annual rate of 6.25 percent can be entered as **.0625/12**. Calc is more than happy to divide or multiply (or perform other computations) in the input boxes.

   Other values that are entered in Figure 12-3 are as follows:

   - NPER: The number of periods for a 30-year loan is 360 monthly periods,

   - PV: The present value is the amount of the loan — from the bank's point of view that is a negative number.

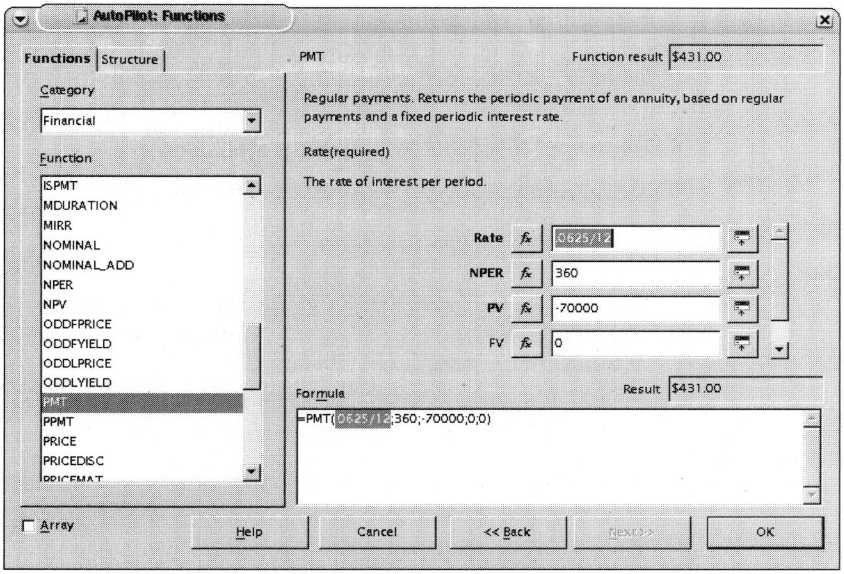

Figure 12-3:
You can
use the
AutoPilot:
Functions
dialog box
to quickly
create
formulas.

- FV: This is the future value. For a mortgage, this is always 0.

- Type: This indicates whether your payment is made at the beginning or end of the period. For a mortgage, this is 0 as well. For other types of investments, 0 indicates that the payment is at the end of the period; 1 means that it's at the beginning. (You need to scroll down to see Type).

Notice the button that's labeled fx next to each argument name in Figure 12-3. Don't click this button unless you want to nest your formulas. Nesting formulas is covered in the section "Creating Magic Formulas," later in this chapter. If you click the fx button, just remember that glorious invention known as the Back button.

When you type your value or cell reference in an input box, do not press Enter, unless it is the last value or address that you need to enter. Calc interprets pressing Enter as if you had clicked OK in the dialog box.

If Err502 — or some other error number — appears in the Result box, you can find out what the error means by clicking the Help button and then click the Index tab and double-click #Ref error messages (fourth line down from the top of the list) to bring up the list of error messages and their corresponding numbers. Most common errors are invalid parameters. For example, Calc displays an error message when it finds an array when it expects to find a single cell, or when the wrong number of parameters is listed. (This can occur if you use a comma instead of a semicolon, use a colon instead of a semicolon, or forget to enter all the parameters.) We often forget to enter all the parameters, because we forget to scroll down the parameter input lines in the AutoPilot:Functions dialog box.

To enter a cell reference instead of typing a value, you can either type the address of the cell or type the name of the range (for more about range names see the section coming up, "Naming ranges") or you can use the Shrink button.

To use the Shrink button, follow these steps:

1. Place your cursor in the input box in which you want to enter the cell reference.

2. Click the Shrink button.

   The AutoPilot:Functions dialog box shrinks to include just the input box, the title bar, close box, and the Maximize button. Your active sheet is now accessible.

3. Click the cell that you want to refer to in your formula. Or click and drag from one diagonal corner to the other corner of a range of cells.

   A colored border surrounds the selected cell(s). This border may turn a different color after you release the mouse button.

4. Click the Maximize button.

   The AutoPilot:Functions dialog box reappears.

6. **Repeat Step 5 until all values have been entered, be sure that the Array check box is deselected, and click OK.**

   The Array check box is an option for creating array formulas. We generally don't use this check box. An easier and just as powerful way of dealing with arrays is listed in the section "Creating formula arrays," later in this chapter.

7. **Click OK.**

   The result that appears in the Result box of the AutoPilot:Functions dialog box now appears in your cell.

Naming ranges

Giving a name to a range is useful for creating formulas. Instead of using the Shrink button or coordinates for a range into the input boxes of the AutoPilot: Functions dialog box, you can just type in a name. Using a range name is often easier and makes the function more readable as well.

After you name a range, whenever you want to select it for any reason, you can simply click the name in the Sheet Area list box on the Formula Bar, and presto, you are transported to your selected range.

To define a name for a range, do the following:

1. **Select the cells for your new range.**

2. **Choose Insert⇨Names⇨Define.**

   The Define Names dialog box appears.

3. **Type a name into the Name input box.**

4. **Click OK.**

   The name of your range now appears in the Sheet Area list box on the Formula Bar.

Editing functions

You can edit functions in the following ways:

✔ Use the AutoPilot:Functions dialog box.

✔ Double-click the cell where the function resides. The function appears and is editable.

✔ Select the cell where the function resides and edit it in the Input line of the Formula Bar.

To edit functions using the AutoPilot:Functions dialog box, select the cell where the function resides and click the AutoPilot:Functions button on the Formula Bar, or choose Insert➪Functions. This opens the AutoPilot:Functions dialog box, allowing you to modify your entries in the input boxes. Notice that the Structure panel is displayed. A graphic representation of your function appears in the Structure panel. This is useful to see what functions are nested. Nested functions are covered in the section "Nesting functions," later in this chapter.

To edit a function manually, perform the following steps:

1. **Select the cell that contains your function.**

   Your formula appears in the Formula Bar's Input line.

2. **Click the Input line on the Formula Bar (or double-click the cell).**

   If you double-click the cell, your formula appears in the cell and becomes editable. If you click the Input line, the Input line is editable. Color-coded borders appear in the spreadsheet surrounding each cell or range that is referred to in your formula. Your formula also becomes a rainbow of colors — one color for each cell or range.

3. **Reposition the colored borders as you desire, or type the new addresses that you want to use.**

   If you reposition the colored borders, the cell and range addresses change in the formula to reflect their new position. If you type the new addresses into the formula, the borders move to reflect your new formula.

4. **Press Enter or click the Accept button on the Formula Bar.**

   This is important. Otherwise, whenever you click in your spreadsheet, you are inadvertently inserting new addresses into your formula and moving colored borders around by mistake. You will feel like you are lost like Alice in Wonderland.

Entering functions manually

Calc also allows you to type functions manually into any cell. If your function has no parameters, such as =NOW() or =TODAY(), why not just type it in? And if your function is more complicated, you can look up the parameters using the AutoPilot:Functions dialog box, and then return to the active sheet and type the function into the cell. Just be careful to follow these rules:

✔ Start with an equal sign.

✔ Place semicolons between the parameters.

✔ Be sure that you list the correct number of parameters between the parentheses.

✔ Don't misspell *anything*.

Copying and pasting formulas

You can copy and paste formulas containing values just like numbers. For example, typing =EASTERSUNDAY(2004) produces the same value no matter where you copy and paste it. The same is true for typing =NOW(), which requires no parameters.

If your formula contains a cell reference, for example =SQRT(A1), which returns the square root of the number in cell A1, to copy that formula, you need to understand *relative addressing*. For the example shown in Figure 12-4, Calc always looks one row up and three columns back to find the value to use in the SQRT formula, no matter what cell the formula is moved or copied to.

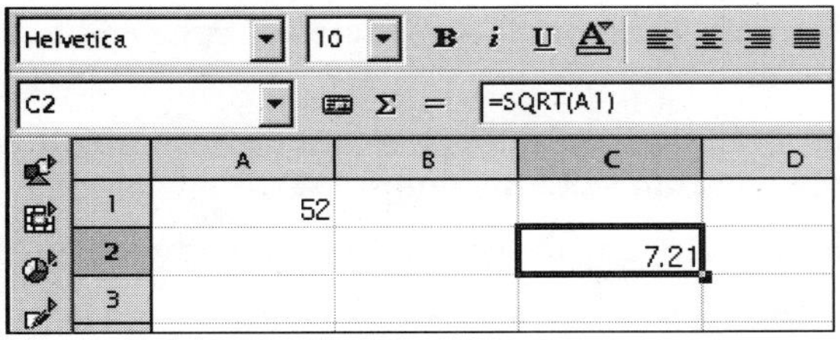

Figure 12-4: Cell references are often relative and change whenever the formula is moved.

To move or copy a formula that contains a relative address, you may want to move or copy the cell that it is addressing as well.

Relative addressing is very useful, especially in extending totals. For example, if you have one formula that totals a column, you can easily copy the formula to other columns.

Creating formula arrays

The mortgage table in Figure 12-5 is a formula array, which was created from a single formula that was copied and pasted into every cell of the table.

Notice how every mortgage payment refers to the column and row headings: number of years and interest rate for its unique value. To create a table that refers to row headings, and/or column headings, you need to understand *absolute addressing*.

An absolute address is easier to understand than a relative address. An absolute address is one that does not change when the formula is moved from one cell to another. For example, in Figure 12-4, if the formula =SQRT(A1) refers to an absolute address of cell A1, whenever you move or copy that formula, it always refers to cell A1 for its value. Calc uses dollar signs to denote absolute addresses. The formula with an absolute address reads =SQRT(A1).

The dollar sign in front of the A fixes column A as nonchanging when the formula is copied or moved, and the dollar sign in front of the 1 fixes Row 1 as nonchanging when the formula is copied or moved.

To create a formula with absolute references, follow these steps:

1. **Select the formula that you want to insert absolute references.**

   The formula appears on the Input line of the Formula Bar.

2. **In the Input line, select the first coordinates of your cell range and do one of the following.**

   • If you want both the row and column to be absolute, then press Shift+F4. (For example, A1 becomes A1.)

   • If you want just the row to be an absolute reference, press Shift+F4 twice. (A1 becomes A$1.)

   • If you want just the column to be an absolute reference, press Shift+F4 three times. (A1 becomes $A1.)

3. **Repeat Step 2 for all your desired coordinates in your formula.**

4. **Click Accept or press Enter.**

Recalculating formulas

Recalculating is generally automatic for formulas. When you change a value in a table, the total automatically changes. But some formulas and functions do not recalculate automatically. For instance, the NOW function places the time and date into a cell. If you want the current time — not the time that you happened to have inserted that function into the cell — you need to recalculate. Also, very large spreadsheets may require recalculation to produce reliable results.

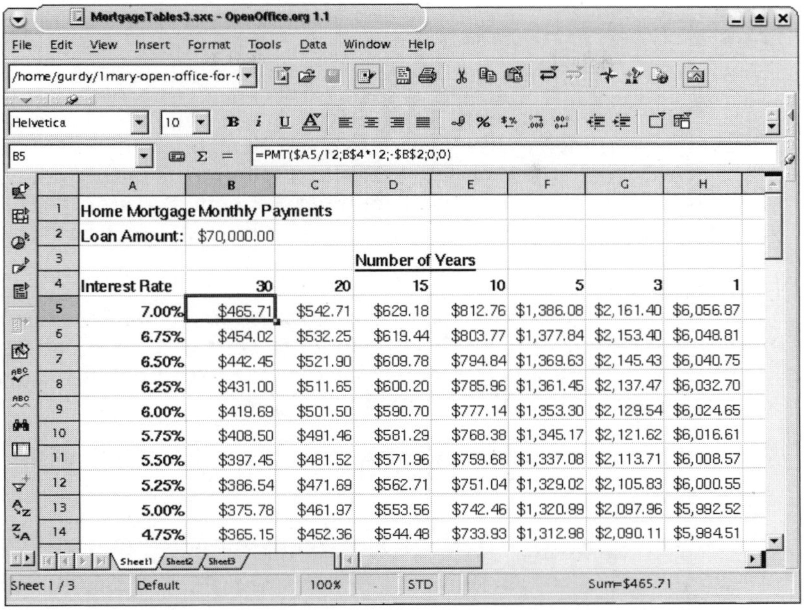

Figure 12-5:
Mortgage
tables are
arrays of
formulas
generated
using
absolute
addressing.

Recalculating is easy. Just choose Tools➪Cell Contents➪Recalculate. Recalculation occurs immediately. Your Now function now shows the correct time and date.

If your spreadsheet is not recalculating automatically, be sure that the Automatic Recalculation feature is turned on. Choose Tools➪Cell Contents, and be sure that the Automatic Recalculation check box is selected.

Creating Magic Formulas

The functions of Calc, which are listed in the AutoPilot:Functions dialog box, are basic formulas. These functions are building blocks that can be placed and stacked together to create more complex formulas that can perform almost any calculation in a spreadsheet. Functions may nest within other functions, making complex formulas, or they may refer to conditions, creating conditional formulas. Regardless of what you call them, formulas and functions are like fairy dust particles that turn your rug into a flying carpet.

Nesting functions

Functions within functions are called *nested functions*. One function's output is the other function's input. For example, to find out what today's week number is — from 1 to 52 — you could use a calendar and count the weeks or your could create the function =WEEKNUM(TODAY();2). The function TODAY returns the current date, and the number 2 specifies to start counting the new week with Monday, not Sunday. The WEEKNUM function then tells you today's week number.

You can nest functions with the AutoPilot:Functions dialog box, or you can just type functions into a cell. Remember to start with an equal sign, use the right number of parameters, use semicolons between parameters, make no spelling mistakes, and drive carefully.

To nest functions using the AutoPilot:Functions dialog box, perform these steps:

1. **Click the empty cell where you want your function to reside.**

2. **Choose Insert⇨Function or click the AutoPilot: Functions button on the Formula Bar.**

   The AutoPilot:Functions dialog box appears.

3. **Choose your category, and double-click the desired function.**

   In the preceding example, you would double-click WEEKNUM. The input boxes appear for your function.

4. **Click in the first input box.**

5. **Click the fx button to the left of the input box.**

   The input boxes disappear, but the Category list box and the Function list box remain.

6. **Choose All for the category, and in the Function list box, double-click the function that you want to insert.**

   For this example, double-click TODAY. The information for the double-clicked function appears and if the function has parameters; the input boxes for the parameters also appear.

7. **Fill in the parameters of your function (if any), and then click the Back button to return to your original function.**

8. **Enter values, cell references, range names, equations, or nested formulas into each input box for the formula.**

9. **Press Enter or click OK.**

   In the example, the number of weeks from the beginning of the year to the current date is entered in your active cell.

Creating conditional formulas

Conditional formulas are commonly used in Calc. Suppose that you sell nursery plants and you give free gifts to customers who buy a certain quantity of plants. If your customer buys over $40 worth of plants, you add a free rhododendron plant to his order. This is a conditional formula. An example of this conditional formula is shown in Figure 12-6.

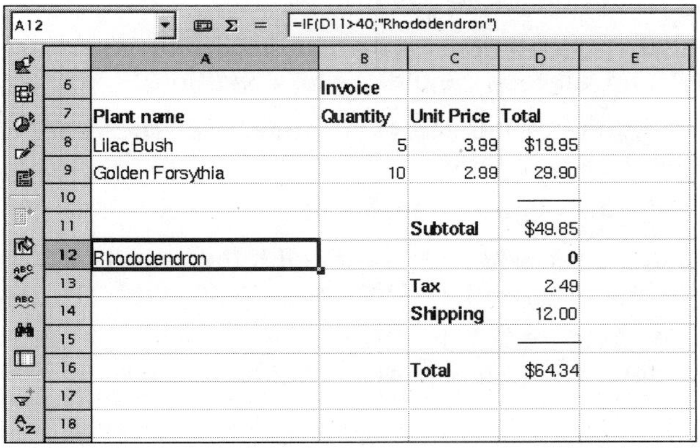

Figure 12-6:
An automated invoice makes use of a conditional formula.

	A	B	C	D	E
	A12	▼ 📼 Σ =	=IF(D11>40;"Rhododendron")		
6		Invoice			
7	Plant name	Quantity	Unit Price	Total	
8	Lilac Bush	5	3.99	$19.95	
9	Golden Forsythia	10	2.99	29.90	
10					
11			Subtotal	$49.85	
12	Rhododendron			0	
13			Tax	2.49	
14			Shipping	12.00	
15					
16			Total	$64.34	
17					
18					

To create a conditional formula, perform the following steps:

1. **Click the cell where you want your result to reside.**

   For example, in Figure 12-6, the formula resides in cell A12.

2. **Choose Insert⇨Function or click the AutoPilot: Functions button on the Formula Bar.**

   The AutoPilot:Functions dialog box appears.

3. **Choose All or Logical from the category list, and double-click** IF **in the function list.**

   The input boxes appear for the parameters of the IF function.

4. **Click in the first input box, labeled Test, and click the Shrink button to the left of the input box. Or type in the cell address containing the data you want to evaluate and skip to Step 8.**

   Your dialog box shrinks, and your spreadsheet is accessible.

5. **Click the cell that contains or will contain the data that you want to evaluate.**

   In Figure 12-6, the cell that contains the subtotal is the desired cell.

6. **Click the Maximize button.**

   The AutoPilot: Functions dialog box reappears. The cell that you chose appears in the Test input box.

7. **Press ←.**

   This deselects the cell address. If you did not press ←, your cell address is replaced by whatever you typed next. The cursor now is blinking to the left of the cell address.

8. **Type your conditional statement.**

   In Figure 12-6, the conditional statement is D11>40. The operators: <, >, >=, <=, and = are all good candidates for conditions.

9. **Click in the input box labeled Then value, and type your value into the box. Use quotes for text.**

   In Figure 12-6, this value is "Rhododendron".

10. **To place a different value into your cell if the condition is not met, click in the input box labeled Otherwise value, and type your value.**

    For example, in Figure 12-6, instead of leaving the cell blank if a customer does not order over $40 worth of goods, you could insert something like, "Sorry, no rhododendrons for you" — or maybe not.

11. **Press Enter, or click OK.**

    The value that your formula returns appears in the active cell.

Part IV

Using Impress — The Presentation Package

The 5th Wave   By Rich Tennant

Okay—you were right, I was wrong. F5 opens the garage door, and F6 backs the car out.

In this part . . .

*T*his part tells you all you need to know about creating a great presentation. Step by step, it starts with the basics, such as starting a presentation, editing a presentation, creating bullets and paragraphs, and helping your audience with graphics, animation, and handouts.

Chapter 13

Creating a Presentation

In This Chapter

▶ Opening a new or existing presentation

▶ Understanding presentation views

▶ Inserting slides

▶ Saving a presentation

1n this chapter, we cover the basics of using Impress, OpenOffice.org's presentation application. You discover how to open a presentation, move around in its various views, add some slides, and save the presentation. These skills are the basis for all your presentation creation.

Starting a Presentation

When creating a new presentation, you can start from scratch or use AutoPilot to help you along the way. Of course, you can also open an existing presentation and continue to work on it.

Using AutoPilot to start quickly

By default, when you open Impress, AutoPilot opens to let you start from scratch, use a template, or open an existing presentation, as shown in Figure 13-1. Impress has two kinds of templates. *Presentation backgrounds,* or design templates, include only a background, and you add all the text. *Presentations,* or content templates, include both a background and suggested ideas for text. The current version has two templates of either kind.

For more templates, go to www.ooextras.org and click Impress.

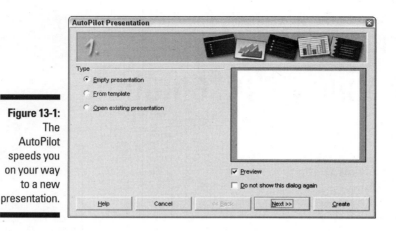

Figure 13-1:
The
AutoPilot
speeds you
on your way
to a new
presentation.

Even if you start from scratch, you get to choose a design or content template, the type of output (such as overheads or on-screen), and a transition type. Using the Template option offers you the additional opportunity to specify the name of your company, a subject, and the specific pages (slides) that you want to include if you choose a content template.

AutoPilot varies depending on your choices. The following steps show you how if you choose the Template option. The Empty Presentation option is similar.

1. **From the drop-down list on the first screen, choose Presentation Backgrounds to start a new presentation with a background, or choose Presentations to choose one of the content templates that provide an outline structure for various kinds of presentations. Choose one of the templates, and click Next.**

   For this step, we chose one of the Presentation options, Recommendation of a Strategy.

2. **On the second screen, choose a slide design.**

   If this sounds repetitive, it is. You can choose the same presentation backgrounds and presentations. However, if you've already chosen a background (see Step 1), you can choose a presentation (content template) here to combine the two; that is, the content on the background that you chose. For this step, we chose a custom template that we created.

   Later in this chapter, we explain how to add a template to the list of presentation backgrounds. In Chapter 14, we explain how to use Master view, where you design repeating elements of a presentation or a template.

3. **In the Select an Output Medium panel of the second screen, choose the type of output that you want to create. Click Next.**

   This selection determines the size and orientation of your slides. The Original option uses a size that is based on the template that you chose.

Use Screen if you plan to use an LCD projector or present from your computer screen. Use Slide to print individual slides (for a carousel projector).

4. On the third screen, choose a slide transition effect and speed from the drop-down lists.

A slide transition effect determines how each slide appears. Select the Preview check box so that when you choose an effect, you can see what the transition looks like in the Preview box.

5. In the Select a Presentation Type panel of the third screen, choose Default, which runs the presentation under your control, or choose Automatic, which loops the presentation repeatedly. Click Next.

If you choose Automatic, set the timing for each slide and the pause after each run-through of the presentation.

6. In the fourth screen, you can add the name of your company, the main subject of the presentation, and other ideas that you want to convey. Click Next.

The items that you enter appear on the title slide of the presentation. You can change them later if you want. This screen does not appear if you chose to create an empty presentation.

7. On the fifth screen, choose the pages that you want and click the Create button.

This screen only appears if you chose a content template.

Figure 13-2 shows the presentation that results from the choices we made.

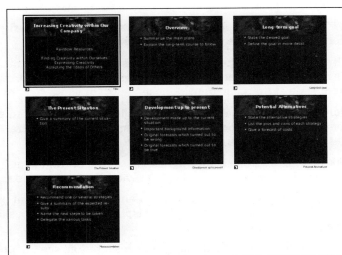

Figure 13-2:
A presentation that uses a custom template background and the Recommending a Strategy content template that comes with OpenOffice.org.

Opening an existing presentation

To open an existing presentation, you can do one of the following, depending on your circumstances:

- ✔ Start OpenOffice.org, and click the File menu. Choose one of the presentations at the bottom of the menu.

- ✔ From any OpenOffice.org application, choose File⇨Open.

- ✔ Start OpenOffice.org Impress and choose File⇨New⇨Presentation. From the AutoPilot screen, choose Open Existing Presentation.

Viewing Your Presentation

When you have a presentation on-screen, you need to know how to display your presentation in the best way to get your work done and how to navigate through it.

Using Impress's views

Impress has six views, each of which displays your slides differently. You choose a view based on what you need to see at the moment. The view buttons are at the upper-right corner of your screen. The various views are described as follows:

- ✔ **Drawing view:** Shows one slide at a time so that you can easily focus on perfecting that slide, as shown in Figure 13-3.

- ✔ **Outline view:** Shows the text of your presentation only so that you can work on your content and see how it flows. To see a small preview of the current slide at the same time, choose View⇨Preview.

- ✔ **Slides view:** Shows small views of your slides so that you can see many of them at once, reorder them, delete them, and so on. Figure 13-2 shows a presentation in Slides view.

- ✔ **Notes view:** Shows one slide with a space at the bottom to add notes for yourself or for someone else who will review the presentation.

- ✔ **Handout view:** Enables you to format handouts that you can print and give to your audience. Handouts can display from one to six slides per page.

For more information on printing your presentation, see Chapter 17.

- ✔ **Slide show view:** Displays the presentation full-screen, slide by slide. You use this view when you deliver your presentation to an audience.

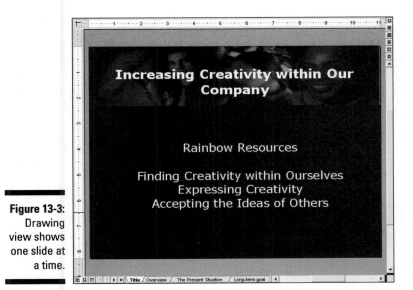

Figure 13-3: Drawing view shows one slide at a time.

Understanding Impress's modes

In addition to views, Impress has three modes that display different aspects of the infrastructure of a presentation. Okay, what does that mean and how do you change from one mode to another? In this section, we explain the modes and how they relate to the views. The mode buttons are at the lower-left corner of your screen. The modes are as follows:

✔ **Slide mode:** This is the mode that you normally use to work on creating your presentation. You can only use Drawing or Notes view when you are in Slide mode, because these views are the only views that let you actually add graphics and objects to a slide.

✔ **Master mode:** This mode formats the overall structure of the presentation. For example, you set the font types and colors for the entire presentation in Master mode. You can also add a graphic, such as a logo, that you want to appear on every slide. Master mode with Drawing view sets the structure for the slides. Master mode with Notes view sets the structure of the Notes view. Master mode with Handout view lays out handouts that you print and give to your audience.

✔ **Layers mode:** This mode enables you to access the layers of a slide. When you enter Layers mode, tabs appear, one for each layer. Click a tab to make its layer current. Layers mode is not exclusive to the other modes — you use the Layers mode button to turn Layers mode on and off with either Slide mode or Master mode active. The default layers are as follows:

  • **Layout:** Contains all the normal objects on a slide, such as text and graphics. You use this layer most often.

- **Controls:** Holds buttons that you have created. You usually create buttons to execute a macro.

- **Dimension Lines:** Holds dimensions that you create to measure objects on the screen.

  You use dimension lines to measure objects. To draw a dimension line, choose the Dimension Line button from the Lines and Arrows toolbar of the Object Bar. Click and drag to draw the line. Press Ctrl to snap to an object, and press Shift to hold the dimension line to an exact multiple of 45 degrees. Figure 13-4 shows an example of a dimension line.

Figure 13-4: Use dimension lines to measure your objects.

You can lock a layer to prevent editing and hide a layer to make it invisible. For example, you may want to measure an object with a dimension line, but you probably don't want that dimension to appear in your presentation. You can also add new layers to help you organize the objects on your slides. Use the following when working with layers:

✔ **Add a layer:** In Layers mode, right-click (Control+click on the Mac) any layer tab and choose Insert Layer from the shortcut menu that appears. Name the layer, set its properties (whether the layer is visible, printable, or locked), and click OK.

✔ **Lock or hide a layer:** In Layers mode, right-click (Control+click on the Mac) any layer tab and choose Modify Layer from the shortcut menu that appears. Select the Locked check box to lock the layer. Deselect the Visible check box to hide the layer. You can also deselect the Printable check box to ensure that the layer is not printed.

✔ **Delete a layer:** In Layers mode, right-click (Control+click on the Mac) any layer tab and choose Delete Layer from the shortcut menu that appears. Click the Yes button to confirm. Deleting a layer deletes any object on that layer.

Click the Layers mode button to leave Layers mode.

Adding a template to an existing presentation

If you start a new presentation using the Empty Presentation option, you can add a template at any time. Follow these steps:

1. **Switch to Master mode.**

   We explain Master mode in the previous section of this chapter.

2. **Choose Format⇨Styles⇨Slide Design.**

   The Slide Design dialog box opens.

3. **Click the Load button.**

   The Load Slide Design dialog box opens.

4. **From the Categories list, choose Presentation Backgrounds.**

5. **Choose one of the templates from the Templates list.**

6. **Click OK twice to close both dialog boxes and return to your presentation.**

7. **Return to Slide mode.**

   The slide design appears on your slides. (We explain Slide mode in the previous section of this chapter.)

Navigating through a presentation

As soon as you have more than one slide, you need to know how to navigate through a presentation. You can navigate in the following ways:

- In Slide mode, each slide has a tab at the bottom of the screen. Click the tab to display the slide. If the tab is not visible, click the left and right arrows to the left of the tabs to scroll through the tabs.

- Display the Navigator (click the Navigator button on the Function Bar). Each slide is listed, as shown in Figure 13-5. Double-click any slide in the Navigator to display that slide.

For details about navigating through a presentation in Slide Show view, when you deliver it, see Chapter 17.

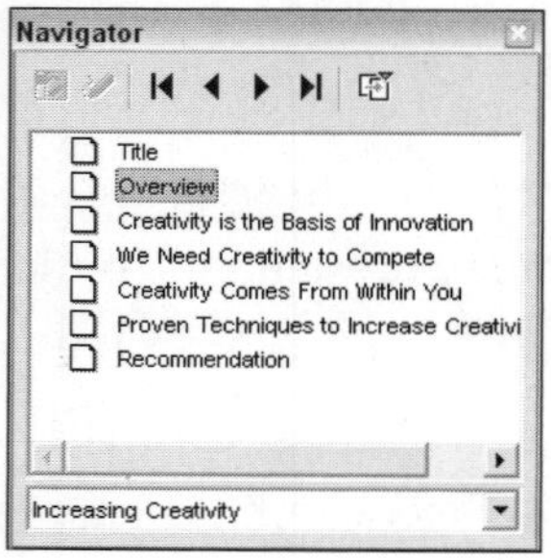

Figure 13-5:
The
Navigator
quickly
whisks you
through
your pre-
sentation.

Adding Slides

To build your presentation, you need to add slides. Usually, you build a presentation slide by slide, so when you finish one slide, you add the next. Of course, if you used AutoPilot to create a presentation using a content template, you may already have the slides that you need. Then again, you may need additional slides.

To add a slide, follow these steps:

1. **Display the slide after which you want to insert a slide.**

2. **Choose Insert⇨Slide.**

   The Insert Slide dialog box appears, as shown in Figure 13-6.

   To display the Presentation toolbar, which contains several often-used commands, include Insert Slide. Choose View⇨Toolbars⇨Presentation.

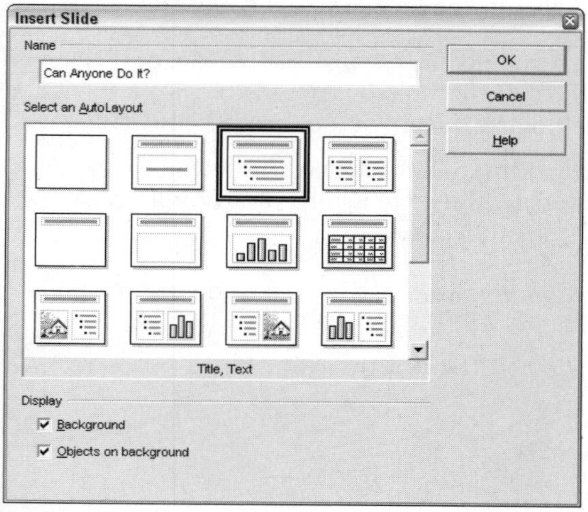

Figure 13-6:
The Insert
Slide dialog
box.

3. **In the Name text box, enter a name for the slide.**

    If you don't enter a name, OpenOffice.org inserts `Slide 2`, depending on the slide number. A name that relates to the topic of the slide, ideally the title of the slide, is more helpful for navigating.

4. **From the Select an AutoLayout panel, choose a layout.**

    A layout provides you with a structure for laying out a slide. Choose the layout that best matches what you want to have on the slide.

5. **Click OK.**

Later in this chapter, we explain how to add text to a slide. Chapters 14 and 15 explain how to edit text and add graphics.

Creating an outline in Impress

To focus on your content at first and go back and fill in the graphics later, create your presentation using Outline view. To create a presentation in Outline view, follow these steps:

1. **Click the Outline view button on the toolbar.**

    You now see a white space where you can start to type. To also see a small view of each slide, choose View⇨Preview. The cursor is next to a slide icon.

2. **Type the title of the slide next to the slide icon, as shown in Figure 13-7.**

3. **Press Enter, and type the next line of text for the slide. Press Enter again.**

    A new slide icon appears at the left of the new line of text, indicating that this text will appear on a new slide. You see a new slide if you have a preview. However, you want this text to be on the same slide as the first line of text.

4. **Select the new line of text and click the Demote button on the Object Bar, or press Tab.**

    The new line of text moves to the right, under the first line of text. If you have a preview, you can see that the new line of text is now on the same slide as the first line.

5. **If you want, continue to type more text for the slide.**

6. **To start a new slide, type the slide title and press Enter.**

    This line of text appears at the end of the previous slide that you were working on.

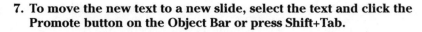

7. **To move the new text to a new slide, select the text and click the Promote button on the Object Bar or press Shift+Tab.**

   The new text now appears on a new slide.

8. **Repeat Steps 4 through 6 to create more slides, as shown in Figure 13-8.**

You can move any slide in Outline view by clicking its slide icon and dragging up or down. You can also use the Move Up and Move Down buttons on the Object Bar.

Creating an outline in Writer

You can create your outline in Writer and then send it to Impress. You may simply find it easier to write in Writer, or you may have an outline that someone already created.

To create the outline in Writer, you need to format it specially so that Impress knows how to divide the text into slides, which text should be a slide title, and which text should be bulleted text on the slide. This is easy:

✔ Text that uses a heading style becomes a slide title and starts a new slide.

✔ Any text that uses a paragraph style, such as Text Body, becomes bulleted text.

If you're not familiar with styles in Writer, see Chapter 4.

If someone gives you an outline that was created in Microsoft Word, open the outline in Writer and format it as we just described. Then save it as a Writer document.

To create the presentation with this outline, follow these steps:

1. **In Writer, choose File⇨Send⇨AutoAbstract to Presentation.**

   The Create AutoAbstract dialog box opens.

2. **In the Included Outline Levels text box, enter the number of levels of heading styles that you want to include.**

3. **In the Subpoints per Level text box, enter the number of bulleted items that you want to include.**

   To include all the text, use a high number here. Use lower numbers to use only the first one or two points in your presentation.

4. **Click OK.**

   OpenOffice.org creates a new presentation from your outline.

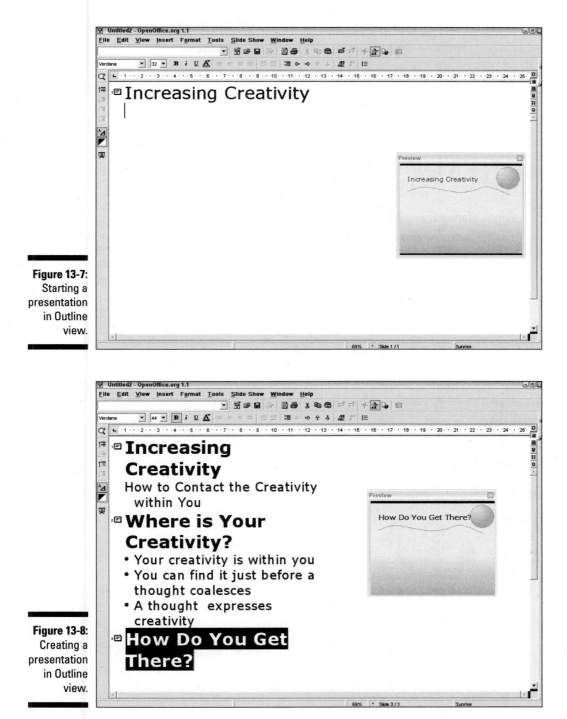

Figure 13-7:
Starting a
presentation
in Outline
view.

Figure 13-8:
Creating a
presentation
in Outline
view.

You can now add a template as described earlier in this chapter, and further refine your presentation.

Adding text to a slide

In the previous section, we explained how to add text to a presentation using Outline view. However, you may prefer to add text to each slide individually. When you add text to each slide, you can see how the text looks on the slide more clearly. If you already have graphics on the slide, you can get a better idea of the entire layout of the slide.

Using text placeholders

The most common way to add text to a slide is to use text placeholders. When you add a slide and choose an AutoLayout, as explained in the section "Adding Slides," earlier in this chapter, you can choose a slide that includes a text placeholder for bulleted text, such as the one that's shown in Figure 13-9.

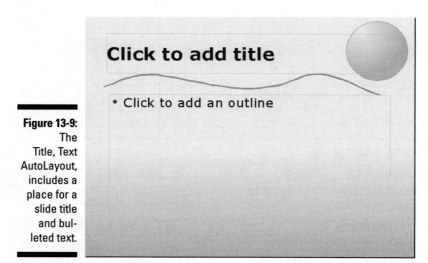

Figure 13-9:
The Title, Text AutoLayout, includes a place for a slide title and bulleted text.

To add the title of the slide, click the *Click to add title* text and start typing. To add bulleted text, click the *Click to add an outline* text and type away. Press Enter to add a new bulleted item.

Inserting a text frame

You don't need to limit yourself to the text placeholders. You can add text wherever you want. OpenOffice.org offers the following types of text frames:

T **Text Frame:** Click the Text Frame button on the Text floating toolbar on the Object Bar. Drag a frame to the desired width. You see a frame that is the width that you dragged but with a height of only one line, no matter how you dragged. Don't worry! Start to type, and the frame increases in height as you type to adjust to the amount of text. If you later adjust the width of the frame, the text rewraps to fit the new width. You should probably use this type of frame most of the time.

T **Fit Text to Frame:** Click the Fit Text to Frame button on the Text floating toolbar on the Object Bar. Drag a frame to the desired width. You see four handles indicating the frame size and a cursor that is the full height of the frame! Plunge ahead and start typing. The text is probably huge, unless you dragged a very short frame. When you think you want a new line, press Enter. To finish, press Esc. Only now does the text adjust to the size of the frame. If you later adjust the size of the frame, the text changes size (both height and width), just as a graphic object scales when you adjust its selection border. Use this type of frame when you want text to act like a graphic object.

Chapter 14 explains how to edit and format text in more detail.

Saving Your Presentation for Posterity

Before you create too many slides — or even after creating the first slide — you should save your presentation. You can save in OpenOffice.org format or save to several other presentation formats. You can also export your presentation to a host of other formats, such as PDF (Adobe Reader), SWF (Flash Player), HTML, and many graphic formats.

Saving in OpenOffice.org format

To save a presentation for the first time, follow these steps:

1. **Choose File➪Save, click the Save button on the Function Bar, or press Ctrl+S.**

   The Save As dialog box opens (but only if you are saving the presentation for the first time).

2. **In the Save in drop-down list, choose a location for the presentation.**

3. **In the File Name text box, enter a name for the presentation.**

4. **Click the Save button.**

After you save your presentation for the first time, you should save every few minutes, using the same method. Now, the Save As dialog box doesn't open because the presentation already has a name and location. The saving process occurs without much fanfare, but you can rest easy knowing that you won't lose your work if your computer crashes or the electricity goes off.

Saving in other presentation formats

To share your presentation with others who don't have OpenOffice.org (is anybody left out there who doesn't have OpenOffice.org?), you can save your presentation in Microsoft PowerPoint format. In fact, you can save in all the following formats:

- ✔ OpenOffice.org presentation (.sxi): Of course.
- ✔ OpenOffice.org Presentation Template (.sti): Save your presentation as a template for future reuse.
- ✔ Microsoft PowerPoint 97/2000/XP (.ppt, .pps): The PPT format is the regular PowerPoint format. The PPS format is the slide show format, which is used when you are delivering a presentation full-screen.
- ✔ Microsoft PowerPoint 97/2000/XP Template (.pot): Save your presentation as a PowerPoint template for future use in PowerPoint.
- ✔ OpenOffice.org Drawing (.scd): Save in OpenOffice.org Drawing format.
- ✔ StarDraw (.sda, .sdd): Save in two possible versions of StarOffice's Draw format.
- ✔ StarImpress (.sdd): Save in two possible versions of StarOffice's Impress format.
- ✔ StarImpress Template (.vor): Save in two possible versions of StarOffice's Impress template format.

To save your presentation in one of these formats, choose File➪Save As. In the Save As dialog box, choose the format that you want from the Save as Type drop-down list. Click the Save button. OpenOffice.org creates a copy of your presentation in the new format.

If you save your presentation as a template, you should save the template in a location that you can easily find when you want to create a new presentation based on the template. Follow these steps:

1. **Choose Tools⇨Options⇨Paths and look for Templates. Write down the location or locations for templates.**

   You'll probably find more than one location. In that case, look in those locations to find out where the templates that are used in AutoPilot reside. On our Windows system, these templates are in the `C:\Program Files\OpenOffice.org1.1\share\template\english\layout` folder. If necessary, start AutoPilot again (choose File⇨New in Impress) and choose the template option to see the names of the templates there. The filenames don't necessarily exactly match the names that appear in AutoPilot, but they are similar.

   To save a content template, look for the location of the presentations that appear in AutoPilot. On our Windows system, the location is the same as that for the design templates, but the last folder is `presnt` instead of `layout`.

2. **Choose File⇨Save As, and choose the OpenOffice.org Presentation Template (`.sti`) option from the Save as Type drop-down list. Give your template an easy-to-recognize name.**

3. **From the Save in drop-down list, choose the desired location for the template.**

4. **Click the Save button.**

5. **Choose File⇨New⇨Templates and Documents.**

   The Templates and Documents dialog box opens.

6. **In the left panel, choose Templates.**

   You see in the template folders in the Title panel.

7. **Double-click the folder that contains your template.**

   The templates appear in the Title panel.

8. **Choose the template that you want, and click the Open button.**

Exporting to other formats

You can also export your presentation to graphic formats. You may want to use a graphic format to insert an image of a slide into a Writer document or onto a Web page. You can also use this format to send a copy of your presentation to other people who don't have a presentation program. Table 13-1 lists the most common export formats.

Table 13-1	Export Formats
Format	**Description**
HTML	Hypertext Markup Language, the format that browsers read. Used to post a presentation to a Web site.
PDF	Adobe's Portable Document Format, a widely used graphic format. Requires the Adobe Reader, which is a free download from www.adobe.com.
SWF	Macromedia Flash Player, a widely used animation format. Requires the Flash Player, which is a free download from www.macromedia.com.
BMP	Windows bitmap, a common bitmap graphic format.
EMF	Enhanced Metafile, a Windows vector format.
GIF	Graphics Interchange Format, a common bitmap graphic format that supports transparency but a limited number of colors.
JPEG	Joint Photographic Experts Group, a common bitmap graphic format that is suitable for photographs as well as other graphic art.
PCT	Mac Pict, a Mac graphic format.
PNG	Portable Network Graphic, an increasingly common bitmap format that supports transparency with a larger color palette than GIF.
SVG	Scalable Vector Graphics, a vector graphic format.
TIFF	Tagged Image File Format, a bitmap format that is often created from scanned images.
WMF	Windows Metafile, a Windows vector format.

Exporting to HTML format

When you export to HTML format, as described in the previous section, the HTML Export AutoPilot opens so that you can specify settings that relate to your HTML file. Follow these steps to export to HTML:

1. **Choose File⇨Export, and choose HTML from the File Format drop-down list. Click the Save button.**

2. **In the first screen of the HTML Export AutoPilot, choose New Design to create a design in the AutoPilot, or choose Existing Design (if any are listed).**

If you choose Existing Design, choose a design and click Next.

The next steps assume that you chose New Design.

3. **On the second screen, choose the publication type, as follows:**

   - **Standard HTML format:** Creates a regular HTML page for each slide, along with navigation tools.

   - **Standard HTML with frames:** Creates HTML pages so that the slides are in the main frame. A frame on the left side contains a table of slides with hyperlinks to each slide.

   - **Automatic:** Creates an HTML presentation that advances automatically. You can use existing timings for each slide or set a timing here. You can also loop the presentation.

   - **WebCast:** Creates Active Server Pages (ASPs) or Perl programming code so that you can deliver the presentation in real-time over the Internet and change the slides in the audience's Web browsers.

     To use the WebCast option, you need access to a server that supports ASPs or Perl.

   Depending on the type of publication that you choose, the options change accordingly. Choose the options that you want. In the steps that follow, we chose the Standard HTML format option. For this option, you can choose to create a title page and decide whether you want to display notes that you have written for each slide.

4. **Click Next.**

5. **On the next screen, choose the type of graphic format you want to use for the slides: GIF or JPEG. Also, choose the desired resolution. Click Next.**

6. **If you chose to create a title page, insert information for the title page. Click Next.**

7. **On the next screen, choose one of the button styles for navigating from slide to slide. Click Next.**

8. **On the next screen, choose colors for text and hyperlinks. Click the Create button.**

   The Name HTML Design dialog box opens.

9. **To save the parameters that you chose for the HTML document so that you can use them again in the future, enter a name and click the Save button. Otherwise, click the Do Not Save button.**

OpenOffice.org creates the HTML presentation in the same folder as your regular presentation. To see the presentation run, find the HTML file and open it. Use the navigation buttons to run through the presentation.

When you create an HTML presentation, you end up with a large number of files. If your presentation is in a folder with many other files, you will probably have a hard time figuring out which files belong to the presentation. Because you need to upload the files to your Web server, you should save your presentation in a new folder before you export it to HTML format.

Exiting Impress

When you finish your working session in Impress and save your presentation, it's time to exit Impress. To exit a presentation, choose File➪Close. Other presentations or other OpenOffice.org files remain open.

To close OpenOffice.org, choose File➪Exit or click the Close button on the toolbar.

Chapter 14

Modifying a Presentation

● ●

In This Chapter

▶ Editing text

▶ Formatting text

▶ Using bullets

▶ Formatting paragraphs

▶ Using Master view

● ●

*A*fter you start a presentation, you always need to edit and change it. In this chapter, we explain how to edit text and make it look good, too. We cover the tricks of the trade for using bullets (the kind that communicate peacefully) and lining up your paragraphs. Finally, we explain how to use Master view to control the design of your entire presentation and give it consistency.

Editing Text

Editing text in Impress is not much different from editing text in Writer, but you should know about the few differences that exist. These differences mainly occur because of the graphical nature of a presentation.

Selecting text

To edit text, you need to select it. You use the same techniques that you use in Writer. You can do any of the following to select text:

✔ Drag across text

✔ Double-click a word to select the word

✔ Triple-click a line to select the entire line of text

When you select text in a text placeholder or a separate text frame that you added to a slide, you also select the placeholder or frame itself — you see a border and square handles, as shown in Figure 14-1.

Most of the techniques for selecting text in Writer also apply to Impress. For a more detailed list of techniques, including keyboard shortcuts, see Chapter 3.

When you select text, you can't see its color because of the highlighting. So sometimes you want to deselect text. The easiest way to deselect text is to simply click on the edge of the slide or even completely off the slide, on the gray background.

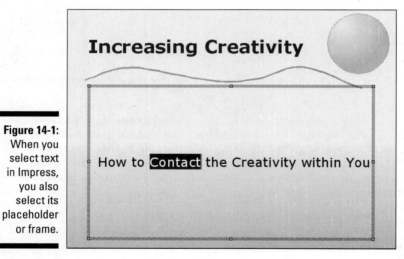

Figure 14-1:
When you select text in Impress, you also select its placeholder or frame.

Changing text

After you select text, you can type over it to replace what is selected. You can also click between words or letters and type to insert text. These techniques are the same as the ones that you use in Writer.

To copy text, you can use the standard techniques of drag and drop and copying to the clipboard, and then pasting. Dragging and dropping text from slide to slide works best in Outline view. Copying and pasting works in Outline view as well as in Slide view. You can also move text by using drag and drop or by cutting to the Clipboard and then pasting.

To delete text, select it and press Delete. You can also place the cursor after the text and press Backspace.

For more details about changing text, see Chapter 3.

If you have text in a placeholder or frame and don't want any text there, you can delete the placeholder or frame instead. By default, when you click in a text placeholder or text frame, you are in text edit mode, so pressing Delete or Backspace deletes only the text. So how do you delete the placeholder or frame? You need to click the border of the placeholder or frame and then press Delete or Backspace. When you click the border, OpenOffice.org understands that you want to deal with the whole object, not just its text.

Using Text with Style

The presentation template and its Master view control the default font type, font size, and font color. (The Master view is explained more fully in the section "Using Master View," later in this chapter.) Overall, you should stay as consistent as possible. Using many fonts and font sizes in a presentation yields a chaotic impression. However, you may want some variety or to make an exception for a particular slide. You can easily change the look of any text.

When you change the font of some text, you should choose a font that looks good with other fonts that you are using. Serif fonts have small horizontal lines added to their edges and are ideal for paragraph text. Most of the text in this book is in a serif font. Sans-serif fonts have simpler shapes — use them for headings. For bulleted text, you can choose either a serif or a sans-serif font. Legibility is the most important principle. However, you may also want to match the look of your font with your overall design.

To change the font, select the text and choose the font that you want from the Font drop-down list on the Object Bar. To change the font's size, choose the size that you want from the Font Size drop-down list on the Object Bar.

On the same Object Bar, you can continue to format your text, adding bold, italic, or underline formatting and changing the color.

In Chapter 16, we explain how you can add animation effects to text in text frames.

Playing with Bullets

The most common type of text in a presentation is a bulleted list. Contrary to popular opinion, these bullets are not dangerous — they don't hurt you, your audience, or even the text.

Why are these benign bullets so popular in presentations? Bulleted lists are usually partial sentences that contain just enough content to remind you and your audience of the concept that you are trying to get across. You don't want your audience to read the slide while you're talking — you want them to listen to you. Use bulleted text to help you keep your presentation on track, but not to read word for word.

Creating a bulleted list

When you create text in a text placeholder by choosing one of the text layouts, your text is automatically formatted with bullets. (Chapter 13 explains how to choose a layout for a slide.) You just type away and press Enter to insert a new bullet.

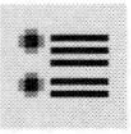

If you create text in a text frame, you need to select the text and click the Bullets button on the Object Bar. To remove the bullets, select the text and click the Bullets button again.

Choosing bullets

You can format the bullets to match your presentation design or bring attention to an item. The bullets automatically follow the style that is used in the Master view, which we explain later in this chapter. To create bullets that differ from those in the Master view, follow these steps:

1. **Select the bulleted text.**

2. **Choose Format➪Numbering/Bullets, and click the Bullets tab.**

   The Numbering/Bullets dialog box, shown in Figure 14-2 with the Bullets tab on top, opens.

3. **Choose the type of bullets that you want.**

4. **Click OK.**

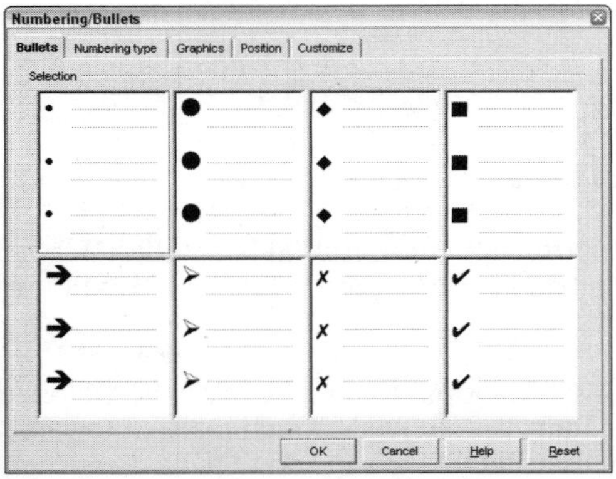

Figure 14-2:
The Bullets
tab of the
Numbering/
Bullets
dialog box.

To further format your bullets, click the Customize tab of the Numbering/Bullets dialog box. On the Customize tab, you can change the color and size of the bullets. You can also create a new bullet by choosing a character from any font set.

Finally, you can click the Graphics tab to choose some graphic bullets. Choose the one that you want, and click OK.

Creating numbered lists

If the text on your slide is part of a sequence, you can number the text instead of bulleting it. Follow these steps to number your text:

1. **Select the text.**
2. **Choose Format⇨Numbering/Bullets.**

   The Numbering/Bullets dialog box opens.
3. **Click the Numbering Type tab.**
4. **Choose the type of numbering that you want.**
5. **Click OK.**

You can click the Customize tab to change the color, size, and format of the numbers.

Formatting Paragraphs

Just as you can format paragraphs in a word processor, you can format paragraphs in Impress. You can change the margins, alignment, and line spacing. Because a presentation is so graphical in nature, you want to make sure that your paragraphs look orderly.

Lining up with the ruler

The easiest and most direct way to set the margins is to use the horizontal ruler that's above each slide. If you don't see this ruler, choose View⇨Rulers to make it appear. You also use the ruler to set indents, as shown in Figure 14-3.

The gray area at the left and right edges of the horizontal ruler defines the slide's margins. You can drag the edges of the gray area to change the margins.

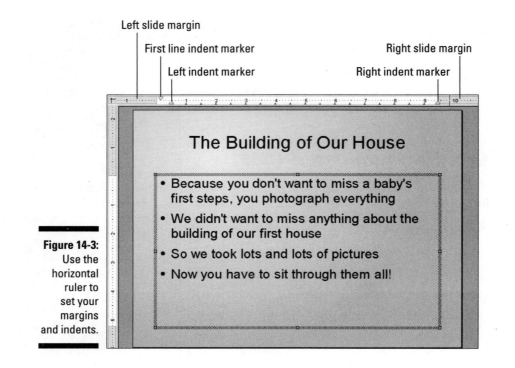

Left slide margin

First line indent marker

Left indent marker

Right slide margin

Right indent marker

Figure 14-3:
Use the
horizontal
ruler to
set your
margins
and indents.

The Building of Our House

- Because you don't want to miss a baby's first steps, you photograph everything
- We didn't want to miss anything about the building of our first house
- So we took lots and lots of pictures
- Now you have to sit through them all!

To change indents, use the indent markers. The top marker sets the indent for the first line only. For bulleted lists, this marker is to the left of the bottom marker and creates a hanging indent. The top marker determines the position of the bullets. To change the bullet position, click and drag the top marker to the left or right.

The bottom marker sets the indent for the rest of the lines of the paragraph. In bulleted text, this marker sets the position of the left side of the text, which is to the right of the top marker. To move the text, press Ctrl and drag the bottom marker to the left or right. Use this technique to move the text in relation to the bullets.

Aligning text

While most text is *left-aligned* — that is, the text along the left margin lines up — headings are often centered. Occasionally, you may want to right-align text. You can also *justify* text. This forces the text to reach both the left and right margins on each line, but justified text sometimes places too much space between the words and may look strange for bulleted text.

To align text, select the text and choose one of the alignment buttons on the Object Bar.

Spacing your lines

If you need to fit just a little more text on a slide or expand your text so that it doesn't look lost, you should adjust the line spacing. Select the text and choose Format➪Paragraph to open the Paragraph dialog box. Click the Indents & Spacing tab, as shown in Figure 14-4.

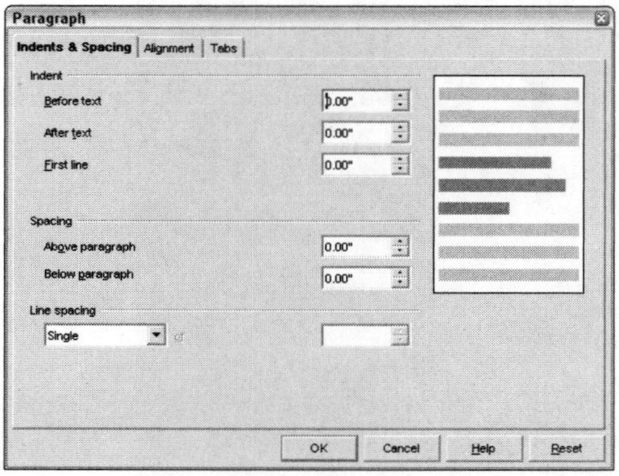

Figure 14-4:
The Indents
& Spacing
tab of the
Paragraph
dialog box.

Use the Spacing section to change the spacing before or after a paragraph. This section affects the spacing between paragraphs.

Use the Line Spacing section to change the line spacing within a paragraph. Choose one of the options from the drop-down list. To set exact line spacing, use the At Least option and enter a distance in the text box. You can experiment with various spacing until you get the look that you want.

Using Master View

The Master view is the key that controls the look of your entire presentation. In Chapter 13, we explain the various modes, one of which is Master view. To enter Master view, click the Master view icon at the lower-left corner of your screen or choose View➪Master➪Drawing. (See Figure 14-5.)

Typically, you specify the following items in Master view:

- ✔ **Background:** Choose Format➪Page and click the Background tab. You can use a solid color, gradient, bitmap image, or *hatch* (repetitive pattern).

- ✔ **Fonts:** Choose Format➪Character or use the Object Bar to choose font type, size, and color. You can separately format the title and the bulleted text.

✔ **Bullets:** Choose Format⇨Numbering/Bullets. We explain how to format bullets in the section "Choosing bullets," earlier in this chapter.

✔ **Graphics:** Choose Insert⇨Graphics to insert logos or other graphics. You can also use the drawing tools to create your own.

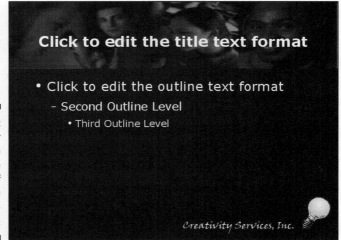

Figure 14-5: Use Master view mode to set up the design of your entire presentation.

In the same way, you can specify the look for title slides, notes pages, and handouts. Choose View⇨Master⇨Title, Notes, or Handout.

When you have completed setting up your master slide, you may want to save the presentation as a template so that you can use it again easily. For detailed instructions on saving a presentation as a template, see Chapter 13.

If you start with a template, your master slide may be just what you need already. If not, go to Master view before you design your presentation to create the overall look in advance. It's better to make changes on the master slide than on individual slides. If you later decide to change the bullets, for example, you can change them once on the master slide, instead of changing them on each slide.

Chapter 15

Making Presentations Picture-Perfect

*T*ext alone is not enough for a presentation. To effectively communicate, you should add graphics and choose color to enhance your message. Most professional presentations include graphics on at least 50 percent of the slides. As you compose your presentation, think about what kind of art, photos, and drawings could add an extra element of interest and detail.

Adding Images

Inserting a photo of a product helps your audience visualize what you're trying to sell them. Placing a colored rectangle behind some text makes the text stand out. Add some clip art of a flower livens up your presentation, especially if you're trying to sell florist's ribbon. Each type of graphic has a different effect, depending on how you use it.

To decide what type of graphics you should use, pay attention to other presentations. Look at brochures and Web sites, and get a feel for the effect of combining various types of art with text.

Clipping art

Clip art is drawn artwork that you can insert onto any slide. You can find clip art on the Web, both for free and for purchase. You can also buy collections of clip art on CD-ROMs or DVDs. Clip art can be humorous, such as when you use a light bulb to represent creativity, or iconic, such as when you use an arrow to depict a process. Clip art can also evoke a theme or certain feelings. For example, if you're selling garden furniture, you may want clip art of flowers and plants on each slide to set the right mood.

You need to be careful that you don't use copyrighted artwork without permission. If you find art on a Web site, be sure to read the terms of use.

If you find clip art on the Web, you can download it to your computer. If you have the clip art on a CD-ROM or DVD, you can insert the clip art directly from the disc. Each image is a separate file.

The procedure for inserting a graphic is the same in Impress as it is in Writer. For detailed steps, see Chapter 5.

When you insert clip art, the image appears at the center of your slide, with eight small square handles around it, as shown in Figure 15-1.

You can immediately drag the image to a new location on the slide and resize the image if you want.

Figure 15-1:
A newly
inserted
graphic
image.

You can use any of OpenOffice.org's editing tools to recolor, rotate, filter, and flip the clip art, among other possibilities. We explain how to edit graphic images in Chapter 5.

Drawing objects

OpenOffice.org has a full complement of drawing objects that you can place on a slide. Impress users often use rectangles, circles, and other shapes behind text to emphasize text and hold text together. Arrows can point out important points, and connectors can create flow charts and other diagrams.

You should adjust the color of these objects to match the colors of your background and text. Always make sure that text is clearly visible on a shape. You can change both the fill and line colors of a shape such as a circle or a rectangle. Of course, arrows and lines don't have a fill color.

You can find all the information you need about creating and editing these drawing objects in Chapter 5. Don't forget to check out Chapter 5 for information on saving your drawing objects for future use.

You can also create objects using OpenOffice.org's Draw program and insert them into your presentations. We cover Draw in Chapter 18 and Bonus Chapter 4 on the CD.

Coloring Backgrounds

An important part of the look of your presentation is the background of your slide. People often think of the background as the main part of the template, although a template also includes font formatting and may include some text content. However, regardless of the background of your template, you can add new backgrounds to your heart's content.

Be careful when adding backgrounds. You typically don't want to use a different background for each slide. However, a little variety can keep your audience awake and emphasize certain slides.

To change a background for the entire presentation, use Master view mode. Choose View⇨Master⇨Drawing. Then follow the directions in the next few sections for changing a slide background. When you change a background in Slide mode, OpenOffice.org asks you if you want to change the background for the entire presentation or for just one slide. If you choose to change the background for the entire presentation, OpenOffice.org changes the master slide for you.

If you change the background for one slide and then change the background for the entire presentation, the background for the one slide that you changed remains unchanged. Changes to individual slides override changes to the master slide.

Creating a plain-colored background

You can simply choose a color as a background for a slide. Maybe it's a little boring, but it's certainly simple. To use a colored background, follow these steps:

1. **Display the slide.**

2. **Choose Format⇨Page, and click the Background tab.**

   The Page Setup dialog box opens, as shown in Figure 15-2.

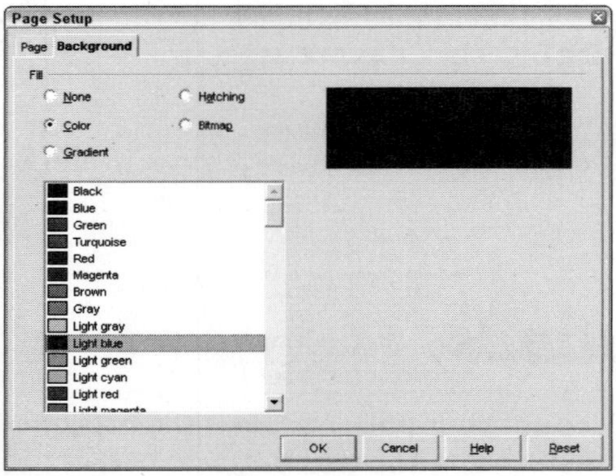

Figure 15-2: The Background tab of the Page Setup dialog box.

3. **In the Fill section, select the Color option button.**

4. **Choose a color from the list of colors.**

5. **Click OK.**

   A message appears asking if you want to use these background settings for all the pages.

6. **To change the background for all the slides, click Yes. To change only the slide that you displayed, click No.**

If you can't find the color that you are looking for, you can define your own color. For detailed instructions on how to define a color, see Chapter 18.

Creating a gradient background

A *gradient* gradually changes from one color to another. Gradients are often used as backgrounds for presentations. However, make sure that your text shows up well against both colors. To use a gradient background, follow these steps:

1. **Display the slide.**

2. **Choose Format⇨Page, and click the Background tab.**

   The Page Setup dialog box opens, as shown previously in Figure 15-2.

3. **In the Fill section, select the Gradient option button.**

4. **Choose a gradient from the list of gradients.**

5. **Click OK.**

   A message appears asking if you want the background settings for all the pages.

6. **To change the background for all the slides, click Yes. To change only the slide that you displayed, click No.**

You can create your own gradients in a number of styles from any two colors. For detailed steps, see Chapter 18. After you create and save your gradient, it appears in the Page Setup dialog box so that you can choose it.

Hatching a background

A *hatch* is a pattern made up of parallel lines. You can change the pattern by changing the spacing, angle, and color of the lines. Hatches rarely work well on a slide because they interfere with the legibility of text. To create a hatched background, follow these steps:

1. **Display the slide.**

2. **Choose Format⇨Page, and click the Background tab.**

   The Page Setup dialog box opens, as shown previously in Figure 15-2.

3. **In the Fill section, select the Hatching option button.**

4. **Choose a hatch from the list of hatches.**

5. **Click OK.**

   A message appears, asking if you want the background settings for all the pages.

6. **To change the background for all the slides, click Yes. To change only the slide that you displayed, click No.**

You can create custom hatches, as explained in Chapter 18. A hatch that you create and save appears in the list of hatches so that you can choose it as a background.

Using a bitmap image as a background

Perhaps the most common type of background is an image or photo. The photo is often recolored to match the presentation's color scheme and softened so that it doesn't take attention away from the text. OpenOffice.org includes a set of repetitive bitmap images that are soft enough to use as slide backgrounds. To use one of these bitmaps as a background, follow these steps:

1. **Display the slide.**

2. **Choose Format⇨Page, and click the Background tab.**

   The Page Setup dialog box opens, as shown previously in Figure 15-2.

3. **In the Fill section, select the Bitmap option button.**

4. **Choose a bitmap from the list of bitmaps.**

5. **To fit the bitmap over the entire slide, in the Position section, deselect the Tile check box and select the AutoFit check box.**

6. **Click OK.**

   A message appears, asking if you want the background settings for all the pages.

7. **To change the background for all the slides, click Yes. To change only the slide that you displayed, click No.**

Importing your own image file as a background

To use your own image file, you need to open the Area dialog box and import the image there. The image then appears in the Page Setup dialog box list. Follow these steps to import a bitmap image for use as a background:

1. **Choose Format⇨Area, and click the Bitmaps tab.**

   The Area dialog box opens, with the Bitmaps tab on top.

2. **Click the Import button.**

   The Import dialog box opens.

3. **Locate the file that you want to use, and click Open.**

   You return to the Area dialog box.

4. **Click OK to return to your presentation.**

Customizing your image

You can use OpenOffice.org to colorize an image so that it works better as a background. For example, you may want to use the floor plan that's shown in Figure 15-3 as a background.

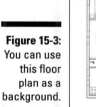

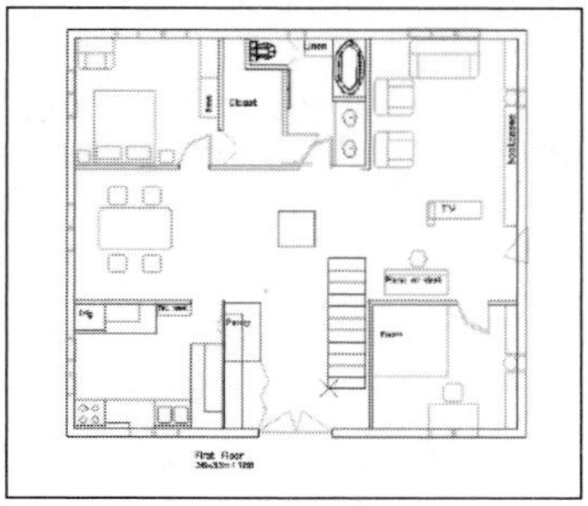

Figure 15-3:
You can use
this floor
plan as a
background.

The problem is that the floor plan has both light and dark areas, so some text won't show clearly. You need to color the image, so that it's mostly blue, and soften it a bit. This procedure involves a number of steps, but they're all easy. Follow these steps to colorize and soften the bitmap:

1. **With any slide displayed, choose Insert⇨Graphics.**

   The Insert Graphics dialog box opens.

2. **Locate the file that you want to use, choose it, and click Open.**

   The image appears on your slide, selected.

3. **Use the following controls on the Object Bar to edit the photo or other image:**

   - **Red RGB:** Adjust the value to vary the amount of red in the image. To make a blue image, reduce this value close to nearly 0%.

   - **Green RGB:** Adjust the value to vary the amount of green in the image. To make a blue image, reduce this value to nearly 0%.

   - **Blue RGB:** Adjust the value to vary the amount of blue in the image. To make a blue image, increase this value to nearly 100%.

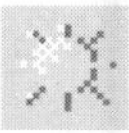

   - **Brightness:** Adjust the value to make the image lighter (brighter) or darker. For a dark blue image, reduce the value below 0%.

   - **Contrast:** Increase the contrast to make the lights lighter and darks darker (more contrast) or decrease the contrast to make the image more monochrome. For a blue image, reduce the value below 0%.

- **Gamma:** Increase the gamma to make the medium and dark tones brighter and decrease it to make them darker. For a dark blue image, decrease the gamma. You need to fiddle with the gamma to get the right value, which varies with the image.

  You can also crop the image. Click the Crop button at the right end of the Object Bar, and use the Crop dialog box to cut off unwanted edges of the image.

- **Filter:** Choose one of the effects from the Filter floating toolbar. You can click the Soften button to get a softer effect for a background. The result of our editing is shown in Figure 15-4.

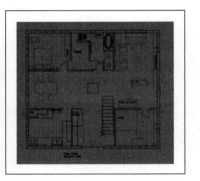

Figure 15-4:
The image
has been
colorized,
darkened,
and
softened.

4. **With your image still selected, choose File➪Export.**

   The Export dialog box opens.

5. **From the File Format drop-down list, choose the file format that you want. Select the Selection check box to export only the selected image.**

   The JPEG format is often used for photographs. Other common bitmap formats are GIF and PNG.

6. **In the File Name text box, enter a name for the image.**

7. **Click Save.**

   Depending on the format that you chose, a dialog box offering save options may appear. These options control the quality and features of the image.

8. **Specify the settings that you want, if applicable, and click OK.**

9. **To import the image into the bitmap list, choose Format➪Area and click the Bitmaps tab.**

   The Area dialog box opens.

10. **Click the Import button, find the file that you want, and click Open.**

    The Name dialog box opens.

11. **Enter a name for the bitmap, and click OK twice to return to your presentation.**

    OpenOffice.org adds the bitmap image to the list of bitmaps. For more information on importing a graphic image, see Chapter 18.

12. **Choose Format⇨Page, and select the Bitmap option button.**

13. **Choose your bitmap from the bitmap list.**

    Set the parameters that you want in the Size and Position sections of the Page Setup dialog box. For example, to fit the image over the entire slide, deselect Tile and select AutoFit.

14. **Click OK.**

    A message appears asking if you want to use the background for all the pages (slides).

15. **Click Yes to place the image on all the slides, or click No to place the image on the displayed slide only.**

You now have a suitable image that you can use as a background for your presentation.

Applying a design template

You can also add a background by applying a different design template. Follow these steps to apply a design template:

1. **Choose Format⇨Styles⇨Slide Design.**

   The Slide Design dialog box opens.

2. **Click the Load button.**

   The Load Slide Design dialog box opens.

3. **From the Categories list, choose a category, such as Presentation Backgrounds.**

4. **From the Templates list, choose the template that you want to use.**

   You can preview the template. Click More, and select the Preview check box.

5. **Click OK.**

   You return to the Slide Design dialog box. The new template is selected.

6. **To use the template for all your slides, replacing any existing templates, select the Exchange Background Page check box. To simply add the template, deselect this check box.**

7. **Click OK to return to your presentation.**

Adding a Coolness Factor with 3-D

OpenOffice.org has a great complement of 3-D objects and features that you can use to make your presentations pop out from its slides. You can use 3-D effects for both text and graphic objects. You can also create shadows to add a subtle 3-D effect.

Creating 3-D text

A shadow on text gives the impression that the text is slightly above the slide. Figure 15-5 shows some text with and without a shadow.

Figure 15-5:
The text
above is
plain. The
text below
sports a
shadow.

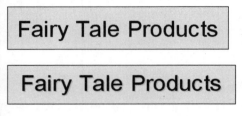

To add a shadow, follow these steps:

1. **Select the text.**
2. **Choose Format⇨Character.**

   The Character dialog box opens.
3. **Click the Font Effects tab.**
4. **Select the Shadow check box.**
5. **Click OK.**

You can also right-click and choose Style⇨Shadow from the shortcut menu that appears.

You can convert text to a 3-D object. However, after you do this, you cannot edit the text — it becomes a graphic object. The text must be in a text frame, not a text placeholder. For more information on creating text in text frames, see Chapter 13. To convert text to 3-D text, follow these steps:

1. **Click the text frame.**

   The text displays a border, and you see the cursor inside the text.

2. **Click the border to remove the cursor and display only the eight handles.**

3. **Right-click the text, and choose Convert⇨To 3D from the shortcut menu that appears.**

Figure 15-6 shows some text before and after converting to 3-D. Be careful — text can be hard to read in 3-D. You can adjust the depth and other features of your 3-D text to help make it more readable. For exact details, see Chapter 18.

Figure 15-6:
You can turn your text into 3-D shapes.

Fairy Tale Products

Fairy Tale Products

Inserting 3-D objects

You can insert 3-D objects, such as boxes and cylinders, onto your slide by using the 3D Objects floating toolbar. Long-click the 3D Objects icon on the Main toolbar to find these objects. Click any 3-D object, and drag on your slide to insert the shape. You can place a text frame on top of a 3-D shape so that the 3-D shape appears to have text on it, as shown in Figure 15-7.

For advanced techniques on using 3-D objects, see Chapter 18.

Figure 15-7:
You can emphasize text by placing a text frame on top of a 3-D object.

Welcome New
Employees!

You can add shadows to your 3-D objects. OpenOffice.org comes with some preset shadow styles that you can quickly apply to your objects. Follow these steps to add shadows to your 3-D objects:

1. **Select the 3-D object.**

2. **Click the 3D Effects button on the Main toolbar, or choose Format⇨ 3D Effects.**

   The 3D Effects dialog box opens, as shown in Figure 15-8.

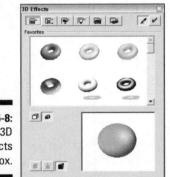

Figure 15-8:
The 3D
Effects
dialog box.

3. **Click the Favorites button (the leftmost button at the top of the dialog box).**

4. **Click one of the effects that includes a shadow.**

5. **Click Apply.**

6. **Close the 3D Effects dialog box.**

   OpenOffice.org applies the shadow effect to your 3-D shape.

Have fun experimenting with other 3D Effects as well! See Chapter 18 for the lowdown on the many ways that you can fiddle with your 3-D objects.

Chapter 16

Animating Impressively

Movement catches the eye and wakes up your audience. Animation can be very effective when used appropriately. You can also add sound or music to a presentation or a specific slide. In this chapter, we explain how to add motion to text, objects, and the transition from slide to slide.

Using Text Effects Effectively

OpenOffice.org offers two types of animation for text. One type creates moving text like you would see in a ticker tape — the text moves across the screen. We explain this type of animation in this section.

The other type of animation applies to both text and objects and governs how these items appear. Text and objects can fly in from the left, simply appear, or dissolve into existence. We discuss this type of animation in the next section.

Text effects are simple but you should use them judiciously. These effects only apply to text in text frames; you can't apply these text effects to text in placeholders. OpenOffice.org offers the following text effects:

 ✔ **Blink:** The text blinks on.

 ✔ **Scroll Through:** Scrolls into view and continues through to the other side, disappearing there.

✔ **Scroll Back and Forth:** Scrolls into view, continues to the other side, and then scrolls back in the opposite direction. You need to specify at least two cycles for this effect to work.

✔ **Scroll In:** Scrolls into view and remains in view.

To add a text effect, follow these steps:

1. **Create text in a text frame.**

2. **With the text frame selected, choose Format⇨Text.**

   This menu item is only available if you have selected a text frame. The Text dialog box opens.

3. **Click the Text Animation tab, as shown in Figure 16-1.**

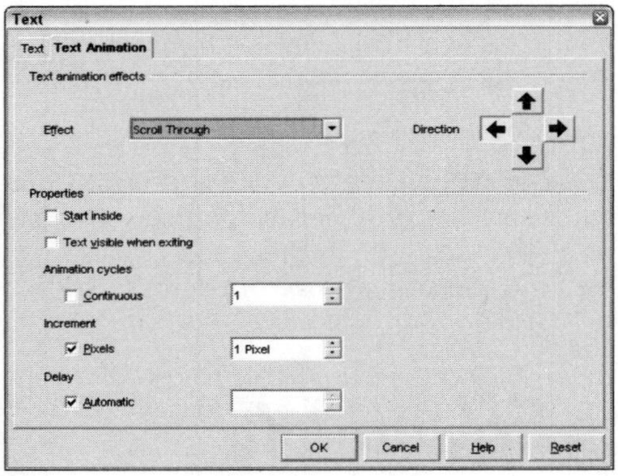

Figure 16-1:
Use the Text
Animation
tab of the
Text dialog
box to
create
blinking and
scrolling
animation.

4. **From the Effect drop-down list, choose one of the effects.**

5. **Click one of the arrows to specify the direction of the scroll.**

6. **In the Properties section, choose the properties that you want for the effect.**

   You may have to test a few property options to get the results that you want. For example, the Scroll Through effect normally starts the text from the edge of the text frame, but if you select the Start inside check box, the text starts from the middle of the frame, completely visible, and then scrolls in the direction that you choose. Under Animation cycles, you can repeat the effect. You can also specify a delay in milliseconds.

7. **Click OK to return to your presentation.**

8. **Click the Slide Show View button to view the animation.**

9. **When you are done previewing the animation, press Esc to return to Drawing view.**

Creating Animation Effects

You can animate how both text and objects appear on a slide. For example, you can make bulleted text appear line by line as you click the mouse so that your audience sees each line as you discuss it. After the animation, you can make the object change color or disappear. You can even move an object along a path. To animate an object, follow these steps:

1. **Select the object that you want to animate.**

   For text in a text placeholder, select the entire placeholder — you don't need to highlight the text itself.

2. **Choose Slide Show⇨Effects or click the Animation Effects button on the Main toolbar.**

   The Animation Effects window opens, as shown in Figure 16-2.

3. **Click the Effects button in the Animation Effects window.**

4. **Choose an effect from the Effects drop-down list or from the icons in the large panel (Favorites), or choose Other from the drop-down list for another set of available effects.**

   When you click an icon, the name of its animation appears at the bottom of the Animation Effects window.

5. **If a set of variations appears in the large panel, choose a variation.**

6. **From the Speed drop-down list at the bottom of the window, choose a speed.**

7. **If you selected text, click the Text Effects button and choose an effect for the text, using the same method as described in Steps 4 through 6.**

   These text effects are like the text effects for objects. They are not the blinking or scrolling effects that you can create for text frames.

8. **To specify sound effects and aftereffects, click the Extras button at the top of the Animation Effects window.**

Many animations automatically come with a sound. If you don't want the sound, click the Extras button to turn off the sound.

9. **To add an aftereffect, in the Extras section, do either of the following:**

   • Click the Object Invisible button to make the object disappear after animation.

   • Click the Fade Object with Color button to change the object's color after animation.

   If you fade the object, choose a color from the drop-down list.

10. **To add a sound that plays during the animation, click the Sound button and choose a sound from the drop-down list. To add your own sound file, click the Open button, locate the sound file, and click Open.**

   OpenOffice.org comes with a good assortment of sounds. When you click the Open button, you are automatically in the folder that contains the OpenOffice.org sound gallery.

11. **To remove a sound, click the Sound button so that it does not appear selected (indented).**

12. **To assign the sound to the selected object, click Assign.**

13. **To view the animation in Slide Show view, click the Slide Show View button in the upper-right corner of your screen.**

   You can go into Slide Show view, view your animation, and return to Drawing view without closing the Animation Effects window. Leaving the window open allows you to go back and make adjustments as you work.

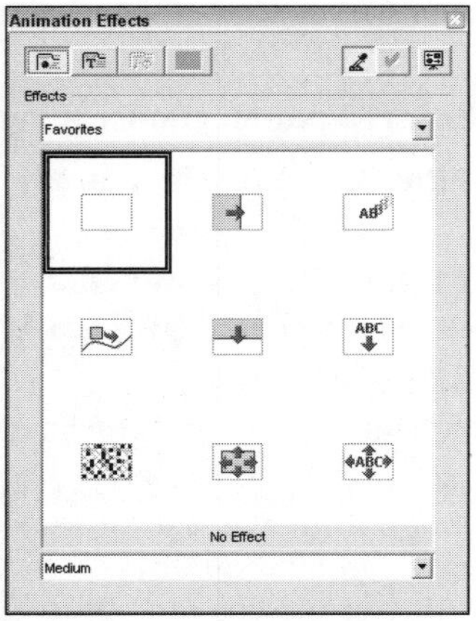

Figure 16-2:
The Animation Effects window allows you to add animation to objects, including text.

To change the order of animation, click the Order button in the Animation Effects window. Select an object and drag it to a new position.

To remove animation from an object, select the object and choose the first icon, called No Effect, from the Favorites collection of icons in the Animation Effects window.

Adding Sound Bytes

Sounds can create a mood or add humor to a presentation. You can add a simple sound or play music. As described in the previous section, you can add a sound to an animation effect. You can also add a sound to a slide transition, as explained later in this chapter. In this section, we explain how to insert a sound object to a slide.

You can add a sound to a slide in the following formats:

- ✔ .au/.snd (SUN/NeXT audio)
- ✔ .wav (Microsoft Windows audio)
- ✔ .voc (Creative Labs/Soundblaster audio)
- ✔ .aiff (SGI/Apple audio)
- ✔ .iff (Amiga audio)

To insert a sound, follow these steps:

1. **Choose Insert⇨Object⇨Sound.**

   The Insert Sound dialog box opens.

2. **Locate the sound that you want, and select it.**

3. **Click the Insert button.**

   A sound icon appears on your slide.

Creating Animated GIF Files

A GIF file is a bitmap graphic file. An animated GIF file is a series of small GIF files that differ slightly from each other. An application or browser displays the GIF files quickly in order, giving the appearance of animation. Many ads that you see on the Internet are created using animated GIF files.

OpenOffice.org contains a GIF animator that you can use to create animations for your presentations. You can create drawing objects by using OpenOffice.org's tools, or you can import bitmap images. The overall process is simple — you put all the images on a slide, add each image in order to the animation, and set the timing for each image. Follow these steps to create an animated GIF for your presentation:

1. **Create or insert all the images that you want to use on a slide.**

   To create an animation effect, the images are usually similar, with just slight differences. You don't have a great deal of control over the placement of the objects, so your animation needs to emphasize shape changes rather than movement.

2. **Choose Slide Show⇨Animation.**

   The Animation window opens.

3. **Select the first object for the animation.**

   You can select objects on your slide while the Animation window is open.

4. **Click the Apply Object button to add the image as one frame in the animation.**

   The object appears in the Preview pane, as shown in Figure 16-3.

   If you line up all your images in the order that you want to insert them in the animation, you can select them all at once by dragging across them all and then clicking the Apply Objects Individually button, which is to the right of the Apply Object button. In this way, you can create an entire animation in one fell swoop.

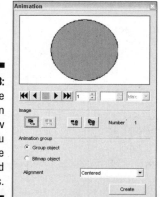

Figure 16-3:
The Animation window allows you to create animated GIF files.

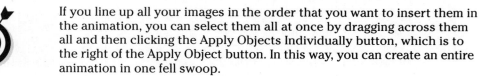

5. **Repeat Steps 3 and 4 to add additional objects to the animation until you have all the objects that you need.**

   As you add objects, you see the frame number increase in the middle of the Animation window.

6. **In the Animation Group section, select the Bitmap Object option button.**

7. **To set the timing for each frame, click the small down arrow to the right of frame number to return to Frame 1.**

8. **Set the timing for Frame 1 in the Duration box to the right of the frame number.**

   The frames must be short to give the appearance of animation. The unit of the Duration box is seconds, so a setting of 1.00 is 1 second. You can try setting each frame to 0.05 or 0.1 as a start.

9. **Increase the frame number by 1, and set the duration for each of the frames in your animation.**

10. **To repeat (loop) your animation, set the number of times in the Loop Count box, which is to the right of the Duration box.**

11. **Click the Create button to create the animated GIF file.**

    The new animation appears on your screen.

12. **You can now delete all the objects that you used for your animation, or you can drag them off the slide if you want to save them.**

13. **To play the animation in the Animation window, set the frame number in the Frame box to 1 and click the Play button. To see the slide in Slide Show view, click the Slide Show View button in the upper-right corner of your screen.**

As you work, you can delete an image in a frame by displaying it in the Animation dialog box and clicking the Delete Current Image button. To change an animation after you have created it, select the animation, choose Slide Show⇨Animation to open the Animation dialog box, make the changes that you want, and resave it (by clicking Create) as a new animation.

Adding Slide Transition Effects

You can add effects that determine how a slide appears. For example, the slide can move in from the left or right or dissolve into view. You can add a different transition to each slide (it's a little nerve-racking!) or add one transition to all your slides. Use discretion with slide transitions, and keep them simple. Follow these steps to add a transition:

1. **To add a transition, use one of these options to select one or more slides:**

   - Switch to Slides view and drag across the slides to select them (or choose Edit➪Select All).

   - Select the slide that you want to work with.

2. **Choose Slide Show➪Slide Transition to open the Slide Transition dialog box, as shown in Figure 16-4.**

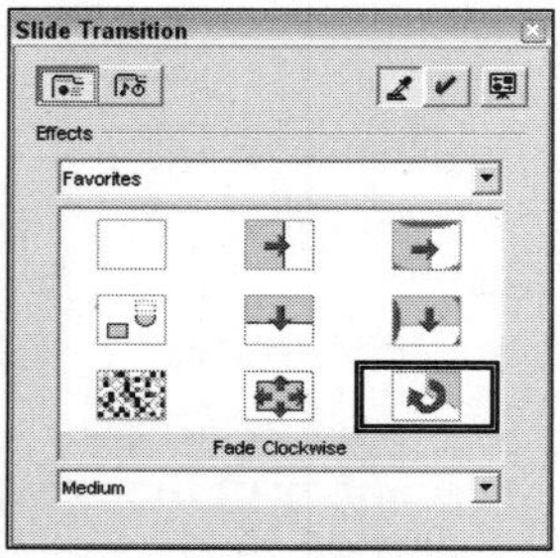

Figure 16-4:
The Slide Transition dialog box.

3. **Click the Animation Effects button in the Slide Transition dialog box.**

4. **Choose an animation by doing one of the following:**

   - Choose one of the animations in the pane.

   - Choose an animation from the Effects drop-down list.

   - Choose Other from the Effects drop-down list, and then choose one of the animations in the pane.

   When you click an animation in the pane, the title appears at the bottom of the dialog box.

5. **If you choose an animation from the drop-down list and variations appear in the pane, choose one of the variations.**

6. **Click the Additional Options button in the Slide Transition dialog box.**

7. **In the Extras section, choose one of the following options:**

   - **Automatic:** The slide advances automatically after the time that you set in the text box. Animation effects for objects also play automatically.

   - **Semiautomatic:** The slide advances automatically after the time that you set in the text box, but animation effects for objects only play when you click the mouse.

   - **Manual:** Both slide animation and object animation occur only when you click the mouse.

8. **To choose a sound for the slide transition, click the Sound button and choose a sound from the drop-down list.**

   Most transitions come with a sound. If the Sound button is selected (indented), you have a sound. To remove the sound, click the Sound button (so that it is no longer indented).

   A sound that plays each time you advance a slide can get annoying. In most cases, you want to remove the sound.

9. **Click the Apply button to apply the slide transition and any effects to the selected slides.**

   If you are in Slides view, you see a small icon at the lower-left corner of each selected slide, indicating that it has a slide transition.

Play your presentation in Slide Show view to check out your new slide transitions.

To delete slide transitions, follow these steps:

1. **Select the slide or slides.**

2. **Choose Slide Show⇨Slide Transition.**

3. **Choose Favorites from the drop-down list.**

4. **Choose the No Effect icon, which is the first icon.**

5. **Click Apply.**

Chapter 17

Showing a Presentation

- -

- -

*Y*ou have worked hard and finally completed a beautiful and compelling presentation. Now you need to deliver it to your audience. Before you jump right in, you should practice several times until your delivery is smooth and comfortable. Only then should you get in front of an audience.

Preparing to Deliver a Slide Show

Practice makes perfect. Your presentation is important, and the quality of your delivery is a major factor in the success of your presentation. (The other two factors are your content, including its organization, and the look/layout of the presentation.)

To practice, start by going into Slide Show view (choose Slide Show⇨Slide Show) and run through the presentation, speaking out loud to your computer, which is your imaginary audience. (Don't worry about what your neighbors think.) The expression *slide show* is often used to indicate a presentation in Slide Show mode but *slide show* and *presentation* can also be used as synonyms.

The second step is to practice with the equipment that you plan to use, including the computer and projector, for example. This step is crucial. We've seen too many disasters, or near disasters (staying up late the night before trying to find a computer that's powerful enough to play a large presentation) that could have been prevented by practicing the entire presentation in advance with the final equipment.

The final step is to practice in your final venue, if possible. This step gives you the opportunity to check out the seating, determine where to put the projector, see where to stand, know how to set the temperature of the room, and so on.

Setting slide timing

If you want your presentation to advance automatically, you need to set the time for each slide to be viewed. If you are delivering a presentation yourself, you may not want to set slide times. You typically set timings for self-running presentations, such as those that you may present at a convention or in lobbies. To set slide timing, follow these steps:

1. **Choose View⇨Workspace⇨Slides View to enter Slides view.**

   If necessary, click the first slide so that you start from the beginning.

2. **Click the Rehearse Timings button on the Object Bar.**

   OpenOffice.org automatically places you in Slide Show view so that you see your presentation full-screen. You see a timer at the lower-left corner of your screen.

3. **Start speaking out loud if you plan to use the automatic timings for a presentation that you plan to deliver. Pretend that you are talking to an audience.**

   To determine the timings for a self-running presentation, you can read the presentation to get an idea of how much time your audience will need to read each slide.

4. **When you think it's time to move to the next slide, click the timer.**

   Don't click the slide — you have to click the timer itself. OpenOffice.org advances to the next slide.

5. **Repeat Steps 3 and 4 until you finish the presentation.**

   You automatically return to Slides view.

You can click any slide and see its timing on the Object Bar. You can manually change the setting for any slide by changing the number in the Time text box of the Object Bar.

You don't need to use the timings that you set. As explained in the section "Specifying slide show settings," later in this chapter, you can decide to advance each slide manually if you want.

Hiding slides

You may want to create variations of your presentation for different audiences or to include slides that you plan to show only if your audience indicates some interest in a specific topic. To hide a slide, follow these steps:

1. **Switch to Slides view (choose View⇨Workspace⇨Slides View).**

2. **Click the slide that you want to hide.**

3. **Choose Slide Show⇨Show/Hide Slide.**

Specifying slide show settings

You can specify a number of settings that determine what happens when you present your slide show. For example, you may have created timings for your slides for practice purposes, but you may not want to use these timings when you actually present. Follow these steps to specify slide show settings:

1. **Choose Slide Show⇨Slide Show Settings.**

   The Slide Show Settings dialog box opens, as shown in Figure 17-1.

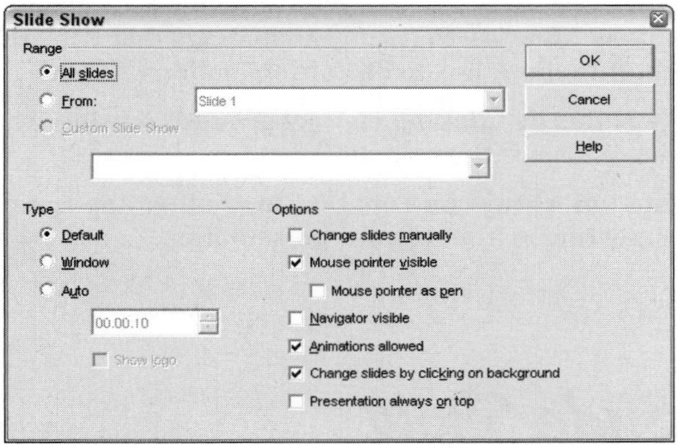

Figure 17-1:
The Slide
Show
Settings
dialog box.

2. **In the Range section, click From and choose a slide if you don't want to start from the first slide.**

   Otherwise, keep the default setting of All Slides.

3. **In the Type section, choose Default, which plays the presentation once full-screen.**

   To play the presentation in the OpenOffice.org application window, choose Window. To automatically loop the slide, choose Auto. If you want a delay between repetitions, enter an amount in the Time text box.

4. **In the Options section, specify the following settings:**

   - **Change Slides Manually:** Select this check box to ensure that OpenOffice.org ignores timings that you have set and only advances slides when you use the mouse or a keyboard shortcut to advance a slide.

   - **Mouse Pointer Visible:** Selected by default, this setting displays the mouse pointer in Slide Show view. Deselect this check box to hide the mouse pointer. If you have hyperlinks or other objects that you need to click, you should leave the mouse pointer visible; otherwise, you may not need it.

   - **Mouse Pointer as Pen:** If you display the mouse pointer, you can initially display it as a pen so that you can annotate a slide. We explain how to annotate a slide in the section "Annotating a slide," later in this chapter.

   - **Navigator Visible:** Starts the slide show with the Navigator visible. We explain how to use the Navigator during a slide show in the section "Navigating through a slide show," later in this chapter.

   - **Animations Allowed:** Plays any animations that you created. Deselect this check box to disable animations.

   - **Change Slides by Clicking on Background:** Advances a slide when you click it. This is the default.

   - **Presentation Always on Top:** Disallows other application windows from appearing in front of your presentation.

5. **Click OK.**

Delivering a Slide Show

You're all ready to go. Now you just need to get up in front of that audience and speak. Easier said than done, yes? Actually, it's not that bad. If you have practiced and are well prepared, everything will go more easily. If possible, spend a couple of minutes chatting with individual members of the audience as they come into the room so that you don't feel like you're addressing a faceless crowd.

Have your presentation already open and in Slide Show view before you start. You can black out the screen by pressing the B key, as we explain later, until you are ready to start. Then press B again to display your first slide.

Using a mouse and keyboard to run your slide show

When you go into Slide Show view to deliver a presentation, you don't have any menus or toolbars, so you need to know how to navigate. Usually, you just need to click the mouse to advance to the next animation or next slide. To go to the previous slide, right-click. You can also use a number of keyboard shortcuts, as described in Table 17-1.

Table 17-1	Keyboard Shortcuts for Delivering a Slide Show
Action	*Shortcut*
Start slide show	F9
End slide show	Esc, Backspace, or the minus key (–) on the number keypad
Go to next animation or slide	Spacebar
Go to next slide	Enter, ↓, →, Ctrl+Page Down, or N
Go to specific slide	Type number of slide and press Enter
Go to previous slide	←, ↑, Ctrl+Page Up, or P (same as right-clicking)
Go to first slide	Home
Go to last slide	End
Open Navigator	F5 (where you can double-click any slide to go to it directly)
Black out screen	B
White out screen	W

Navigating through a slide show

You can also use the Navigator when you present. Press F5 to open the Navigator, as shown in Figure 17-2.

First slide   Next slide

Live mode   Drag mode

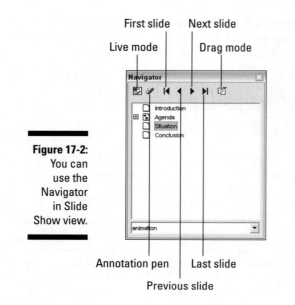

Figure 17-2:
You can
use the
Navigator
in Slide
Show view.

Annotation pen   Last slide

Previous slide

To go to any slide listed, double-click the slide. If you plan to use the Navigator, you should name your slides. Slide 1, Slide 2, and so on are not helpful names. To name a slide, right-click a slide's tab in Drawing view and choose Rename Slide from the shortcut menu that appears. A good practice is to name the slide based on its title text.

You probably don't want to use the Navigator all the time because it obstructs part of your slides, but for special situations, the Navigator can be a lifesaver.

Annotating a slide

You can temporarily draw on a slide to emphasize a point, as shown in Figure 17-3. Okay, making it look good is hard, but maybe your audience doesn't mind. This type of annotation doesn't last — if you go to the next slide and then return to the annotated slide, your annotation marks are gone.

Editing in Slide Show view

To annotate a slide, click the Annotation Pen button in the Navigator. You can then close the Navigator if you want. However, to get rid of the pen cursor, you need to reopen the Navigator and click the Annotation Pen button again.

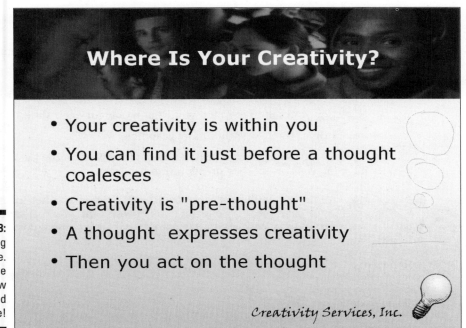

Figure 17-3:
Annotating
a slide.
Someone
can't draw
a round
circle!

A nice feature enables you to edit slides while in Slide Show view. You may find this invaluable in an informal situation such as a brainstorming session. For example, you can include a slide with a text placeholder and start writing down the ideas that your group comes up with.

Because you don't have menus or toolbars, your options are somewhat limited. For example, you can't insert a new text frame. But you can edit what's already on the slide, and if you have a slide with an empty placeholder, you can add text to the placeholder. Just click to select the placeholder and start typing.

You can access the shortcut (context) menu, however. The shortcut menu contains commands to cut, copy, and paste as well as commands for many formatting options. For example, you can change the font of the text that you entered.

To edit in Slide Show view, click the Live Mode button in the Navigator. You don't need to keep the Navigator open while you edit your slide. Press F5 to close the Navigator.

Printing presentations

You may never need to print a presentation. On the other hand, printing a presentation has many uses. You can print

- ✔ Handouts to give to your audience that contain images of each slide.
- ✔ Notes for yourself to help tell you what to say for each slide.
- ✔ The outline (the text without any graphics).
- ✔ A paper presentation to give to someone for review, if the person doesn't have Impress or another presentation program.

For information on saving your Impress presentation in another format, see Chapter 13. For example, if a colleague has PowerPoint, you can save a copy of the presentation in PowerPoint format and e-mail the presentation as an attachment instead of printing and mailing the presentation.

Printing slides

You can simply print your slides. To print one or more slides in your presentation, follow these steps:

1. **Choose File⇨Print.**

   The Print dialog box opens. By default, OpenOffice.org prints the entire presentation, one slide on each sheet of paper.

2. **To specify individual slides for printing, click Pages in the Print Range section of the Print dialog box and enter the pages that you want to print.**

3. **To set print options, click the Options button in the Print dialog box to open the Printer Options dialog box, as shown in Figure 17-4.**

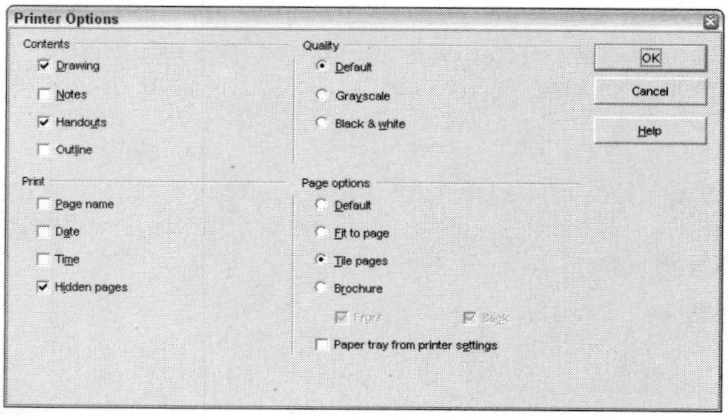

Figure 17-4:
The Printer
Options
dialog box.

   4. **In the Contents section, choose what you want to print, as follows:**

      - **Drawing:** Prints the slides.

      - **Notes:** Prints the presentation as it looks in Notes view. This includes the slide at the top and an area for text at the bottom.

      - **Handouts:** Prints one or more handouts on a page. To change the number of slides that print on a page, choose Format⇨Modify Layout while you are in Handouts view.

      - **Outline:** Prints only the text.

   5. **In the Quality section of the Printer Options dialog box, choose whether to print in color (the default mode), in grayscale, or in black and white.**

   6. **In the Print section, choose whether to add the page name, date, and time to each slide.**

      You can also choose whether to include hidden slides. (We explain hidden slides in the section "Hiding slides," earlier in this chapter.)

   7. **In the Print Options section, choose whether to print one slide per page, scale slides to fit the page, tile pages (if your slides are larger than your paper), or create a brochure.**

   8. **Click OK when you are finished setting the printer options to return to the Printer dialog box.**

   9. **Click OK to print.**

Part V
Using Draw: The Graphics Program

The 5th Wave   By Rich Tennant

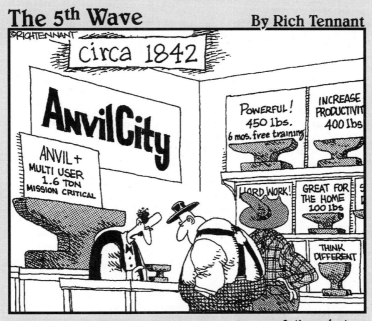

"Now, if you travel a lot, you'll want one of these laptop anvils. This one's nice and light, but you're limited in how much work you can get done on it..."

In this part . . .

OpenOffice.org Draw is a serious drawing program for serious artists, yet it's easy enough even for a child to use. With Draw, you can make those images that are crystal clear in your mind become a reality on the computer screen. It's never been easier to become an artist.

Draw has an enormous number of uses. It can be used for Web design, graphic design, architectural drawings and so much more. You can use it to create and edit 3-D images and map textures onto them. You can design your own logo. You can import and manipulate photographic images. You can choose from millions of colors and create customized lists of colors, or use ready-made lists of colors. You can also specify your own gradient colors and use them to make your art look so real you feel you can reach in and touch it. Or generate gradient transparencies to create glowing effects. You can animate text and use the cross-fade tool to create images that can be animated in Impress. You can use layers, which enable you to trace shapes and objects. The uses of Draw are infinite. And the best thing about it is that it's all easy, and in this part we show you how.

Chapter 18

Unleashing the Artist Within

In this chapter, you enter the amazing world of Draw. Even if you have no training in art, with Draw you can create beautiful graphics for memos, presentations, or brochures; for posters or Web sites; or even for books. You don't need to buy disks of clip art and search through huge piles of images. You don't need to feel guilty about swiping an image from someone's Web site for your own use. Make your own images! It's easy. Even combining a few lines, shapes, and colors or gradients is enough to make some beautifully expressive designs.

In this chapter, we show you how to use Draw to "get graphic," using lines and arrows and shapes, and how to combine, subtract, and intersect shapes to make complex images. We show you how to use the Distort tool to create wavy curves without even touching the curve tool, and we show you the secret powers of the Duplication tool and many others.

Finally, we discuss how to define your own colors and how to use gradients, bitmaps, hatchings, glows, and transparencies to give a polished, professional look to your art.

Getting Graphic

A great way to get acquainted with Draw is to start playing around with lines and arrows.

Lines and arrows

Draw offers you the ability to draw almost any kind of line or arrow that you could possibly imagine. You can specify the thickness, color, and transparency of each line, and you can choose whether you want the line to be continuous, dotted, or dashed. You can even choose the exact number of dots/dashes/ spaces combinations and transparencies of your lines or arrows.

- ✔ When you *long-click* (click and hold for a moment) the Lines and Arrows button on the Main toolbar, the floating Lines and Arrows toolbar appears with two line-option buttons and several arrow-option buttons. (If the Main toolbar is not visible, choose View⇨Toolbars⇨Main Toolbar.)

- ✔ The Line button lets you draw lines at any angle you want. Click this button, and then click and drag in the drawing window to create your line.

    To make your line larger or smaller, just select it and pull the handles to readjust the size of the line.

- ✔ The size and position of the line are shown on the status bar at the bottom of the Draw document. If the status bar is not visible, choose View⇨Status Bar.

If you want straight lines, choose the Line (45°) button. This is definitely a timesaver if you just want some straight lines that go across, up, or down — or slanted halfway between. Arrows can be one-directional or two-directional, they can begin or end with a circle or square, or they can be special architectural *ticks* that are useful for blueprints, as shown in Figure 18-1.

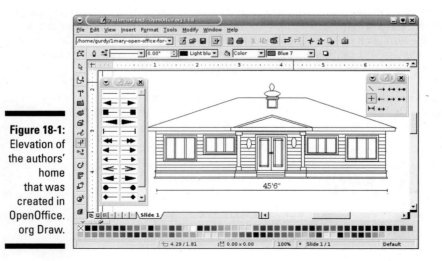

Figure 18-1: Elevation of the authors' home that was created in OpenOffice. org Draw.

Lines and arrows are especially useful for drawing blueprints. We drew most of the plans for our home in OpenOffice.org Draw. We worked with design experts, but we drew almost everything ourselves, and it saved us a lot of expense. And it was easy!

Do you want to change the look of your lines and/or arrows? Make them fatter? Make them more colorful? Make them dots or dashes or both? Just draw the line or arrow, and then select it and use the list boxes on the Object Bar to adjust the line style, width, and color.

Swapping arrowheads

Do you want to customize your arrows? Notice that the dimensions in Figure 18-1 do not contain double arrows like the default dimension line button. Draw offers an easy way to edit the arrows and customize them to the precise look that you need.

To edit arrows, perform the following steps:

1. **Long-click the Lines and Arrows button on the Main toolbar.**

    The floating Lines and Arrows toolbar appears.

2. **Choose the button that most closely suits your needs and draw your line in the Draw document.**

    For instance, if you want to have a dimension line without the arrows, click the Dimension Line button and draw your dimension line.

3. **Click the Arrow Style button on the Object Bar.**

    The floating Arrow Style toolbar appears.

4. **From the left column of arrow styles, click the style that you want to use for the left part of the arrow. And from the right column, click the style that you want for the right part of the arrow.**

    The new style takes effect after each click. (If the new style does not take place, then make sure your line is selected by clicking on it, and re-do Step 4.)

Changing arrow styles can be perplexing if you inadvertently change a Lines and Arrow tool instead of a selected line or arrow,. For instance, when we first started, we clicked on the line tool, then, opened the Arrow Style toolbar and made a few clicks. Afterward, every time we tried to draw a straight line, we got a square on one end and a circle on another! Aargh! To undo your arrow styles, click the button on the Lines and Arrows toolbar that needs fixing and open the Arrow Style toolbar. Then click the correct line or arrow styles from both the left and right columns.

Drawing to scale

To make sure that everything is correctly proportioned you need to select a unit of measure and a drawing scale. You only need to do this if you are creating plans or blueprints, such as drawings for a house.

To select a drawing scale and unit of measure for the status bar, choose Tools⇨ Options. Then when the Options dialog box appears, expand the Drawing menu and click on General. The Options-Drawing-General panel appears. Select the drawing scale from the 23 options that are available in the list box. We used a scale of 1:100 so that our drawing would fit on 8½×11-inch paper and be faxable. Select a unit of measurement from the list box. For our home drawing, we selected Foot.

When you create a line, the size of each line is shown in the Status bar. When drawing your lines to scale, remember that the Status bar shows feet, tenths of feet, and hundredths of feet — not feet and inches.

The dimension line automatically inserts the scaled dimension to the nearest foot and no inches. (Mac users may need to draw the line precisely horizontal.) To add inches, click the dimension and type. You can even change the "ft" to """. (Mac users need to select the dimension line, then click the Text button, and then type.)

Changing the look of your lines, arrows

To do something more fancy, such as adding transparency to your lines or arrows or varying the size of the arrowheads independent of the line thickness, as shown in Figure 18-2, you use the Line button on the Object Bar. Transparency can also be adjusted by using the Line button.

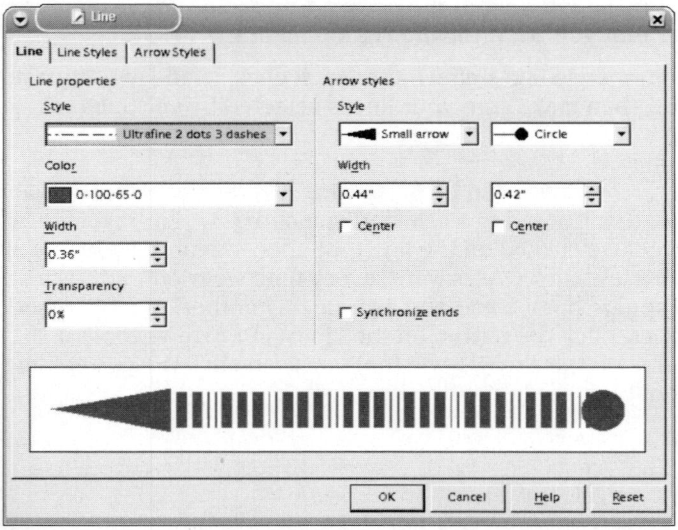

Figure 18-2:
Editing lines
and arrow
styles.

To modify line and arrow thickness, color, transparency, or style using the Line button, perform the following steps:

1. **Draw or select the line that you want to modify, and click the Line button on the Object Bar.**

   The Line dialog box appears, as shown in Figure 18-2. The line that is selected in the main drawing window also appears in the Line dialog box.

2. **Choose a color, width, and/or transparency from the list boxes.**

   Watch the image change in the display box as you do so.

3. **From the Line properties Style list box, choose a style for your line. If you can't find a style that suits your needs, click the Line Styles tab and create a unique line style.**

   In Figure 18-2, we wanted a striped pencil, so we chose Ultrafine 2 dots 3 dashes.

4. **Click the Arrow styles options and set them to your liking.**

5. **Click OK.**

   The line or arrow that you had originally selected is now transformed to your specifications.

The trick to getting those fine details looking good is to use the Zoom tool. Long-click the Zoom button to see the floating Zoom toolbar. The Zoom In tool is useful for adding those fine touches, and then you can use the Zoom Out tool to see the finished product. Other buttons include Zoom 100 percent, Zoom Previous (which takes you to your previous zoom setting), Zoom Next, Zoom Page, Zoom Width (which fills the width of the window with the width of the page), and Optimal Zoom (which is great when some of your page is empty). Also, Object Zoom is ideal when you have an object or objects selected.

Rectangles and squares

Rectangles and squares are your basic building blocks. Draw provides eight options. Long-click the Rectangle button to view the four buttons of rectangles and four buttons of squares, each with straight or rounded corners or filled. These buttons are used just like the line and arrow buttons. Click the button, and then click and drag in the drawing page to create your rectangle. And if you want to edit the rectangle, select it and pull the handles to resize.

The color of the lines and the fill color are both changeable. Just select the square or rectangle and use the list boxes on the Object Bar. You can also change the line size of your box or make it dotted — or even invisible. And you can fill your rectangle with an interesting gradient, hatching, bitmap, and so on. You can also make the fill invisible.

Circles and ellipses

The Ellipse button on the Main toolbar offers some fun options on its floating Ellipses toolbar. You have the choice of filled or unfilled circles and ellipses. These are used and modified just like the rectangles and squares that we discussed in the previous section. Draw also offers a Circle Pie, Ellipse Pie, Circle Segment, and Ellipse Segment. These tools require two extra clicks to define your segments and pies.

To create a circle or ellipse pie, perform the following steps:

1. **Click the Circle Pie or Ellipse Pie button, either filled or unfilled, and draw your circle or ellipse.**

   A radius line appears from the center of the circle or ellipse to the edge. When you move your mouse around the outside of the circle or ellipse, the radius line moves.

2. **Position the radius line at the angle that you want and then click.**

   The circle or ellipse disappears, and when you move the mouse, either a wedge or a Pacman (if you used a circle) appears. You can move the mouse and watch the Pacman's mouth open wider or close.

3. **Position the mouse so that the pie is as small or large as you want, and click.**

   Your pie is complete. You can apply different colors, fills, line sizes, or styles from the list boxes on the Object Bar.

Circle and ellipse segments are created just like pies, but instead of being wedge-shaped or Pacman-shaped, they are bowl-shaped or globe-shaped and slightly flat on one side.

Arcs are also created like pies and segments.

Polygons

Use the Polygon buttons on the Curves toolbar to create triangles, stars, and octagons. Draw gives you four options for drawing polygons: regular, 45-degree, filled, and unfilled. You can use the Filled 45-Degree option to make nice cityscape silhouettes with just a few clicks of the mouse. The 45-degree angle is perfect for rooftops. Use it when you want to make triangles, too.

To create a polygon, perform the following steps:

1. **Long-click the Curve button on the Main toolbar.**

   The floating Curves toolbar appears which contains the four Polygon.

2. **Click the polygon button of your choice.**

3. **Click and drag in the Draw document.**

   A line appears.

4. **Release the mouse button and move the mouse.**

   The line from Step 3 stays put, and another line starts from the end of that line.

5. **Stop moving the mouse where you want to create the next corner for your Polygon. Then click and release the mouse, and start moving the mouse again.**

   Each time you click, you create another corner point for your polygon, and each time you move the mouse after clicking, a new side of your polygon appears.

6. **Repeat Step 5 until all but the last corner of your polygon are defined. For the last corner, double-click the mouse.**

   Double-clicking ends the process and closes the polygon if you chose a filled polygon. (It does not close an unfilled polygon.)

Natural selection

You may want to select two or more objects at the same time. For instance, to merge two or more shapes, as described in the section "Merging Shapes" later in this chapter, you need to select all the shapes. You can accomplish this feat in two ways:

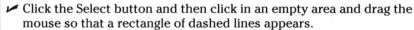

- ✔ Shift+click the objects that you want to select.

- ✔ Click the Select button and then click in an empty area and drag the mouse so that a rectangle of dashed lines appears.

   Keep dragging the rectangle to surround the objects that you want to select. Objects that are only partially encompassed in the selection area are not selected.

Terrific Text

Well-designed text can make your words jump off the pages of your brochures, posters, Web pages, and more. Draw allows you to create text boxes anywhere and resize them and move them around. With Draw you can automatically shrink or expand your text to fill any space you have available. And you can generate *callouts,* which are text boxes with pointers on them to describe objects at a distance. Draw also provides you with all the great formatting tools available in Writer. In other words, Draw has awesome powers to transform any boring old text into fabulous-looking text.

Creating and using text boxes

To insert text into your Draw document, perform the following steps:

1. **Long-click the Text button on the Main toolbar to open the floating Text toolbar.**

   The floating Text toolbar has three text buttons: the Text button, the Fit Text to Frame button, and the Callouts button.

   Did you notice that the Draw Object Bar changed to the Text Object Bar? (If the Object Bar is not visible, choose View⇨Toolbars⇨Object Bar.)

2. **Click the Text button.**

3. **Choose the font, size, style (bold, italic, or underline), and color from the Text Object Bar.**

4. **Click in the document**

   A blinking cursor appears surrounded by six small green squares, called handles.

5. **If you want to fix your right margins so that your text will wrap, then pull the handles to expand your text box to the size you want. If you do not want your text to wrap, then skip this step.**

   Notice that when you pass your mouse over the handles, the mouse changes to a two-directional arrow.

6. **Type your text.**

   If you have resized your text box, then your text wraps. If you have not resized it, then your text box expands to the right as you type until you press Enter. Whether you resized it or not, your text box expands vertically as you enter more text than it could otherwise hold.

7. **If you want to reposition your text box, pass your mouse over the borders between two handles and, when the mouse changes to a four-directional arrow, click and drag the text box wherever you like.**

8. **If you want to use any options on your Text Object Bar, such as centering text, line spacing, and so on, feel free to do so. For complete information about all that, refer to Chapter 4.**

You can toggle between the Draw Object Bar and the Text Object Bar using the little triangle button on the far right of the Object Bar.

Fitting your text to a frame

What if you want your text box to remain a fixed size and never expand when you add more text? That means the more text you enter into the text box, the smaller the text becomes. OpenOffice.org has just the tool for that. It's called the Fit Text to Frame feature.

To use the Fit Text to Frame feature, do the following:

1. **If the floating Text toolbar is not visible, then long-click the Text button on the Main toolbar.**

2. **Click on the Fit Text to Frame button.**

3. **Click and drag in the Draw window to create a text box of whatever size you want.**

   A box appears that resizes as you drag. When you release the mouse, the lines of the box disappear and six handles appear, along with a blinking cursor the size of the text box. You can always resize the box, using these handles.

4. **Type your text. Press Enter wherever you want line breaks. Your text does not wrap automatically.**

   The text appears huge, but don't be alarmed, because it resizes itself when you reach Step 5.

5. **When you have finished typing your text, click in the Draw document outside the text box.**

   Doing so deselects the text box, and the text resizes to fit the text box.

If you want your text box to have a frame, perform the following steps:

1. **Click in the text box to select it.**

   Green handles appear and a blinking cursor.

2. **Click the triangle on the far right of the Text Object Bar to bring up the Draw Object Bar.**

3. **Change "Invisible" in the Line Style list box to the line style of your choice**

   Lines appear to border your text box. Feel free to adjust the Line size and Line Color, as well.

Creating callouts

Callouts are a particularly useful tool for text. You can use callouts to point to an object in your document and describe it with text by using a framed text box and pointer.

To create callouts, follow these steps:

1. **If the floating Text toolbar is not visible, then long-click the Text button on the Main toolbar.**

2. **Click the Callouts button. (It's the one that looks like it belongs in a comic book.)**

3. **Click and drag, in the Draw document, starting from the "pointing" part of the callout and ending where you want the text box to be located.**

4. **Adjust the size of the text box by clicking and dragging the handles on the text box.**

5. **Double-click the text box frame or pointer.**

   A cursor appears inside the text box.

6. **Type your text.**

Draw also allows you to animate text. Check out Chapter 16 for more about that. Also, you can add shadows by selecting your text and choosing Format⇨ Fontwork. Then click on the shadow button of your choice and use the list boxes below to choose its angles and color.

If you want to get really fancy, try wrapping your text on to a 3-D object, like a sphere or cone — or your own 3-D creation. Just select your text and choose Modify⇨Convert⇨To Bitmap; then export it as a jpeg file. Check out Chapter BC04 on the CD for details on importing 3-D Textures.

Building with Shapes

A powerful feature of Draw is its ability to merge, subtract, and intersect shapes. These features enable you to use basic shapes as building blocks to create your own +skyscraper of artwork. Figure 18-3 shows an image of flowers in a flowerpot; the image uses these shapes features. The flowerpot is made up of three rows of the same repeated Pacman shape (the unfilled circle pie), all merged together. The stems of the flowers are each made of two ellipses, one subtracting the other. And the flowers are a single petal shape that was created by simply intersecting two ellipses. The same petal is used repeatedly. In other words, just two shapes — a Pacman pie and an ellipse — are the basis of the entire image.

Figure 18-3:
The vase
and flowers
are all
merged,
subtracted,
and
intersected
shapes.

Merging shapes

Merging shapes is a fantastic feature for creating complex images in a simple way. Merging shapes allows you to have a single border line around multiple shapes, allowing you to select your new shape with the ease of a single click.

To merge shapes, perform the following steps:

1. **Select the two or more shapes and/or lines that you want to merge.**

   Your shapes can be either filled or unfilled. Your Lines and Arrows must be at least .02 inch thick in order to merge properly. And, oddly enough, the objects you select, whether shapes, lines, arrows, or combinations of the three, don't have to be touching each other.

2. **Choose Modify⇨Shapes⇨Merge.**

   If the shapes overlap, the outline of the top shape disappears at the area of intersection, and the two shapes appear and function as if they were one shape. Also, if the original shapes are two different colors, the merged shape is transformed into the color, gradient, and so on of the bottom shape.

After you merge shapes, you can merge the new shape with other shapes, building more complex shapes, such as the flowerpot shown in Figure 18-3, which is essentially a single unfilled circle pie.

To apply a gradient, hatching, or bitmap to lines, such as straight lines, arrows, or the lines of unfilled shapes, choose Modify⇨Shapes⇨Merge to transform the lines and/or unfilled shapes into fills. The lines must be at least .02 inch thick to transform into a fill.

Subtracting shapes

You may have noticed that Draw doesn't have an eraser tool, as do many art programs. The apparent lack of the eraser tool is no problem, though, because you can create an eraser simply by positioning any filled object over the shape or object that you want to erase (or subtract). Select both shapes and then choose Modify⇨Shapes⇨Subtract. The stems of the flowers in Figure 18-3 were created by overlapping one oval with another oval, just leaving a sliver uncovered, and then selecting them both and choosing Modify⇨Shapes⇨Subtract.

Intersecting shapes

The Intersect feature of the Shapes tool is fun to use when you are searching for imagery that is really striking. Intersecting can create unusual and appealing shapes. The petals of the flower in Figure 18-3 are a simple intersection of two ovals. To create a new shape from the intersection of two shapes, select the shapes and then choose Modify⇨Shapes⇨Intersect.

Combining shapes and lines

The Combine feature is basically the opposite of the Intersect feature. Instead of having the intersections of two shapes remain, the intersections disappear. The Combine feature is not just limited to shapes; it can also be used for intersecting lines and arrows.

  ✔ To combine shapes or lines, select your shapes and then choose Modify⇨Combine.
  ✔ To undo your combination, select it and then choose Modify⇨Split.

Editing Exceptionally

Draw has exceptional abilities to edit basic shapes. Transforming shapes by distorting them or using the Set in Circle tool or the Set to Circle tool produces a variety of unique shapes. And those unique shapes — or even ordinary shapes — can be duplicated, rotated, and manipulated in various ways to create fascinating fractal images of varying simplicity or complexity.

Moving, flipping, and rotating

Now that you know the basic shapes that Draw offers, you're ready to do something with them. Moving, rotating, and flipping are the three most basic, yet powerful options. Rotating an object is described later in this section. Moving and flipping are accomplished as follows:

- ✔ To move a shape that you created (or any object), simply click and drag. To move the shape more precisely in a single direction, click to select it and use the arrow keys.

- ✔ To flip an object vertically, select it and choose Modify⇨Flip⇨Vertically.

- ✔ To flip an object horizontally, select it and choose Modify⇨Flip⇨Horizontally.

    You can also use the Flip button on the Effects floating toolbar of the Main toolbar. To use this button, select the object that you want to flip and then click the Flip button. A red line indicates where Draw intends to flip the object. If that line is not to your liking, you can move it. To perform the flip, drag a handle of the object from one side of the red bar to the other side.

To rotate an object, perform the following steps:

1. **Select the object or objects that you want to rotate.**

2. **Long-click the Effects button on the Main toolbar to bring up the Effects floating toolbar. (If the Effects toolbar is already visible, then skip this step.)**

3. **Click the Rotate button or choose Modify⇨Rotate.**

    The handles of the selected object or objects change from green to red. A dot with short lines projecting horizontally and vertically appears in the center. This indicates the center of the rotation. Feel free to move this dot to wherever you want the center of rotation to be.

4. Click a corner handle and drag.

The cursor changes to a horseshoe shape, and the object rotates around the center dot in the direction that you drag. The number of degrees of rotation is shown in the Status bar at the bottom of the Draw window.

To achieve a 3-D effect for your rotation, click and drag on a side handle instead of a corner handle.

Arranging, aligning, and grouping

Three handy ways of moving and grooving in Draw are arranging, aligning, and grouping. These terms are described as follows:

- ✔ **Arranging** allows you to specify what image goes on top and what stays underneath.

- ✔ **Aligning** allows you to align your objects for the professional look that they deserve. (A wise person once told us that half of good graphic design is simply getting everything lined up perfectly.)

- ✔ **Grouping** makes it easy to move complex shapes around with a single click. Grouping is similar to choosing Modify⇨Shapes⇨Merge, but slightly different.

Arranging

You probably already noticed that your artwork can get lost if you have too many shapes and things piled on top of each other. The natural order of stacking is that the first object that's placed on the page stacks on the bottom, the last object stacks on the top, and everything else stacks in order of its arrival on the page.

If that order does not suit you, Draw offers ways to change it by using the floating Arrange toolbar, keyboard shortcuts, or the Arrange options of the Modify menu.

Open the Arrange toolbar by long-clicking the Arrange button on the Main toolbar. On the Arrange toolbar are the Bring to Front button, the Bring Forward button, the Send Backward button, the Send to Back button, the In Front of Object button, the Behind Object button, and the Reverse button. The Bring to Front and Bring Forward buttons perform the same function when only two objects are involved. The same is true of the Send to Back and Send Backward buttons.

The In Front of Object and Behind Object buttons are great when you want to specify an object that you want the selected object to be in front of or behind. You specify which object the selected object needs to be in front of or behind by clicking the object after you click the In Front of Object or Behind Object button.

The Reverse button requires that more than one object be selected, and it simply reverses their order.

These options are all accessible from the main menu as well as the Arrange toolbar. Choose Modify⇨Arrange and then choose the desired option. Most of the arrange options also have keyboard shortcuts, which are listed on the drop-down Arrange menu.

Sometimes, the simplest way to bring an object to the front is to just cut and paste the object. Doing so makes your object the most recent on the page and gives it top billing.

Aligning

To align your objects on the page, long-click the Alignment button on the Main toolbar. The floating Alignment toolbar appears. (Alternatively, you could choose Modify⇨Alignment from the main menu.) The alignment options are Left, Centered, Right, Top, Center, and Bottom. Select all the objects that you want to align and then choose the alignment option that suits you best. (Do each row and each column separately, unless you want one big mishmash.)

To evenly space objects horizontally or vertically, select the objects and choose Modify⇨Distribution to open the Distribution dialog box. Choose one of the vertical or horizontal options and click OK.

You can also find the position of an object by choosing Format⇨Position and Size. Figure 18-4 shows the Position and Size dialog box. The added benefit of using this dialog box is that you can also type a new position for the object into the text boxes and your object moves to the location that you specify. This gives you pinpoint accuracy.

Grouping

Grouping allows you to combine objects so that you can manipulate them as if they were a single object. Grouping is very handy when dealing with complex objects and it's also reversible. Notice that the Modify menu contains the Ungroup option as well as the Group option. These options are disabled (they are hard to read and they don't function) until you select multiple objects or a grouped object.

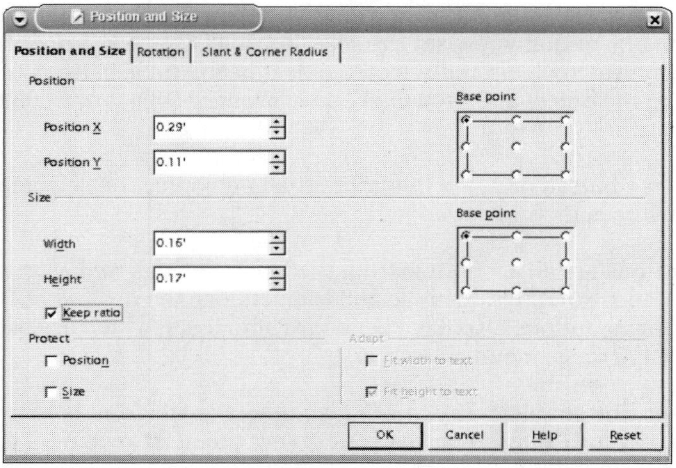

Figure 18-4:
The Position
and Size
dialog box
can place
your objects
on the
drawing
page with
pinpoint
accuracy.

To group two or more objects, select the objects and choose Modify⇨Group, or press Control+Shift+G. To ungroup the objects, select the grouped object and choose Modify⇨Ungroup, or press Alt+Control+Shift+G.

You don't have to ungroup a set of objects to edit a single component. Just double-click the grouped object, and the objects that comprise the group appear normally on-screen (whereas all ungrouped objects appear faded). Edit the grouped objects as you want and then choose Modify⇨Exit Group, or press Control+F3 to return to normal editing mode.

When you double-click a group, you may be surprised to find that not all the objects are ungrouped. This is because groups may be contained within other groups. If you grouped an object in several grouping sessions and you wish to edit that object, you may need to ungroup the object in the reverse order that you grouped it in until you free the group that you want to edit.

Duplicating

In addition to duplicating an object, the Duplicate feature also allows you to rotate your object a specific number of degrees and to move your object left or right, up or down, or a specific distance per duplication. You can enlarge the object or make it smaller. You can morph from a starting color to an ending color. And you can specify the number of duplications of your object. Using this tool can easily add beauty and complexity to your art. And if you just want to resize your object with precision, you can also use the Duplicate tool.

Figure 18-5 shows the values that we entered to create the flower shown back in Figure 18-3. The original shape that we duplicated was a two-petal, propeller-like shape. When rotating with the Duplicate tool, the rotation occurs around the center of the object. You can't change the center of rotation, so a single petal does not rotate into a flower.

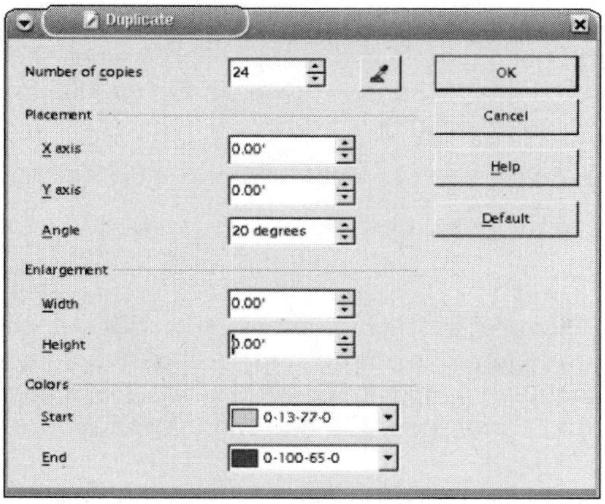

Figure 18-5:
The values
in the
Duplicate
dialog box
were used
to create
the flower
effect in
Figure 18-4
using two
merged
petals as
the selected
shape.

To duplicate objects, perform the following steps:

1. **Create and select the object or objects that you want to duplicate.**

   Remember, if you plan to rotate the object, it will rotate around its center, so you may need to duplicate and flip your object and then select both objects if you want them to appear to rotate around an edge instead.

2. **Choose Edit⊏⟩Duplicate.**

   The Duplicate dialog box appears, as shown in Figure 18-5.

3. **Enter the number of copies into the list box.**

   For the flower in Figure 18-3, we entered 24 copies.

4. **Enter the distance that you want the X axis of the rotation and Y axis of the rotation to move after each duplication, and enter the angle of rotation.**

   Entering 0 in the X- and Y-Axis list boxes fixes your image in place and allows your image to rotate around a constant point. Entering nonzero values in these list boxes sometimes creates a spiral-like image when you rotate. To duplicate in a straight line at any angle that you choose, enter nonzero values in the X- and Y-Axis list boxes and enter 0 in the Angle list box. For instance, entering a nonzero value in the X-axis list box, 0 in the Y-axis list box, and 0 in the Angle list box simply duplicates your image in a horizontal line.

5. **In the Width and the Height list boxes, enter the increment by which you want each successive duplication to enlarge or reduce.**

   To maintain the scale as the image size changes, be sure that the width and height that you choose are in the same proportion as the width and height of your selected image. For the flower in Figure 18-3, we did not change the width or height setting.

6. **Select the colors that you want to start and end with in the list boxes.**

   Gradations of colors can give a nice effect.

7. **Click OK.**

   Check out your duplication. Is it what you expected? If not, press Ctrl+Z to undo the duplication and give it another try. It usually takes a few tries to get it exactly how you like it. To get the effect of a flower, we copied the top double petal, pasted it, and then flipped it horizontally.

If duplication does not work as expected, the scale of your Draw window may not be 1:1. The values in the list boxes are sensitive to the scale that is set when you choose Tools⇨Options, then expand the Drawing menu of the Options dialog box and click General. For example, if your scale is 1:10 you need to type 10 instead of 1 into the list boxes to create the desired effect.

Using the Distort, Set in Circles, and Set to Circles tools

Do you ever feel like your artwork is sometimes a little too neat and tidy? No problem. Draw has tools to change all that: the Distort, Set to Circle (Slant), and Set in Circle (Perspective) tools. Each of these tools distorts your image and creates interesting curves in different ways. Using any or all three of these tools allows you to easily warp all that unwanted symmetry out of existence. Figure 18-6 shows an image that was created by subtracting and merging ellipses and then applying the Distort tool to get a more organic look and feel.

Figure 18-6:
Break the symmetry and create interesting curves by using the Distort tool.

To use the Distort, Set to Circle (Slant), or Set in Circle (Perspective) tool, perform the following steps:

1. **Select the object or objects that you want to distort.**

2. **Long-click the Effects button on the main menu to view the floating Effects toolbar. Then click the Distort button, the Set to Circle (Slant) button, or the Set in Circle (Perspective) button.**

   A dialog box sometimes appears asking if you want to convert your selected object to a curve. If this dialog box appears, click Yes. If you click No, almost no effect will take place when you use the tool.

3. **Click and drag a handle of the object to achieve your desired shape.**

   The cursor changes when the mouse passes over a handle, either to a tiara-like shape (Set in Circle or Set to Circle), or a finger-pointing hand (when using Distort on corner handles), or two arrow halves pointing in opposite directions (when using Distort on side handles).

   When you click and drag any corner handle a grid appears over your object Dragging your mouse distorts the grid. When you release the mouse button, your image maps itself according to the final shape of the grid.

   When you click on side handles, a grid also appears over your object (unless you're using Distort, in which case no grid appears). But dragging your mouse distorts your object regardless of whether a grid appears or not.

Using these buttons involves a bit of trial and error. If you use Distort or the other two tools and your result is not what you hoped, choose Edit⇨Undo and try again. After some practice, you'll be able to better visualize the final result when you view the warping of the grid.

Cross-fading

Cross-fading offers yet another tool for creating appealing and complex images. With the Cross-fading tool, you select two images and specify how many iterations you want. The Cross-fading tool then creates copies that gradually change from the first image into the second image. One major use of cross-fading is to create animations within Impress. These animations can add pizzazz to your Web site or presentation.

To cross-fade two objects, perform the following steps:

1. **Position both shapes where you want your cross fade to start and end, and select both shapes.**

   Cross fades can be performed on normal shapes and on merged, intersected, and subtracted shapes. Grouped shapes and lines and arrows do not cross-fade, and shapes must either be unfilled or filled with color, not with a gradient, bitmap, or hatching.

2. **Choose Edit⇨Cross-fading from the main menu.**

   The Cross-fading dialog box appears.

3. **Enter the number of increments in which you want the cross-fading to take place. Also, select the Cross-fade attributes and Same Orientation check boxes, if they do not already have check marks.**

   The Cross-fade attributes option allows the attributes such as line widths and colors to cross-fade properly. The Same orientation option keeps your cross fade from twisting and turning in a way that seems unnatural.

4. **Click OK.**

   The cross fade appears in your drawing page as a grouped object. To select a single shape in the cross fade, you need to ungroup it.

Coloring Your World

A wide range of colors are provided in the Area Style/Filling list boxes on the Object Bar, as well as gradients, bitmaps, and hatchings. But these colors are just small drops in the ocean of possibilities, and they may or may not suit your needs. You may want pastel colors or different shades of colors.

Fortunately, Draw allows you to choose from millions of colors and to choose the precise colors that suit your needs.

Draw also allows you to modify your list of colors, or your *palette*. You can create and save different palettes for different types of artwork and then load them whenever you like. Draw also provides some alternative ready-made palettes, such as a Web-safe palette for when you are creating art for your Web site. This all adds up to infinite flexibility for your artwork.

To apply a different color to a line, arrow, curve, or to the borders of a shape, select the object and then select the line color from the Line Color list box on the Object Bar.

To apply a different color to an area, select the object, choose Color from the Area Style list box on the Object Bar, then choose your color from the Area Filling list box. Your object changes color immediately. You could also pick your color from the Color bar (refer to Figure 18-1). This Color Bar only works for areas, not lines. To view the Color Bar, choose View⇨Toolbars⇨Color Bar. If you can't find the color that you're looking for, you can define your own color by using the RGB (Red-Blue-Green) model, the CMYK (Cyan-Magenta-Yellow-Black/Key) model, the HSB (Hue-Saturation-Brightness) model, or by using a color spectrum box. Follow these steps to create a color definition:

1. **Choose Format⇨Area and click the Colors tab, or click the Paint can on the Object Bar.**

   The Area dialog box opens to the Colors panel.

2. **In the Name box, enter a name for your new color or choose the color from the Color List that you want to modify..**

3. **To define a color using the RGB or CMYK model, choose RGB or CMYK from the Color Model drop-down list and then enter the values that you want in the color text boxes.**

   • The RGB model mixes red, green, and blue light to create colors. Values range from 0 to 255. If all three colors are set to 0, you get black. If all three colors are 255, you get white.

   • The CMYK system, often used for printing, mixes cyan, magenta, yellow, and black. Values range from 0 to 100 percent. If all colors are set to 0 percent, you get white. If all colors are 100 percent, you get black.

You can first choose a color that is similar to the color that you want and then start experimenting by changing the values in the color boxes.

4. **To define a color using the HSB model or in a color spectrum, click Edit.**

   The Color dialog box opens, shown in Figure 18-7.

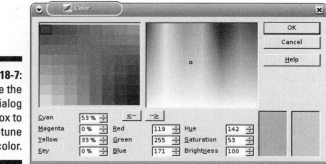

Figure 18-7:
Use the
Color dialog
box to
fine-tune
your color.

5. **In the Color dialog box, do one or more of the following and then click OK.**

   • Enter numbers in the CMYK, RGB, or HSB text boxes to define your color.

   • Click anywhere in the color spectrum on the right.

   • To focus the color spectrum on the right around the color that you want, click a color tile in the left pane and click the right-arrow button. To focus the tiles in the left pane around a color on the right, click an area in the right pane and click the left-arrow button. You can then more easily choose the color that you want.

   When you click OK, you are returned to the Area dialog box.

6. **Click Add if you are adding a new color, or modify if you are modifying an existing color.**

   OpenOffice.org adds your new color to its color palette. You see a swatch for the color at the bottom of the other color swatches.

7. **Click OK.**

After you create your own color, you can find it among the other color swatches on your Color bar and on the Object Bar list boxes.

Adding Great Gradients

Gradients are great for creating amazingly real-looking 3-D objects and adding flourish to your creations. Figure 18-8 shows two examples gradients. Draw offers some ready-made gradients in the Area Style/Filling list box on the Draw Object Bar, but the actual number of possible gradients is, of course, infinite. And, because finding the particular gradient that you need for your masterpiece in the Gradient list is unlikely, it's fortunate that Draw allows you to create your own gradients.

With Draw, you can specify the increments of the gradation. That means, if you want your gradient to take place in 5 or 6 steps — instead of the 60 or so steps that Draw may use automatically — you can produce an interesting effect. In Figure 18-8 is an example of a gradient that has only eight increments. It is made from four triangles that have the same gradient applied to them.

Figure 18-8:
This glowing sun and modern design are both produced using gradients.

To add or modify a gradient, perform the following steps:

1. **Select the object to which you want to apply the new or revised gradient.**

2. **Click the Paint Can on the Object Bar, or choose Format⇨Area. When the Area dialog box appears, click the Gradients tab.**

   The Gradients panel of the Area dialog box appears.

3. **Select the gradient that you want to modify from the list box, or if you want to add a new gradient, select a gradient that most closely resembles the gradient that you want to create.**

4. **Choose the type of gradient you want from the Type list box (if it's different from the gradient that you already selected).**

   Draw offers Linear, Axial (slanted linear), Radial, Ellipsoid, Square, and Rectangular gradients. If you're not sure what each of these do, select each type one at a time and watch how the gradient changes in the Preview window.

5. **Enter values into the Center X, Center Y, Angle, and Border boxes to modify the gradient.**

   Watch how your gradient changes with the different values that you enter. The Center X and Center Y boxes are only active for Radial, Ellipsoid, Square, and Rectangular gradient types. The Angle box, of course, has no effect on Radial gradient types.

6. **Choose the starting and ending colors as well as their intensity values.**

   Keep your eyes on the Preview window to see if you like what you choose. Also, if the exact color that you need doesn't exist on the list, feel free to click the Colors tab and add your color to the list box's list.

7. **Click Add if you are adding a gradient, or click Modify if you are modifying an existing gradient.**

   A Name dialog box appears, requesting a name for your new gradient. If you clicked Modify, the name of the gradient that you are modifying is in the name input box.

8. **Type in a new name, if desired, and click OK.**

   The Name dialog box closes.

9. **Repeat Steps 3 through 8 to add new or modify gradients.**

10. **After you finish, click OK.**

    The Area dialog box closes. The gradient of the item that you selected in Step 1 changes to the last gradient that you added. If you click Cancel, the gradient of your selected item does not change, but the gradients that you added or modified are still listed in the list box.

 If you like the colors but want to modify the way the colors blend into each other, then try out the Gradient button on the Effects toolbar. Select an object with the gradient you want to modify, then click the Gradient button and move and drag the two squares that appear. Notice how the gradient changes? It's a cool way to get your art just how you want it.

To change the increments of gradation, as in Figure 18-8, do the following:

1 **Select the object with the gradient that you want to modify.**

2. **Click the Paint Can on the Object Bar.**

   The Area dialog box opens with the Area panel showing.

3. **Select Gradient in the Fill section of the Area panel. (Don't select the Gradients tab!)**

   The Gradient list appears as well as a check box labeled Automatic.

4. **Deselect the Automatic check box.**

   A number appears in the list box next to it.

5. **Choose the number of Increments from the list box.**

   Watch the gradient change in the Preview window as the numbers get lower.

6. **Click OK.**

   The Area dialog box disappears and the new gradient fills the selected object.

Hatching Handily

Hatching is a great way to get lots of lines in your artwork without having to draw them. Remember that hatchings don't have to be devoid of color. You can either put your hatched object on top of a background with a gradient fill or color of your choice, or you can specify a background color. Figure 18-9 is an example of a handy use for hatching. Creating the tennis racket strings would be a tedious chore without the hatching tool.

Figure 18-9:
Tennis strings are drawn with ease by creating a customized hatching.

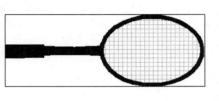

You can use the hatchings supplied by OpenOffice.org by choosing Hatching from the Area Style list box, then choosing your hatchings from the Area Filling list box beside it. But, often you may want to tweak the ready-made hatchings, or add a new hatching for a whole new look of your own.

To create a customized hatching, perform the following steps:

1. **Select the object to which you want to apply the hatching and then click the Paint Can on the Object Bar.**

   The Area dialog box appears.

2. **Click the Hatching tab.**

   The Hatching panel appears in the Area dialog box.

3. **Select the hatching from the list box that you wish to modify. Or if you're creating a new hatching, then it doesn't matter what hatching is selected by default or selected by you from the list box.**

4. **Fill in the Spacing, Angle, Line Type, and Color input boxes to generate your new or modified hatching.**

   Watch the hatching change in the Preview window as you modify the parameters. If you want a horizontal, vertical, or 45-degree angle, you can click the line of your choice below the Angle input box, instead of entering the number of degrees.

5. **Click the Add button and type in a new name for your hatching. Or if you are modifying a hatching, then click the Modify button.**

   Both the Add and Modify buttons open the Name dialog box. The Add button suggests a new name in the Name field, whereas the Modify button suggests the name of the already existing hatching that is selected.

6. **Click OK.**

   The new hatching is applied to the selected object and added to (or modified in) the list of hatchings in the list box.

To assign a background color to a hatching, select the object that you want to hatch with a background and click the Paint Can on the Object Bar to open the Area dialog box. Click the Area tab, and select the Hatching option button. The hatchings list and the Background color check box appear. Select this box, choose the background color from the list box list of colors, select the hatching of your choice, and click OK.

Glorious Glows and Transparencies

Transparencies can add fascination and sophistication to your work, and you can use transparencies in a myriad of ways. Transparencies can be used to allow layers to show through other layers, as shown in Figure 18-10. A Christmas tree is depicted with simple see-through triangles. Another use for transparencies is *glows*. Glows are created by applying a gradual transparency to a color. Glows are similar to gradients, but glows involve the color becoming more transparent instead of gradually changing to another color. The glow on the sun in Figure 18-8 was created by using yellow changing to white. But it could also have been created by fading out the yellow.

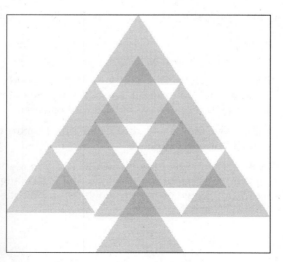

Figure 18-10:
A simple decoration is created using transparent triangles.

To apply a transparency to a selected object, click the Paint Can or choose Format➪Area to open the Area dialog box. Click the Transparency tab. In the Transparency panel, select Transparency as the Transparency mode and choose the amount of transparency that you want. The higher the number, the more transparent your object is.

To create a glow, perform the following steps:

1. **Select the object or objects that you want to fill with a glow.**

   Your object may already be filled with a color, gradient, bitmap, or hatching. (Yes, even a hatching can have a glow applied to it.)

   You probably want the lines of your shape(s) to be invisible. To do so, choose Invisible from the Line Style list box on the Object Bar.

2. **Click the Paint Can or choose Format➪Area to open the Area dialog box, and click the Transparency tab.**

   The Transparency panel of the Area dialog box appears. The fill of your selected object appears in the Preview window.

3. **Select Gradient as the Transparency mode, and select the Type, Angle, Border, Start value, and End value from the list boxes.**

   Watch your fill change as you specify the parameters. You should choose a high start value and a low-end value for a nice glowing effect. And check out the Quadratic gradient type, along with a 45-degree angle. Keep changing the values until you achieve the desired result.

4. **Click OK.**

   The transparency gradient fills your selected shape — hopefully in the way you expected. If not, try again. With a little practice, your work will be glowing with perfection.

If you want to fiddle with your transparency using a graphical interface, try out the Transparency button of the Effects toolbar. Just select your object, and click the Transparency button, then move the two squares around on the object to create different effects. Try it with gradients, too, to create super realistic-looking stuff.

Bitmapping Brilliantly

Draw offers some interesting bitmaps, such as water, fire, metal, and so on. These are found in the Area Style/Filling list boxes on the Object Bar. You can use these to map textures onto your selected objects. These ready-made bitmaps are nice, but Draw also allows you to do a lot more with bitmaps, such as:

- ✓ Import bitmaps as graphics or for mapping textures
- ✓ Adjust colors, contrast, brightness, crop using the Bitmap Object Bar
- ✓ Customize texture mapping
- ✓ Create unique bitmaps using pixels
- ✓ Convert almost anything into a bitmap
- ✓ Apply filters

Importing bitmaps

Draw allows you to import almost any bitmap format. To insert a bitmap into your Draw document, choose Insert⇨Graphics and open your bitmap file using the Insert Graphics dialog box. Your bitmap appears in the Draw document. Notice, also that the Draw Object Bar changes to the Bitmap Object Bar, as shown in Figure 18-12. The Bitmap bar contains many options, such as filters, choosing Greyscale, or modifying colors, brightness, contrast, transparency, and cropping. For information on filters, see below. For other information regarding the Bitmap Object Bar, refer to Chapter 15.

To import a bitmap for mapping as a texture, perform the following steps:

1. **Select the object to which you want to apply the bitmap, and click the Paint Can on the Object Bar or Choose Format⇨Area.**

   The Area dialog box appears.

2. **Click the Bitmaps tab.**

3. **Click the Import button.**

   The Import dialog box appears.

4. **Browse your files until you find the file that you want to import.**

   To show only the folders and files of the same type that you are looking for, select the file type from the File Type list box; otherwise select All Formats (the default). Be sure that the Preview box is marked so that you can see your image in the Preview window.

5. **Click Open.**

   The Name dialog box appears, requesting a name for your bitmap.

6. **Type in a name and click OK.**

   The image appears in the Preview window.

7. **Click OK.**

   The image is applied to the object(s) that you selected and the name and image of the bitmap is added to the Bitmap list.

Customizing the sizing and tiling of your bitmap

If you import an image, and the image is not exactly how you expected it to look when you apply it, it's easy to size, position, and tile the image to your liking. Even the bitmaps that are provided by Draw may need a bit of editing to work for you.

To customize the sizing and tiling of your bitmap, perform the following steps:

1. **Select the object that contains the bitmap.**

2. **Choose Format⇨Area, or click the Paint Can on the Object Bar.**

   The Area dialog box appears.

3. **If the Area tab is not selected, click it and select Bitmap from the Fill section. (Do not select the Bitmaps tab!)**

   Your bitmap appears in the Preview window. Underneath your bitmap are check boxes and list boxes for various parameters.

4. **Deselect the Original Size check box to adjust the size, and select the Relative check box. Then adjust the size according to the percentage of width and height.**

   The bitmap adjusts accordingly in the Preview window.

5. **If you do not want to tile the bitmap, deselect the Tile check box. If tiling is not marked and you want the bitmap to fit the size of your object, select the Autofit check box and go to Step 6. However, to tile the bitmap, select the Tile check box and adjust the tiling to your liking.**

   Click the X Offset and Y Offset list boxes to offset the tiling, or select the row or column boxes and choose a percentage in the offset list box to stagger the tiling. The changes are shown in the Preview box. These changes may be more or less obvious with different bitmaps.

6. **Click OK.**

   Your bitmap fills the selected area in the manner that you specified.

Creating a unique bitmap

Draw allows you to fill in each pixel of an 8×8–pixel grid with two different colors of your choice. This grid is then repeated to make a new bitmap. Figure 18-11 shows an example of a customized bitmap. The sunflower seeds are created by using this 8×8–pixel grid.

Figure 18-11:
A custom-
ized bitmap
fills the
center
circle of this
sunflower.

To customize a bitmap, perform the following steps:

1. **Select the object to which you want to apply the bitmap and then click the Paint Can on the Draw Object Bar.**

   The Area dialog box appears.

2. **Click the Bitmaps tab.**

   Notice that an 8×8 grid, labeled Pattern Editor, appears in the left side of the panel.

3. **Select the colors that you want for your foreground and background and click in the grid.**

   Each click changes a cell from the background color to the foreground color. Or, if the foreground color is already in the cell, clicking the cell reverts the color to the background color.

   Watch the pattern develop and change in Preview window.

4. **Click Add.**

   The Name dialog box appears, requesting a name for your bitmap.

5. **Type in a name, and click OK.**

   The image appears in the Preview window.

6. **Click OK.**

   The image is applied to the object(s) that you selected.

Your bitmap pattern can be resized using the Area panel of the Area dialog box. Suppose that you want your 8×8 grid to be the letter *T* and you want it large enough to be seen. Just create your *T*, and use the Area panel to resize and tile the *T* according to your needs, as previously described.

Filtering bitmaps (and everything else, too)

OpenOffice.org Draw comes complete with a toolbar of bitmap filters; these filters are incredibly powerful and fun to use. Filters are cool because they do so much with so little effort from you. For example, the pot of flowers that's shown in Figure 18-12 is the same pot of flowers that is shown in Figure 18-2, except that Figure 18-12 has been converted to a bitmap and had some filters applied to it.

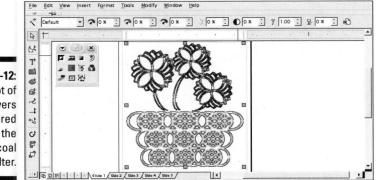

Figure 18-12: A pot of flowers is filtered with the Charcoal Sketch filter.

To apply one or more filters to an object, perform the following steps:

1. **Select your object, and choose Modify⇨Convert⇨Bitmap.**

   The Draw Object Bar changes to the Bitmap Object Bar, as shown in Figure 18-12. Using this toolbar, you can modify the percentage of red, green, or blue; the brightness; the contrast; and the transparency of your bitmap. You can also choose Black/White or Greyscale, etc. from the Graphics mode list box.

2. **Click the Filter button on the Bitmap Object Bar.**

   This brings up the floating Filter toolbar, which contains these filters: Invert, Smooth, Sharpen, Remove Noise, Solarization, Aging, Posterize, Pop Art, Charcoal Sketch, Relief, and Mosaic.

3. Click the appropriate filter to apply it to the bitmap.

As you click, the bitmap changes to the new filtered image. To achieve the effect that's shown in Figure 18-12, we clicked the Sharpen filter four times and then clicked the Charcoal Sketch filter.

Filters can be a lot of fun, so have fun!

If you want to use the Bitmap Object Bar, including filters, on any object that is not a bitmap — no problem! Draw lets you convert almost any object to a bitmap, including text. Just select your object and choose Modify⇨Convert⇨To Bitmap.

If you want to use the Bitmap Object Bar for an object that you selected and filled with a ready-made Bitmap provided by Draw, oddly enough, you first need to change it into a bitmap. Choose Modify ⇨Convert⇨To Bitmap, and the Bitmap Object Bar becomes available to you.

Customizing your Color, Gradient, Hatching, and Bitmap Lists

Do you want to have your colors list contain just those colors that are optimized for the Web? Or do you want your gradient list to be more colorful and outrageous? You can specify your own colors and add them to the lists, or you can use the different color lists, gradient lists, and hatching lists that Draw offers.

To load a different color, gradient, or hatching list, choose Format⇨Area or click the Paint Can to open the Area dialog box. Then click the Colors tab, the Gradients tab, or the Hatching tab. Each of these three tabs contains a Load List button. Click the button to open the browser to view the available lists. The color lists use the suffix .soc, the gradients end with .sog, and the hatchings use the suffix .soh. Select your new list and click Open. Notice that the colors, gradients, or hatchings in the Area dialog box are now changed to the new lists.

To save a different color, gradient, hatching, or bitmap list, perform the steps described above in the section "Coloring Your World" to customize your colors, gradients, hatchings, or bitmaps. Notice that you can delete items from the lists by clicking the Delete button. When your list is complete, click the Save button and type in a new name. Then click OK, and you now have a new list to access as you please.

Part VI
The Part of Tens

The 5th Wave   By Rich Tennant

THE SECRET ROOM AT EVERY INTERNET SERVICE PROVIDER

KNOCK FIRST

DISCONNECT

"I'll be right there. Let me just take care of this user. He's about halfway through a 3-hour download."

In this part . . .

The arguments for using OpenOffice.org are exciting and compelling, and here we explain the top ten reasons why. No more worrying about restrictive licenses. No more feeling guilty about using any unauthorized copy. No need to pay for frequent upgrades, or even the program itself. And this just scratches the surface.

The technical support you can get for OpenOffice.org is also amazing, and in this section we show you how. Imagine having thousands of people ready and willing to help you with any problem you may have — and all for free. That sums up the support that you can expect from the OpenOffice.org community. The e-mail lists and online forums are awesome with their experienced volunteers providing deep insight into the nuts and bolts of the entire program. Everyone is excited about this ground-breaking, new open source program, and eager to welcome newbies and give them a helping hand, if they need it.

Chapter 19

Ten Reasons to Use OpenOffice

*W*hy use OpenOffice.org? Maybe this question should be why not use OpenOffice.org? In fact, so many reasons abound for using this program that once you read this chapter, you may wonder why anyone would want to use anything else.

It's Free!

OpenOffice.org is free to all users. It's free now, and it's free forever. Every time a new version of OpenOffice.org is released, that upgrade is free (unlike almost all proprietary software, which forces you to pay every year or so to keep up with the most current version).

If you want to have an extra copy for your home or office, that's free. If you want to give a copy to a friend, that's free. If you need 1,000 copies for everyone in your company, they're all free. It also costs nothing to upgrade those 1,000 copies.

Compare that to the cost of acquiring Microsoft Office XP Standard, which is currently being sold at Amazon.com for $354.99. Even if you have an older version of Microsoft Office, the upgrade to Microsoft Office XP Standard costs $200! All this adds up to lots of money now and lots of money later (and for some, lots of money already spent in the past).

We can think of other ways to spend all that money, can't you?

You're Free!

You're free from any guilty conscience that you may have if you accidentally — or purposely — install some extra copies and violate an end-user license agreement (EULA).

You're free from worrying about your version being too old and incompatible because you don't want to shell out money for upgrades.

You're free from wondering if the proprietary software that you just purchased contains spyware that permits a company to eavesdrop on your activities (or audit your license compliance) without you being aware of it.

You're free from worrying about violating an EULA that is too long, too boring, and too legalized to read, yet may contain unusual clauses such as the one that Microsoft included in its FrontPage 2002 software: "You may not use the Software in connection with any site that disparages Microsoft, MSN, MSNBC, Expedia, or their products or services . . ." In this case, you're free to use your freedom of speech.

You're free from having to choose between your bank account and your reputation or conscience when deciding whether to use a bootleg copy of proprietary software.

You're free from the guilt of not being a good example to your children and insisting that they buy their own copies (or that you buy more copies) of a proprietary program, instead of making illegal copies of your software for them.

You are free from the peer pressure of being asked by friends to borrow your copy of a proprietary program to install on their computer. They may even insist that you help them install it!

You're free from trying to remember where you put your activation code for your installation disk when you need to reinstall a proprietary program on your new computer.

Because the source code is freely available, you're free from being at the mercy of a single company to fix bugs that you find. You are free because you can hire any programmer of your choice to fix these bugs. Okay, you probably aren't going to hire someone to fix bugs, but you could, and some companies will.

Sun Powers It

One of the world's largest computer manufacturers and software developers, Sun Microsystems, Inc., bought the StarOffice code from StarDivision in 1999 and launched it as a free Microsoft Office alternative in May 2002. Sun is a multibillion dollar international corporation that is heavily committed to making OpenOffice.org a success. Sun provides training for OpenOffice.org and support in the form of migration assistance. It also sells StarOffice, an office suite that is based on the source code for OpenOffice.org, with a few extra proprietary features. According to an interview with Danese Cooper from Sun Microsystems, Inc. that was published on the OpenOffice.org Web site, Sun is pleased with the success of OpenOffice.org. OpenOffice.org has "wildly exceeded distribution projections."

Sun views OpenOffice.org as a way to break Microsoft's ever-expanding grip on the world software market. OpenOffice.org also runs on Solaris, Sun's proprietary operating system, and on GNU/Linux, which Microsoft Office does not.

Upgrades and Reinstallations Are Easy

To upgrade your copy of OpenOffice.org, follow these steps:

1. **Pay no money now. (Also, pay no money later.)**

   You don't need to order the product (and you obviously don't need to get a purchase order approved). Furthermore, you don't need to worry about product activation. (So far, you haven't had to do anything.)

2. **Wait for the right moment. That can be any time you like.**

   In the middle of the night, if you decide that you want to upgrade, you can do it right then and there.

3. **Go to** www.openoffice.org/download, **and click a few items.**

   Refer to our installation instructions in Appendix A for more details. Follow the same easy instructions to upgrade OpenOffice.org as you would to install it.

   OpenOffice.org downloads on its own; it may take anywhere from 15 minutes to two and a half hours, depending on which version you need for your operating system, and if you have a fast connection, such as DSL or a slower dial-up modem. You then click a few more things and it's done.

If you're in a hurry, skip all these steps except Step 3.

Commercial Support Is Available, If You Want It

If you want to convert a medium-sized or large business, educational institute, or even an entire government to OpenOffice.org and need some help, Sun Microsystems, Inc. is a good place to start looking for commercial support. Sun, the company that launched OpenOffice.org as a free open source program, provides training and migration assistance for OpenOffice.org as well as its proprietary version, Star Office. Sun offers on-site support during the installation and importation process as well as training for employees, all with minimal disruption to an organization. With Sun's help, even large companies can easily convert to OpenOffice.org. And training can be tailored to the needs of your company (or your government, for example). The URL for Sun's training and support is www.theofficeworkshop.com.

If you need someone to help you work out any problems with OpenOffice.org, you can hire a consultant. OpenOffice.org is widely used, with an estimated 8 million users at this writing, and its usage is growing by leaps and bounds. Many computer consultants use it themselves and are fully experienced with it. Also, if you want to modify the program to your liking, you can do that as well. OpenOffice.org uses easy-to-understand XML-based file formats, and the source code is freely available. Also, OpenOffice.org has a community of 100,000 people, many of whom are volunteer programmers working on the code. Hiring someone to do something that he is already doing for free should be no problem.

Community Support Is Excellent

One of the main reasons for the success of OpenOffice.org is its community support. Since the launch of the OpenOffice.org Web site on May 1, 2002, an estimated 8 million people have adopted the product and 100,000 people have joined the community project. Sun Microsystems substantially funds the project, but the volunteer community controls most of the coding and documentation contributions. The community also provides free online support in the form of documentation, e-mail discussion lists, and forums on the Web. Support comes readily from this active community. Also, OpenOffice.org has gained much success around the globe because the community helps translate it into many different languages.

The OpenOffice.org community is made up of generous volunteers who are willing to give their time and energy to further the cause of free software. A large and very active segment of the community is even devoted to marketing OpenOffice.org, even though this segment has nothing to gain from the endeavor — because it's free!

The volunteer spirit that abounds around OpenOffice.org is a boon to every OpenOffice.org user.

File Formats Are Open Standards

OpenOffice.org uses XML-based file formats that are easy for programmers to understand and easy for computer programs to interoperate with. Unlike Microsoft Office and other proprietary office suites, the OpenOffice.org file formats are publicly documented instead of being trade secrets. As a result, you never have to worry about a file format becoming obsolete or being unable to access your data. With open source software, you can always access your data.

Not only are the file formats open standards, but you can also acquire the source code for the entire program. The source code allows you to reconfigure and recompile the program to suit your own tastes. All the tools that are needed to build a new version of the software are free and open to everyone. However, OpenOffice.org is a huge program with over 75 million lines of code, so few people attempt to substantially redesign the software.

Anyone can redistribute OpenOffice.org for free, or sell it in any format, for example, on a CD. Also, anyone can modify the program and sell the modified version. In short, anyone can do whatever they want with the program as long as that person complies with the terms of the licenses under which it is distributed. These licenses basically require you to allow anyone else to modify, distribute, and sell any copies of OpenOffice.org that you publish.

The availability of the source code also ensures that no secret back doors or spyware is built into your program that could permit a company to eavesdrop on your activities.

It's on Every Major Platform

What if you want to communicate seamlessly with people who work on other platforms?

OpenOffice.org works on every Windows and every UNIX platform, plus Linux, Solaris, Mac OS X (via X11), FreeBsd, LinuxPPC, IRIX, Linux S/390, and TRU64.

Microsoft Office only works on Windows and Mac operating systems. And at any time, Microsoft could decide to discontinue its versions for the Mac, just as it has decided to discontinue making new versions of Internet Explorer for the Mac.

To date, OpenOffice.org has been translated into 23 languages, and it uses internationally standardized technology that is reported to be remarkably robust. It can also import and export virtually every major word processing, spreadsheet, presentation and graphics file format. In fact, according to one testimonial on the OpenOffice.org site, someone who was unable to open his corrupted Excel file with Excel could open it with OpenOffice.org!

With 16 million downloads of OpenOffice.org and operation on so many platforms, what other software package is poised to become so ubiquitous?

Lock In Is Locked Out

Microsoft Office uses proprietary file formats that it often changes when it publishes major new versions of its programs. Older versions of Office are often unable to read the formats that are created by newer versions. Therefore, even if you don't care about (or need) the new features of Microsoft Office, you must constantly buy the upgrades, just to be able to read other people's files (unless they take pity on you and export their files to a previous file format). In this way, you are locked in to always buying the most current upgrade of Microsoft Office. As one Microsoft Office user remarked, "Microsoft's office suite seems less and less like a suite and more and more like a tollbooth."

Using OpenOffice.org breaks the cycle of everyone having Microsoft Word, thus requiring you to have it, too. You can almost flawlessly import from and export to Microsoft Word formats, although some styles and macros could be lost. And other formats can just as easily be read by Calc, Impress, and Draw. You don't need to worry about having to buy new upgrades just to read new files. The volunteers at OpenOffice.org can supply new upgrades to import and export any new Word file formats. With 8 million people currently using OpenOffice.org and depending on this service, it will happen.

Choice Is Good

For years, Microsoft has systematically worked to become the de facto standard in as many software categories as possible. This strategy has been immensely profitable for the company, but do you really want all your software to come from a single monopoly?

OpenOffice.org competes in a way that's very difficult for Microsoft to crush, because OpenOffice.org is free. Thanks in no small part to the power of the Internet, OpenOffice.org can incorporate the good ideas, the development and debugging talents, and the marketing skills of tens of thousands of volunteers from around the world to create a product with an amazing range of features.

You never have to fear that the product will become extinct because its source code will always be available, and programmers even in the distant future will always be able to revise and revive it. Growth and evolution occur in a marketplace when people can make choices, and in a monopoly market, no choice exists. And choice is good.

Chapter 20

Ten Places to Look for Support

*Y*ou can always get by with a little help from your friends. Of course, you need to know how to locate your friends before you can get help from them. As we show you in this chapter, a variety of helpful sources are right at your fingertips. Don't tear your hair in frustration when a problem's got you down; the answers are out there, whether they're online, in the classroom, or even waiting for you on your very own desktop.

Getting Help on Your Desktop

By now, you have probably noticed that almost every dialog box in OpenOffice. org has a Help button. These buttons take you straight to the appropriate section in the Help system.

You can also access Help by choosing Help⇨Contents. Click the Contents tab to look through the table of contents, click the Find tab to search for your topics, or click the Index tab to find your topic in the index. Help covers a wide range of topics and is quite "help"ful. See Chapter 2 for more information on getting help.

Searching the E-Mail Archives at OpenOffice.org

The best way to find support for OpenOffice.org, besides hiring someone to fix your problem for you, is to check out the e-mail lists. These lists involve thousands of people and are extremely active. Since joining in September, 2002, we've received 33,751 messages each to date. That's about 3,000 per month. So keep in mind the fact that your question may have already been asked before. Rather than immediately posting questions to an e-mail list, the proper etiquette is to check the archives first.

To search the e-mail lists archives, perform the following steps:

1. **In your Web browser, go to Open.Office.org's home page,** www. openoffice.org.

2. **Click Mailing lists on the main menu, which is in a column in the left side of the window.**

   The Mailing Lists Guidelines page appears. If you are considering posting to an e-mail list, read these guidelines.

3. **Click Mailing Lists.**

   The General & Project Mailing Lists page appears.

4. **Scroll down to General Mailing Lists, and locate the list of your choice.**

   The lists include users, announce, and discuss. Other lists in the general mailing lists are devoted to the project of developing the program. You probably want to search the users or the discuss lists. The users list addresses specific problems that need fixing, whereas the discuss list is more general and provides a broader discussion of topics that pertain to OpenOffice.org.

   If English is not your native language, check out the foreign language lists in the Project section.

5. **Click Search for the mailing list of your choice.**

   The Search Messages window appears, with a Search field.

6. **Choose whether you want to summarize your search results by date, author, subject, or thread.**

   Unless you are searching for time-sensitive material, we recommend summarizing by subject or thread.

7. **Enter your topic in the Search field.**

   You can type in a general one-word description of your topic and then browse through the results. Or, you can choose a more specific description with multiple words, by using the plus sign (+) as a logical AND between words or by placing multiple words in quotation marks.

8. **Select whether you want to search the subject or the body of the messages.**

9. **Click Search.**

   Your results are listed.

Posting to the E-Mail Lists at OpenOffice.org

If you searched the archives and didn't find the answer to your question, try posting your question on a list. You don't have to join any list in order to post a question, although e-mails sent by non-subscribers are moderated to avoid spam.

To post a message, send an e-mail to the address of the list. The address of the users list is users@openoffice.org, and the address of the discuss list is discuss@openoffice.org. Then search or browse the archives periodically for your answer. Expect to wait at least 24 hours for a response. If you don't receive one after a few days, your question was probably passed over because it had been asked many times before and the answer lies in the archives. Or, it may have been vague or not readily understandable. Check the archives again, and rewrite the question as clearly as you can.

Searching the Newsgroups

You can also find the OpenOffice.org e-mail lists in the newsgroups that are carried by Google Groups. The newsgroup is called mailing.comp.open-office. Google has a different search engine than the one at OpenOffice.org, and you may want to use it instead. To access the OpenOffice.org mailing lists at Google, perform the following steps:

1. **In your Web browser, surf over to** www.google.com.

2. **Click the Groups tab.**

3. **Click Advanced Groups Search.**

4. **Type in search criteria that briefly describe your question in one of the four input fields.**

5. **In the Newsgroup text box, type** `mailing.comp.open-office`.

6. **Click Sort by relevance (unless your question is time-sensitive, in which case you may wish to sort by date instead).**

   If you get too many answers, you can repeat the procedure from Step 3 and narrow your search criteria.

Newsgroups, of course, are also accessible by newsgroup readers, which are sometimes bundled with your e-mail software. If you haven't already set up a newsgroup reader, using Google is easier.

Using Online Forums

In addition to the e-mail lists (which also post to Newsgroups), online forums are very helpful. They are available at `www.oooforum.org`. The forums are as follows:

- ✔ Setup and Troubleshooting
- ✔ OpenOffice.org Writer
- ✔ OpenOffice.org Calc
- ✔ OpenOffice.org Impress
- ✔ OpenOffice.org Draw
- ✔ OpenOffice.org Math
- ✔ OpenOffice.org Macros and API

Questions that are posted on the forums are often answered within just a few hours.

Before you post your question, it is proper etiquette to search the archives to see if the question has already been answered. Type a keyword into the search box, or click Advanced Search. In the Advanced Search window, type your search query, set your search options, and then click Search. If too few or too many results appear, either browse through the results or click the Search button at the top of the window and change your search criteria.

If the answer to your question is not in a previous thread, consider posting a new topic. To post a question on the forum, click the forum that you want to post to and then click the New Thread button. A Post a new topic page appears. Type in a user name, a topic, and your message. Try to formulate your question clearly and completely. Spend some time on it, because lots of people may read it. When you're satisfied with your message, click Preview to preview the message or click Submit to submit your message.

Surfing the OpenOffice.org Web Site

The OpenOffice.org Web site primarily provides downloads of OpenOffice.org and organizes the community for refining and improving the program. The site also hosts the wonderful e-mail lists. But some other goodies exist as well. If you're excited about OpenOffice.org, and want to make other people excited about it too, direct them to the <u>Product Description</u> link on the Home page. This Web page, along with its links, thoroughly describes the features of each program in the suite in a fascinating way, and also offers reviews, case studies, and testimonials. Links to fifteen foreign language sites are accessible by clicking the Site Map link on the Home page. And, if you need some extra guidance installing the program, the Setup Guide for OpenOffice.org 1.1 offers detailed installation instructions at `documentation.openoffice.org/setup_guide/index.html`.

For more information on installing OpenOffice.org, see Appendix A.

OO Extras: Extras for OpenOffice.org

The Extras Web site, located at `http://ooextras.sourceforge.net/`, offers clip art galleries such as the Flow Chart Symbol gallery as well as some nice icons and graphics. It also offers Impress templates and has some foreign language goodies. Everything is community generated and free to use.

Using Other Online Resources

Because OpenOffice.org is free, it inspires others to give freely as well. The following sections outline some goodies that are available from the Web.

The OpenOffice.org Unofficial FAQ v0.1.5a

A nice list of FAQs for OpenOffice.org is available at `www.bytebot.net/openoffice/faq.html`.

This site has useful frequently asked questions, including "Is there a grammar checker?" and "How do I get my scanner to work under OpenOffice.org?" If you don't want to type in the entire URL, you can find a link to it at `www.oooforums.org`.

Useful macro information for OpenOffice by Andrew Pitonyak

This free 241-page online book can be found at `www.pitonyak.org/oo.php`. The book is in OpenOffice.org's sxw format, of course. Pitonyak's Web site also has lots of good stuff about macros and some great links.

Community-based tech support: How to get help with OpenOffice.org

You can find a nice online reference, in PDF format, at `www.mackmoon.com/OOoHelpOutline.html`.

This 19-page document covers mailing lists, forums, and other useful topics.

Signing Up for Classes and Training

Training for OpenOffice.org is offered by many consultants. You'll probably want to find someone in your area — or at least in your country. If you live in the United States or Canada, you can visit `http://getOpenOffice.org` for information on training by Solveig Haugland, the author of *OpenOffice.org Resource Kit* and *The StarOffice 6.0 Companion*.

You may find training through these resources:

- Search the Web for OpenOffice.org training.
- Post a message on the e-mail list at OpenOffice.org and see if anyone in your area gives lessons, especially if you are searching for individual training.
- Inquire at your local computer store.

Make sure that you get references and recommendations before you sign up for training.

For languages other than English, check out the e-mail lists at OpenOffice.org that are in your language. You can always check the archives and see who is offering training, or you can post an e-mail.

Getting Commercial Support

Third-party commercial support is widely available as well for migration assistance or for general support. To find commercial support in your area, use the same techniques as you would to find training instructors. In fact, your training instructor may also offer commercial support. You can search the Web, post a message on the e-mail list, or even inquire at your local computer store. Lots of programmers use OpenOffice.org and know its ins and outs. Someone who lives near you may volunteer with the community OpenOffice.org project and be a veritable expert. Again, always check references.

Part VII

Appendixes

The 5th Wave   By Rich Tennant

In this part . . .

OpenOffice.org is a great deal, but you may not already have it installed on your system. If you're looking for a source, the appendixes of this book show how to install and configure OpenOffice.org from the handy CD that comes with this book.

Appendix A

Installing OpenOffice.org

● ●

In This Appendix

▶ Installing for Windows

▶ Installing for the Mac

▶ Installing for Linux

▶ Downloading upgrades

● ●

*I*nstalling OpenOffice.org is easy and simple. You can either download the program from the OpenOffice.org Web site, or you can find it on the CD-ROM that accompanies this book — how much more convenient can you get?

OpenOffice.org is an ongoing project, so it is always changing and evolving. As a result, you may want to download the latest beta version from the Web site to get the newest features. But because beta software is not finalized and formally released, you can expect it to have a few bugs. Many OpenOffice.org users are the adventurous type and like participating in testing the software and reporting bugs so that the programmers can improve OpenOffice.org.

If you don't like taking risks, you can stick to version 1.1, on the CD-ROM, or version 1.0.3 for the Mac. Then, you can always update to the next fully tested version when it is released.

Installing on Windows

If you install OpenOffice.org from the CD-ROM that accompanies this book, you should check the system requirements, discussed in the next section, and then skip to the section "Starting installation." To download OpenOffice.org from the Web site (www.openoffice.org), keep reading.

System requirements

You should make sure that your system can handle OpenOffice.org. If you have another office suite up and running, you shouldn't have any problem. However, if you have an older, rickety computer, be sure that you have the following items:

- A Pentium-compatible processor.
- Microsoft Windows 98, NT, 2000, or XP (2000, Me, or XP is required for Asian/CJK versions).
- 64MB of RAM (more is recommended).
- 250MB of hard drive space. The OpenOffice.org file is a little more than 60MB.
- An Internet connection, if you intend to download the program from the OpenOffice.org Web site.
- A decompression utility, such as WinZip, if you intend to download the program from the OpenOffice.org Web site (and even if they take from the cd if it's zipped on the CD).

Downloading from the Web site

Download OpenOffice.org from the Web site if you want the latest beta version. To download OpenOffice.org, follow these steps:

1. **Go to** www.openoffice.org.

2. **Click the hyperlink for the version of the software that you want.**

   You are sent to the download page of the version that you chose. Here you can find download and installation instructions.

3. **Scroll down and read the information on this page.**

   Partway down, you see the list of all the language versions of OpenOffice.org. It's pretty impressive.

4. **Scroll to the bottom of the page, where you can see the download sites.**

   If you click the Windows link on the home page, you go directly to these download sites.

5. **Click a link under the geographic area and language that you want. If you see several links, you can choose any one.**

   Your browser starts the download. You may have to choose a location in which to save the file. If you are given a choice to open or save the download file, choose to save. Now all you have to do is wait! When the download is complete, you may see your decompression utility (such as WinZip) open.

6. **If your decompression utility is open with a list of all the files, choose File⇨Copy and copy the downloaded file to a temporary folder.**

   Create a temporary folder for the purpose of decompressing all the files. Later, you can delete all these files and keep only the compressed (.zip) file. If you saved the downloaded file to a specific location, you can skip this step.

7. **Navigate to the file that you downloaded, and decompress it.**

   For example, in Windows Explorer, double-click the file to open it in your decompression program. Then follow the instructions for your decompression program to extract all the files to a temporary folder.

You are now ready to install OpenOffice.org.

Starting installation

After you decompress the installation file, you are ready to start installation. You should have a long list of files in your temporary folder. Follow these steps to begin the installation:

1. **From all the files that you extracted, find the** readme.txt **file and double-click it.**

   The readme document opens. This document contains information that didn't make it into the formal Help system or other information that you should read *before* installing. When you're done reading this document, you can close it.

2. **Find the** setup.exe **file, and double-click it.**

   The OpenOffice.org installation program opens. The first installation screen appears. At this point, you should close other programs that you have open.

   To perform a multiuser installation, go to the following Web site for instructions:

   www.openoffice.org/dev_docs/instructions.html

3. **Click Next.**

   The next screen appears, displaying some information about OpenOffice.org. For example, OpenOffice.org encourages you to register your software and tells you that you can register at any time at the following Web site:

   www.openoffice.org/welcome/registration-site.html

A list of mailing lists also appears. We recommend that you at least subscribe to the users' group, because that's a great way to get help when you need it.

Subscribe to the digest version only; otherwise you'll get dozens of e-mails a day.

 4. Read the information, and click Next.

The Software License Agreement screen appears. You're supposed to read it! Scroll down or press Page Down as you read.

 5. When you finished reading the agreement, click the I Accept the Terms of This Agreement button. To check the agreement in more detail later, click the Print button. Then click Next.

The Enter User Data screen appears.

 6. In the Enter User Data screen, complete the information about yourself and click Next.

Some of this information may already be filled in, taken from the user information on your computer. OpenOffice.org uses this information for templates (such as your name and address at the top of letterhead), to identify who makes changes to documents, and for other similar, legitimate purposes. You don't have to fill out all the information. When you click Next, the Select Installation Type dialog box appears.

 7. In the Select Installation Type dialog box, choose the type of installation that you want and click Next.

Most people can choose Typical installation. Choose Custom if you're picky, and choose Minimal if you're short on hard drive space. The screen informs you how much space each type of installation requires. When you click Next, the Select Installation Directory dialog box appears.

 8. In the Select Installation Directory dialog box, accept the default, type a new directory, or click the Browse button to navigate to a new location. Click Next.

Directory is geek talk for *folder.* If your folder doesn't exist, OpenOffice.org asks permission to create the folder. It's fine to say yes. OpenOffice.org displays the Start Copying dialog box.

 9. Click the Install button.

The Setup Program dialog box appears.

Pay attention here. Some people end up making the wrong decision in this dialog box. It's not easy to change this decision later on.

 10. If you have Microsoft Office documents on your computer and you want OpenOffice.org to open these documents when you double-click them in Windows Explorer, select the xxx check boxes. If not, deselect these check boxes. If you want OpenOffice.org's HTML editor to be your default editor, select the Default HTML Editor check box. If not, deselect the check box. Click OK.

You can always open Microsoft Office documents in OpenOffice.org by opening OpenOffice.org first and then choosing File➪Open. At some point, the Java Setup dialog box appears.

11. **If you have a Java Runtime Environment listed, choose it. If not, select the Do Not Use Java with OpenOffice.org check box. Click OK.**

So what is a Java Runtime Environment? Java is a programming language. OpenOffice.org uses Java for advanced features such as database connectivity and form creation. You don't need Java, but it's nice to have it if you want to use OpenOffice.org's advanced capabilities. You can always get it later, at `http://java.sun.com`. Double-click the `jvmsetup.exe` file, which is located in your OpenOffice.org `Program` folder. When you click OK, the installer starts to copy files.

12. **When you see the message** `Installation Complete`, **click OK.**

You're done! Now choose Start➪Programs➪OpenOffice.org 1.1 and have fun with your new, full-featured, free office suite!

Installing on the Mac

In June 2003, OpenOffice.org 1.0.3 was released for the Mac OS X (pronounced *Mac O S Ten*) operating system. However, OpenOffice.org is not written as a native program for the Mac. It requires an open source program called X11, which is a layer of graphics software that most Unix and Linux graphics applications use. Using X11 made it easier for programmers to adapt OpenOffice.org for the Mac. The native version for the Mac that does not require X11 is being developed but is probably a year or two away from being released.

To run OpenOffice.org 1.0.3 on the Mac, you need to first install X11. It's an easy program to install and run. X11 makes OpenOffice.org look more like a Linux program than a Mac program, so it may be a little disorienting at first, but you get used to it quickly. The biggest challenge may be remembering to press Control+C, Control+X, and Control+V instead of ⌘+C, ⌘+X, and ⌘+V.

X11 is not included on the CD-ROM, but your computer may already have it. It is included as an optional install in recent versions of the Macintosh operating systems such as the Mac OS X version 10.3 (Panther). If you use Panther and did a custom install and selected the X11 package, then you already have X11. Otherwise, it's a free and easy download.

System requirements

OpenOffice.org 1.0.3 for the Mac OS X operating system using X11 requires the following to run:

✔ Mac OS X 10.2 or higher or Darwin 6.0 or higher

✔ 256MB of RAM (memory) (512MB is recommended)

✔ 300MB free hard drive space

✔ 600MB additional hard drive space for installation of auxiliary applications that are required to run OpenOffice.org

✔ 1GB additional free space on your system drive for use as a swap file during installation and execution

✔ G4/400 or higher processor

Downloading X11

If you don't already have X11, downloading and installing X11 is a piece of cake. Follow these steps to do so:

1. **Open your browser window, and go to** `www.apple.com/macosx/x11/`.

   The X11 for Mac OS X page appears.

2. **Click the Download X11 Public Beta button.**

   The Get X11 for Mac OS X page appears. Read this for additional information on X11.

3. **Scroll down to the Tell Us Who You Are (Optional) xxx. Either deselect the I Would Like to Receive Apple News, Software Updates check box or enter your e-mail address in the input box. (You can also enter your name.)**

4. **Scroll down, and click the Download X11 button.**

   It takes about 10 minutes to download X11 through our DSL connection. To monitor the download progress, open the Download Manager window on Internet Explorer (or the equivalent on the browser that you are using). In Internet Explorer, choose Window➪Download Manager.

Installing X11

To install X11, perform the following steps:

1. **If you downloaded the X11 file, double-click the** `X11UserForMacOSX.dmg` **file. Internet Explorer places the file on the desktop. Otherwise, search for the file on your computer.**

   A few copying progress bars appear and disappear. Then a folder window opens that contains the following two files: `Readme.rtf` and

`X11UserForMacOSX.mpkg`. You don't need to read `Readme.rtf`. That information is incorporated into the installer program. You get to see it later.

2. **Double-click the Open Box icon.**

   An Authenticate dialog box appears, asking you for the password of the administrative user. If you install software on your Mac, you're probably the administrative user, so this is typically the same password that you type to log on.

3. **Type your password, and click OK.**

   The Welcome to the Mac OS X X11 Installer window appears. Okay, you can breathe a sigh of relief now, especially when you see the message `You will be guided through the steps necessary to install this software`. It's always nice when your computer takes good care of you.

4. **Click the Continue button.**

   The Important Information window appears. This is where you find the Readme file. It's always fun to see what's considered "important," but don't worry if it sounds too technical. You don't need to know most of this material.

5. **Click the Continue button.**

   The Software License Agreement appears. Fortunately for us, it is a great license agreement. And if you actually read every word of it, you should seriously consider a career in law.

6. **Select the Agree check box.**

   The Destination dialog box appears. If you have more than one hard drive, more than one icon appears from which you can choose your destination drive. However, if you have just one hard drive, this is a no-brainer.

7. **Click the icon of the hard drive where you want to install X11, and click the Continue button.**

   The Easy Install dialog box appears.

8. **Click the Install button.**

   A progress bar appears. On our computer it takes about 5 minutes to install X11. You then see the message `Software was successfully installed`.

9. **Click the Close button.**

   Congratulations! Now you have X11 installed. It's time to download and install OpenOffice.org.

Downloading OpenOffice.org 1.0.3

Skip this section if you plan to use the enclosed CD-ROM for your installation.

To Download OpenOffice.org 1.0.3 for the Mac OS X (X11) operating system, follow these steps:

1. **Using your browser, go to** www.openoffice.org.

   The Web page appears as shown in Figure A-1.

2. **Under the Download OpenOffice.org 1.1 heading, click the Mac OS X (X11) (1.0.3) link.**

   Don't be surprised when the download does not take place. Instead, a new window appears, with a list of links to News, Notes, FAQs, and Screenshots. This is worth reading only if you're interested.

3. **Click the Download link.**

   A list appears with different countries and various bits of information. Because OpenOffice.org is so big (173MB) and so popular, one location can't handle all the downloads. So computers around the world share the job. (If English is not your native language, scroll down and notice that the Localizer programs are here, too. After installing OpenOffice.org, you can return here to get your translation program.)

4. **Click a location that's near you. (Don't worry about whether the Type is HTTP or FTP. For now, either of them is okay.)**

   Another window appears with links to some files and various greetings and technical information. Don't spend much time reading it. All you need is the link to the file to be downloaded.

5. **Click the download link,** ooo103darwingm.dmg.gz.

   Your download begins.

6. **If you are using Internet Explorer, choose Window⇨Download Manager if the Download Manager window is not visible. If you use another Web browser, open the equivalent of the Download Manager window to see how long your download is expected to take.**

   If your Download Manager reports a lengthy download — 6 hours or so — cancel the download and delete the partial file that you downloaded. Then click the Back button in your browser to choose another site from which you can download the file.

   With a DSL connection, our computer downloads the 170MB file in about an hour.

Starting installation for OpenOffice.org 1.0.3

To install OpenOffice.org for the Mac OS X operating system, perform the following steps:

1. **Close all programs that you have running on your computer.**

   If other programs are running, they may interfere with the installation.

2. **If you are using the enclosed CD-ROM, follow these steps:**

   • Insert the CD-ROM into your CD-ROM drive.

   • Double-click on the CD-ROM icon on your desktop to view the folders on the CD-ROM.

   • Double-click on the OpenOffice.org folder.

   • Double-click the file ooo103darwingm.dmg.gz.

   • Click Choose in the Stuffit dialog box that appears.

   Stuffit decompresses the files and creates and opens a OOo 1.0.3 X11 folder on the desktop.

   If Stuffit crashes, then drag the file ooo103darwingm.dmg.gz from the CD-ROM onto your desktop and double-click on it.

   If you downloaded the program, follow these steps:

   • Locate the OOo 1.0.3 X11 folder on your desktop. This folder contains the Install_OpenOffice.org icon.

   • If you can't find this folder, locate the ooo103darwingm.dmg file, which is probably on the desktop, and double-click it.

3. **Yep, you guessed it. Double-click the Install_OpenOffice.org icon.** The Introduction dialog box appears, and the following message is displayed: ZeroG Install Anywhere will guide you through the installation of OpenOffice.org. Okay, go ahead and breathe a sigh of relief here.

4. **Click Next.**

   The Software License Agreement dialog box appears.

5. **Click the I Accept the Terms of the License Agreement button. (Feel free to read the license agreement, of course.) Click Next.**

   The Important Information Window opens.

6. **Read through the important information (or skip it, if you're not interested).**

Don't worry when you see the following message: `Who should use this build? It is ideally targeted to developers and advanced Mac OS X and Darwin users who are comfortable using X11.` You don't have to know anything about X11.

7. **Click Next.**

The Choose Install Folder dialog box appears.

8. **You should probably click the Restore Default Folder button, but if you want to place OpenOffice.org somewhere else, click the Choose button. Then designate the folder of your choice in the Choose a Folder dialog box, and click OK.**

9. **Click Next.**

The Choose Default Paper Size dialog box appears.

10. **Select the US Letter check box or the A4 check box, and click Next.**

The Choose Subcomponents dialog box appears.

11. **Select Typical and click Next.**

You don't really have to select Typical, because it is already selected. Just click Next.

Wait patiently here. It takes a few seconds, then the Preinstallation Summary window appears, showing a summary of what you requested and how much space it will take as well as how much hard drive space is available on your computer.

12. **Click the Install button.**

A window appears stating that the Darwin PPC version is intended for users who are comfortable using the X11 program. This is just a reminder that it's not going to look like a normal Mac program — but you already knew that.

13. **Click OK.**

The XDarwin Not Found dialog box may appear which informs you that "the default AppleScripts for launching OpenOffice.org will not function." If this happens, it's okay! Just proceed on! If the Xdarwin Not Found dialog box does not appear, then some progress bars appear and disappear as the program installs.

14. **If the Xdarwin Not Found dialog box appears, click OK.**

Some progress bars appear and disappear as the program installs. After a few minutes the Install Complete dialog box appears.

15. Click the Done button.

Hurray! You did it! Now see if it works. (Don't worry — it will.)

To start OpenOffice.org for the first time, perform the following steps:

1. Open the file Applications/OpenOffice.org1.0.3/Start OpenOffice.org.

The Choose Application dialog box may appear, displaying the question `Where is your preferred XWindows Server?` (If this dialog box does not appear, your computer is smarter than ours and you can expect OpenOffice.org to appear. It may take a few minutes, so be patient.)

2. If the Choose Application dialog box appears, then in the Applications list box, scroll down and select X11. Click the Choose button.

The X11 menu appears and a strange-looking window, labeled xterm, appears. Fortunately, the only thing that you need to do is to close this window (and only if the sight of it really annoys you).

After a couple minutes, a blank OpenOffice.org Writer document appears, and the OpenOffice.org Registration dialog box appears.

If OpenOffice.org does not appear, but the menu bar at the top of the screen has the menus, "Start OpenOffice.org" and "File", then choose File⇨New⇨Text Document (or Spreadsheet, Presentation, or Drawing). Then wait a few moments for the program to start.

3. If the OpenOffice.org Registration dialog box appears, then mark whatever box you want and Click OK.

By now you are probably so tired of installing the program that you most likely want to mark the "Never register button." But maybe the "Remind me to register later" button is a more rational choice.

That's it! Now you have OpenOffice.org on your Mac! It's a great program! Enjoy!

Installing on Linux

Most people who run the Linux operating system also use OpenOffice.org. The two go together like pizza and pineapple. (Or pizza and sauerkraut, or pizza and olives, extra cheese, peppers...)

To install OpenOffice.org using the enclosed CD-ROM, first review the system requirements that are presented in the next section. Then skip to the section "Installing OpenOffice.org on Linux."

Some Linux systems require single-clicks to open files, whereas others require double-clicks. If you only need to click once to open files, then wherever we tell you to double-click, be sure to single-click only.

System requirements

If you are running Linux on a newer computer, probably you don't have to worry about meeting the requirements for OpenOffice.org. For the record, these requirements are as follows:

- ✔ Linux Kernel version 2.2.13 or higher
- ✔ Glibc2 version 2.2.0 or higher
- ✔ Pentium-compatible processor
- ✔ 64MB RAM (memory)
- ✔ 300MB available hard drive space (350MB for the CJK version)
- ✔ X Server with 800×600 or higher resolution, with at least 256 colors
- ✔ Gnome 2.0 or higher required for Assistive Technology Tools
- ✔ Window Manager

Downloading OpenOffice.org for Linux

You can skip this section if you plan to use the enclosed CD-ROM.

To download OpenOffice.org from the Web site, follow these steps:

1. **Go to** www.openoffice.org.

   The OpenOffice.org Web page opens, as shown in Figure A-1.

2. **Under the Download OpenOffice.org 1.1 heading, click Linux.**

   A new page opens, with a list of links to sites that offer the OpenOffice.org Linux download.

3. **Click a link that's close to your location.**

   A window appears from your browser asking whether you want to open or save the download.

4. **Click the Save As button.**

   The Save As dialog box appears, with the name of the download, OOo_1.1.0_LinuxIntel_install.tar.gz, in the Location input box.

5. **Navigate to any directory using the up arrows and/or list box at the top of the dialog box, and then click the Save button.**

   The Save As dialog box closes. The Download Manager window appears, showing the progress of the download. (If the Download Manager window does not appear, you can open it, for example, in Mozilla by choosing Window⇨Download Manager.)

   The `OOo_1.1.0_LinuxIntel_install.tar.gz` file is downloaded to your computer. (At about 77MB, the download takes 15 minutes on our computer with a DSL connection.)

6. **When the Download Manager indicates that your download is complete, open the Ark KDE utility application (or some other application that decompresses files).**

   If you are using Ark, a blank window appears, displaying the message `No files in current archive.`

   The following steps assume that you are using Ark.

7. **Choose File⇨Open.**

   The Open dialog box appears.

8. **Navigate to the folder in which you saved the download. Then select the `OOo_1.1.0_LinuxIntel_install.tar.gz` file and click OK.**

   A number of files appear in the Ark window.

9. **Click the Extract icon.**

   A window dialog box appears

10. **Enter the folder name that you want to extract to, or choose the default. In the Files to be Extracted panel, select the All check box and click OK.**

    The files are extracted into a new folder, called `OOo_1.1.0_LinuxIntel_install` (which Ark creates), and Ark places the new folder within the folder that you specified (or the default that is specified).

Installing OpenOffice.org on Linux

Now that you have downloaded and uncompressed the OpenOffice.org files, you can install the program. Or, if you plan to use the CD-ROM that accompanies this book, you already saved yourself the trouble of downloading the file, but you still need to decompress the files.

To decompress the files on your CD-ROM, do the following:

1. **Insert your CD-ROM into the drive.**

2. **Double-click the CD-ROM icon on the desktop.**

3. **Double-click the OpenOffice.org folder.**

4. **Double-click the** `OOo_1.1.0_LinuxIntel_install.tar.gz` **file.**

   In most systems, a decompression program appears with a dialog box requesting you to choose the location for the decompressed files. If a decompression program does not appear, then launch the decompression program yourself. Refer to steps 6-10 in the above section.

5. **Perform the steps required by your decompression program to extract the files from the** `OOo_1.1.0_LinuxIntel_install.tar.gz` **file on your CD-ROM and place them in a folder on your hard drive.**

   Our decompression program named the folder, `OOo_1.1.0_LinuxIntel_install` "

To install OpenOffice.org, follow these steps:

1. **Open the** `OOo_1.1.0_LinuxIntel_install` **folder by double-clicking it. (The folder is in the directory that you specified in Step 10 of the "Downloading OpenOffice.org for Linux" section, or Step 5 of the previous steps.) Please note that this is a folder and not a file. Some file managers sort the folders first and then the files, so be sure to look in the folders section.**

   The open folder contains a number of files, from f0001 to f426, plus some Readme, and Setup, and Install files.

2. **Double-click the** `Setup` **file.**

   Several progress bar windows appear and disappear. Then the "Installation program for OpenOffice.org 1.1.0" dialog box appears, displaying the message `Welcome to the OpenOffice.org 1.1.0 Setup.`

3. **Click Next.**

   The Important Information window appears. This may or may not be important information to you.

4. **Click Next.**

   The Software License Agreement appears. (Read the agreement if you choose.)

5. **Scroll down, click the Accept the License Agreement button, and click Next.**

   A window appears that requests personal information. (No, this is not online dating.)

6. **You can fill in the information or leave the text boxes blank. Then click Next.**

   The Select Installation Type dialog box appears.

7. **Select the Standard option button (which is the default), and click Next.**

   The Select Installation Directory dialog box appears. This dialog box suggests a new directory: `/home/myDirectory/OpenOffice.org1.1.0`. (This varies according to your directory arrangement.)

8. **Click Next.**

   A dialog box appears, indicating that the folder does not exist. You see the message `Create it now?` If this message does not appear, skip to Step 10.

9. **Click the Yes button.**

   The Start Copying dialog box appears.

10. **Click the Install button.**

    The Java Setup dialog box appears.

11. **Follow one of these steps:**

    - If you do not have a Java Runtime environment on your computer, select the Install New Java Runtime Environment check box or if that is not available, then select the Do Not Use Java Runtime Environment check box. Click OK.

    - If you already have a Java Runtime Environment, select a version in the list box and click OK.

    If you already have a Java Runtime Environment, if you chose not to install a Java Runtime Environment, or if you have already proceeded through the Java Runtime Environment installer, a progress bar appears in the Installation dialog box. On our computer, this process takes 2 to 3 minutes.

    A Confirm File Replacement dialog box may appear if a file already exists. Otherwise, after a few moments, the Installation Completed dialog box appears with the good news and you can skip to Step 13..

    So what is a Java Runtime Environment? Java is a programming language. OpenOffice.org uses Java for advanced features such as database connectivity and form creation. You don't need Java, but it's nice to have it if you want to use OpenOffice.org's advanced capabilities. You can always get it later, at `http://java.sun.com`.

12. **If you selected a version of Java Runtime and the Confirm File Replacement dialog box appears, click the Replace All button.**

    After a few moments, the Installation Completed dialog box appears with the good news.

13. **Click the Complete button.**

    Now celebrate! Take a break, and help yourself to a bowl of your favorite ice cream!

You launch applications in a variety of ways in Linux, depending on which window manager you have, such as Gnome, KDE, or Window Maker. If you are using KDE, for instance, click the Start Applications button on the KDE panel to view the applications list. Then choose OpenOffice.org 1.1.0 ⇨ OpenOffice.org 1.1.0 Writer (or Calc, Draw, Impress, etc.).

Downloading Upgrades

Upgrading OpenOffice.org is not much different from downloading and installing it in the first place. For Windows and Linux versions, the installation program of the new version creates a new folder and installs everything into the new folder, just like it did in the previous version. When the installation is complete, just click the new version to start your program.

Upgrading the Mac is also similar to installing on it, although you can most likely skip the downloading and installing of X11, unless the new version of OpenOffice.org requires a new version of that, too.

After you download and install the program once, it is much easier to do it again. And once you do it a second time, it becomes a snap to do it a third time — and so on. All in all, it's much easier to download and upgrade OpenOffice.org than it is to order and buy an upgrade of any other leading office program. And it's easier on your bank balance, too.

Appendix B

What's on the CD-ROM

*I*nstead of going to OpenOffice.org to install your program, feel free to use the CD-ROM that's included with this book. It will save you some time, and the program is easy to install.

CD-ROM Contents

The CD-ROM includes OpenOffice.org software, plus plenty of extra information about that friendly, free software

OpenOffice.org software

We've included the following versions of OpenOffice.org on the CD-ROM:

- OpenOffice.org 1.1 RC3 for Windows
- OpenOffice.org 1.1 RC3 for Linux
- OpenOffice.org 1.0.3 for the Mac OS X (using X11)

Before installing OpenOffice.org, make sure that your computer has the necessary system requirements. Refer to Appendix A for the system requirements for the version that you are installing.

Place the CD-ROM into your computer's CD-ROM drive.

If you are installing OpenOffice.org 1.1 for Windows, refer to the subsection "Starting installation" in the section "Installing on Windows" in Appendix A.

If you are installing OpenOffice.org 1.0.3 for the Mac, refer to the section "Starting installation for OpenOffice.org 1.0.3" in Appendix A. You can skip the downloading section, of course, but everything else applies and is clearly explained.

If you are installing OpenOffice.org 1.1 for Linux, refer to the section "Installing OpenOffice.org on Linux" in Appendix A.

Bonus chapters

The CD-ROM has a complete .pdf copy of this book, plus five bonus chapters with extra information on these subjects:

- ✔ Fine-Tuning Your Preferences
- ✔ Manipulating Data
- ✔ Setting Up Impress
- ✔ Getting More Graphic
- ✔ Configuring OpenOffice.org

Adobe Acrobat Reader

The Adobe Acrobat Reader is the utility you need to read the bonus chapters from the CD-ROM. If your system doesn't have the reader, you can install it from this CD-ROM.

Resolving Your CD Problems

If you try installing OpenOffice.org from the CD-ROM and it won't install, then assuming that your 3-year-old is not using your CD-ROM as a Frisbee, the most likely reasons for the installation problems are as follows:

- ✔ You don't have enough RAM or hard drive space.
- ✔ Other programs are running that are affecting the installation of OpenOffice.org.
- ✔ Your antivirus software thinks that OpenOffice.org is a virus.

Use the following methods to fix these problems:

- ✔ Check out the system requirements for your version of OpenOffice.org, and if you need more RAM or more hard drive space, take a trip to the local computer store. Maybe it's time to upgrade to something more powerful.

- ✔ Close all running programs. The more programs that you run, the less memory is available and the slower things go. Furthermore, the running programs may interfere with the installation of OpenOffice.org.

- ✔ Turn off any antivirus software that you have on your computer before installing the OpenOffice.org. Software installers sometimes mimic virus activity and make your computer think that it is under a massive viral attack. Don't forget to turn the virus software back on after installing OpenOffice.org.

If you still have trouble installing the items, try downloading them from the Internet using the instructions in Appendix A and installing that version. Support for installing OpenOffice.org can be found in the General Setup online forum at www.ooodocs.org.

If you believe that your CD-ROM is defective, call the Wiley Customer Care Center at (800) 762-2974 (outside the United States, call (317) 572-3994). You can also e-mail the Wiley Customer Care Center at techsupdum@wiley.com. Technical support is provided only for general quality-control items. For technical support on installation or running OpenOffice.org, visit www.ooodocs.org or consult the mailing lists at www.openoffice.org.

Index

Wiley Publishing, Inc.
End-User License Agreement

READ THIS. You should carefully read these terms and conditions before opening the software packet(s) included with this book "Book". This is a license agreement "Agreement" between you and Wiley Publishing, Inc."WPI". By opening the accompanying software packet(s), you acknowledge that you have read and accept the following terms and conditions. If you do not agree and do not want to be bound by such terms and conditions, promptly return the Book and the unopened software packet(s) to the place you obtained them for a full refund.

1. **License Grant.** WPI grants to you (either an individual or entity) a nonexclusive license to use one copy of the enclosed software program(s) (collectively, the "Software" solely for your own personal or business purposes on a single computer (whether a standard computer or a workstation component of a multi-user network). The Software is in use on a computer when it is loaded into temporary memory (RAM) or installed into permanent memory (hard disk, CD-ROM, or other storage device). WPI reserves all rights not expressly granted herein.

2. **Ownership.** WPI is the owner of all right, title, and interest, including copyright, in and to the compilation of the Software recorded on the disk(s) or CD-ROM "Software Media". Copyright to the individual programs recorded on the Software Media is owned by the author or other authorized copyright owner of each program. Ownership of the Software and all proprietary rights relating thereto remain with WPI and its licensers.

3. **Restrictions on Use and Transfer.**

   (a) You may only (i) make one copy of the Software for backup or archival purposes, or (ii) transfer the Software to a single hard disk, provided that you keep the original for backup or archival purposes. You may not (i) rent or lease the Software, (ii) copy or reproduce the Software through a LAN or other network system or through any computer subscriber system or bulletin- board system, or (iii) modify, adapt, or create derivative works based on the Software.

   (b) You may not reverse engineer, decompile, or disassemble the Software. You may transfer the Software and user documentation on a permanent basis, provided that the transferee agrees to accept the terms and conditions of this Agreement and you retain no copies. If the Software is an update or has been updated, any transfer must include the most recent update and all prior versions.

4. **Restrictions on Use of Individual Programs.** You must follow the individual requirements and restrictions detailed for each individual program in the "What's on the CD" appendix of this Book. These limitations are also contained in the individual license agreements recorded on the Software Media. These limitations may include a requirement that after using the program for a specified period of time, the user must pay a registration fee or discontinue use. By opening the Software packet(s), you will be agreeing to abide by the licenses and restrictions for these individual programs that are detailed in the "What's on the CD" appendix and on the Software Media. None of the material on this Software Media or listed in this Book may ever be redistributed, in original or modified form, for commercial purposes.

5. **Limited Warranty.**

   (a) WPI warrants that the Software and Software Media are free from defects in materials and workmanship under normal use for a period of sixty (60) days from the date of purchase of this Book. If WPI receives notification within the warranty period of defects in materials or workmanship, WPI will replace the defective Software Media.

   (b) WPI AND THE AUTHOR OF THE BOOK DISCLAIM ALL OTHER WARRANTIES, EXPRESS OR IMPLIED, INCLUDING WITHOUT LIMITATION IMPLIED WARRANTIES OF MERCHANTABILITY AND FITNESS FOR A PARTICULAR PURPOSE, WITH RESPECT TO THE SOFTWARE, THE PROGRAMS, THE SOURCE CODE CONTAINED THEREIN, AND/OR THE TECHNIQUES DESCRIBED IN THIS BOOK. WPI DOES NOT WARRANT THAT THE FUNCTIONS CONTAINED IN THE SOFTWARE WILL MEET YOUR REQUIREMENTS OR THAT THE OPERATION OF THE SOFTWARE WILL BE ERROR FREE.

   (c) This limited warranty gives you specific legal rights, and you may have other rights that vary from jurisdiction to jurisdiction.

6. **Remedies.**

   (a) WPI's entire liability and your exclusive remedy for defects in materials and workmanship shall be limited to replacement of the Software Media, which may be returned to WPI with a copy of your receipt at the following address: Software Media Fulfillment Department, Attn.: *OpenOffice.org For Dummies,* Wiley Publishing, Inc., 10475 Crosspoint Blvd., Indianapolis, IN 46256, or call 1-800-762-2974. Please allow four to six weeks for delivery. This Limited Warranty is void if failure of the Software Media has resulted from accident, abuse, or misapplication. Any replacement Software Media will be warranted for the remainder of the original warranty period or thirty (30) days, whichever is longer.

   (b) In no event shall WPI or the author be liable for any damages whatsoever (including without limitation damages for loss of business profits, business interruption, loss of business information, or any other pecuniary loss) arising from the use of or inability to use the Book or the Software, even if WPI has been advised of the possibility of such damages.

   (c) Because some jurisdictions do not allow the exclusion or limitation of liability for consequential or incidental damages, the above limitation or exclusion may not apply to you.

7. **U.S. Government Restricted Rights.** Use, duplication, or disclosure of the Software for or on behalf of the United States of America, its agencies and/or instrumentalities "U.S. Government" is subject to restrictions as stated in paragraph (c)(1)(ii) of the Rights in Technical Data and Computer Software clause of DFARS 252.227-7013, or subparagraphs (c)(1) and (2) of the Commercial Computer Software - Restricted Rights clause at FAR 52.227-19, and in similar clauses in the NASA FAR supplement, as applicable.

8. **General.** This Agreement constitutes the entire understanding of the parties and revokes and supersedes all prior agreements, oral or written, between them and may not be modified or amended except in a writing signed by both parties hereto that specifically refers to this Agreement. This Agreement shall take precedence over any other documents that may be in conflict herewith. If any one or more provisions contained in this Agreement are held by any court or tribunal to be invalid, illegal, or otherwise unenforceable, each and every other provision shall remain in full force and effect.

GNU GENERAL PUBLIC LICENSE

TERMS AND CONDITIONS FOR COPYING, DISTRIBUTION AND MODIFICATION

0. This License applies to any program or other work which contains a notice placed by the copyright holder saying it may be distributed under the terms of this General Public License. The "Program", below, refers to any such program or work, and a "work based on the Program" means either the Program or any derivative work under copyright law: that is to say, a work containing the Program or a portion of it, either verbatim or with modifications and/or translated into another language. (Hereinafter, translation is included without limitation in the term "modification".) Each licensee is addressed as "you".

Activities other than copying, distribution and modification are not covered by this License; they are outside its scope. The act of running the Program is not restricted, and the output from the Program is covered only if its contents constitute a work based on the Program (independent of having been made by running the Program). Whether that is true depends on what the Program does.

1. You may copy and distribute verbatim copies of the Program's source code as you receive it, in any medium, provided that you conspicuously and appropriately publish on each copy an appropriate copyright notice and disclaimer of warranty; keep intact all the notices that refer to this License and to the absence of any warranty; and give any other recipients of the Program a copy of this License along with the Program.

You may charge a fee for the physical act of transferring a copy, and you may at your option offer warranty protection in exchange for a fee.

2. You may modify your copy or copies of the Program or any portion of it, thus forming a work based on the Program, and copy and distribute such modifications or work under the terms of Section 1 above, provided that you also meet all of these conditions:

    a) You must cause the modified files to carry prominent notices stating that you changed the files and the date of any change.

    b) You must cause any work that you distribute or publish, that in whole or in part contains or is derived from the Program or any part thereof, to be licensed as a whole at no charge to all third parties under the terms of this License.

    c) If the modified program normally reads commands interactively when run, you must cause it, when started running for such interactive use in the most ordinary way, to print or display an announcement including an appropriate copyright notice and a notice that there is no warranty (or else, saying that you provide a warranty) and that users may redistribute the program under these conditions, and telling the user how to view a copy of this License. (Exception: if the Program itself is interactive but does not normally print such an announcement, your work based on the Program is not required to print an announcement.)

    These requirements apply to the modified work as a whole. If identifiable sections of that work are not derived from the Program, and can be reasonably considered independent and separate works in themselves, then this License, and its terms, do not apply to those sections when you distribute them as separate works. But when you distribute the same sections as part of a whole which is a work based on the Program, the distribution of the whole must be on the terms of this License, whose permissions for other licensees extend to the entire whole, and thus to each and every part regardless of who wrote it.

Thus, it is not the intent of this section to claim rights or contest your rights to work written entirely by you; rather, the intent is to exercise the right to control the distribution of derivative or collective works based on the Program.

In addition, mere aggregation of another work not based on the Program with the Program (or with a work based on the Program) on a volume of a storage or distribution medium does not bring the other work under the scope of this License.

3. You may copy and distribute the Program (or a work based on it, under Section 2) in object code or executable form under the terms of Sections 1 and 2 above provided that you also do one of the following:

a) Accompany it with the complete corresponding machine-readable source code, which must be distributed under the terms of Sections 1 and 2 above on a medium customarily used for software interchange; or,

b) Accompany it with a written offer, valid for at least three years, to give any third party, for a charge no more than your cost of physically performing source distribution, a complete machine-readable copy of the corresponding source code, to be distributed under the terms of Sections 1 and 2 above on a medium customarily used for software interchange; or,

c) Accompany it with the information you received as to the offer to distribute corresponding source code. (This alternative is allowed only for noncommercial distribution and only if you received the program in object code or executable form with such an offer, in accord with Subsection b above.)

The source code for a work means the preferred form of the work for making modifications to it. For an executable work, complete source code means all the source code for all modules it contains, plus any associated interface definition files, plus the scripts used to control compilation and installation of the executable. However, as a special exception, the source code distributed need not include anything that is normally distributed (in either source or binary form) with the major components (compiler, kernel, and so on) of the operating system on which the executable runs, unless that component itself accompanies the executable.

If distribution of executable or object code is made by offering access to copy from a designated place, then offering equivalent access to copy the source code from the same place counts as distribution of the source code, even though third parties are not compelled to copy the source along with the object code.

4. You may not copy, modify, sublicense, or distribute the Program except as expressly provided under this License. Any attempt otherwise to copy, modify, sublicense or distribute the Program is void, and will automatically terminate your rights under this License. However, parties who have received copies, or rights, from you under this License will not have their licenses terminated so long as such parties remain in full compliance.

5. You are not required to accept this License, since you have not signed it. However, nothing else grants you permission to modify or distribute the Program or its derivative works. These actions are prohibited by law if you do not accept this License. Therefore, by modifying or distributing the Program (or any work based on the Program), you indicate your acceptance of this License to do so, and all its terms and conditions for copying, distributing or modifying the Program or works based on it.

6. Each time you redistribute the Program (or any work based on the Program), the recipient automatically receives a license from the original licensor to copy, distribute or modify the Program subject to these terms and conditions. You may not impose any further restrictions on the recipients' exercise of the rights granted herein. You are not responsible for enforcing compliance by third parties to this License.

7. If, as a consequence of a court judgment or allegation of patent infringement or for any other reason (not limited to patent issues), conditions are imposed on you (whether by court order, agreement or otherwise) that contradict the conditions of this License, they do not excuse you from the conditions of this License. If you cannot distribute so as to satisfy simultaneously your obligations under this License and any other pertinent obligations, then as a consequence you may not distribute the Program at all. For example, if a patent license would not permit royalty-free redistribution of the Program by all those who receive copies directly or indirectly through you, then the only way you could satisfy both it and this License would be to refrain entirely from distribution of the Program.

   If any portion of this section is held invalid or unenforceable under any particular circum-stance, the balance of the section is intended to apply and the section as a whole is intended to apply in other circumstances.

   It is not the purpose of this section to induce you to infringe any patents or other property right claims or to contest validity of any such claims; this section has the sole purpose of protecting the integrity of the free software distribution system, which is implemented by public license practices. Many people have made generous contributions to the wide range of software distributed through that system in reliance on consistent application of that system; it is up to the author/
   donor to decide if he or she is willing to distribute software through any other system and a licensee cannot impose that choice.

   This section is intended to make thoroughly clear what is believed to be a consequence of the rest of this License.

8. If the distribution and/or use of the Program is restricted in certain countries either by patents or by copyrighted interfaces, the original copyright holder who places the Program under this License may add an explicit geographical distribution limitation excluding those countries, so that distribution is permitted only in or among countries not thus excluded. In such case, this License incorporates the limitation as if written in the body of this License.

9. The Free Software Foundation may publish revised and/or new versions of the General Public License from time to time. Such new versions will be similar in spirit to the present version, but may differ in detail to address new problems or concerns.

   Each version is given a distinguishing version number. If the Program specifies a version number of this License which applies to it and "any later version", you have the option of fol-lowing the terms and conditions either of that version or of any later version published by the Free Software Foundation. If the Program does not specify a version number of this License, you may choose any version ever published by the Free Software Foundation.

10. If you wish to incorporate parts of the Program into other free programs whose distribution conditions are different, write to the author to ask for permission. For software which is copy-righted by the Free Software Foundation, write to the Free Software Foundation; we sometimes make exceptions for this. Our decision will be guided by the two goals of preserv-ing the free status of all derivatives of our free software and of promoting the sharing and reuse of software generally.

NO WARRANTY

11. BECAUSE THE PROGRAM IS LICENSED FREE OF CHARGE, THERE IS NO WARRANTY FOR THE PROGRAM, TO THE EXTENT PERMITTED BY APPLICABLE LAW. EXCEPT WHEN OTHERWISE STATED IN WRITING THE COPYRIGHT HOLDERS AND/OR OTHER PARTIES PROVIDE THE PROGRAM "AS IS" WITHOUT WARRANTY OF ANY KIND, EITHER EXPRESSED OR IMPLIED, INCLUDING, BUT NOT LIMITED TO, THE IMPLIED WARRANTIES OF MERCHANTABILITY AND FITNESS FOR A PARTICULAR PURPOSE. THE ENTIRE RISK AS TO THE QUALITY AND PERFOR-MANCE OF THE PROGRAM IS WITH YOU. SHOULD THE PROGRAM PROVE DEFECTIVE, YOU ASSUME THE COST OF ALL NECESSARY SERVICING, REPAIR OR CORRECTION.

12. IN NO EVENT UNLESS REQUIRED BY APPLICABLE LAW OR AGREED TO IN WRITING WILL ANY COPYRIGHT HOLDER, OR ANY OTHER PARTY WHO MAY MODIFY AND/OR REDISTRIB-UTE THE PROGRAM AS PERMITTED ABOVE, BE LIABLE TO YOU FOR DAMAGES, INCLUDING ANY GENERAL, SPECIAL, INCIDENTAL OR CONSEQUENTIAL DAMAGES ARISING OUT OF THE USE OR INABILITY TO USE THE PROGRAM (INCLUDING BUT NOT LIMITED TO LOSS OF DATA OR DATA BEING RENDERED INACCURATE OR LOSSES SUSTAINED BY YOU OR THIRD PARTIES OR A FAILURE OF THE PROGRAM TO OPERATE WITH ANY OTHER PROGRAMS), EVEN IF SUCH HOLDER OR OTHER PARTY HAS BEEN ADVISED OF THE POSSIBILITY OF SUCH DAMAGES.